Routledge Revivals

British Public

CW00818795

First published in 1984, *British Public Schools* is a collection of empirically based articles written by sociologists of education who have conducted research into public schools. Studies are presented on why parents sent their children to public schools, on the experiences of pupils and teachers, on aspirations and attitudes of pupils towards higher education, on the increasing emphasis of schools on examination successes, and on the relationships between public school education and educational and occupational successes. This book is an essential read for scholars and researchers of sociology of education and education.

British Public Schools

Policy and Practice

Edited by Geoffrey Walford

First published in 1984
by The Falmer Press

This edition first published in 2022 by Routledge
4 Park Square, Milton Park, Abingdon, Oxon, OX14 4RN

and by Routledge
605 Third Avenue, New York, NY 10017

Routledge is an imprint of the Taylor & Francis Group, an informa business

Publisher's Note
The publisher has gone to great lengths to ensure the quality of this reprint but points out that some imperfections in the original copies may be apparent.

Disclaimer
The publisher has made every effort to trace copyright holders and welcomes correspondence from those they have been unable to contact.

A Library of Congress record exists under ISBN: 0905273842

ISBN: 978-1-032-25345-9 (hbk)
ISBN: 978-1-003-28277-8 (ebk)
ISBN: 978-1-032-25347-3 (pbk)

Book DOI 10.4324/9781003282778

British Public Schools
Policy and Practice

Edited by

Geoffrey Walford

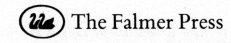 The Falmer Press

(A member of the Taylor & Francis Group)
London and Philadelphia

94515

UK   The Falmer Press, Falmer House, Barcombe, Lewes, East Sussex,
            BN8 5DL

USA   The Falmer Press, Taylor & Francis Inc., 242 Cherry Street,
            Philadelphia, PA 19106-1906

First published in 1984

Library of Congress Cataloging in Publication Data

Main entry under title:

British public schools.

   Includes bibliographies and index.
   1. Public schools—Great Britain—Addresses, essays,
lectures. I. Walford, Geoffrey.
LA632.B75   1984   371′.01′0941   84-13521
ISBN 0-905273-84-2
ISBN 0-905273-83-4 (pbk.)

Typeset in 11/13 Bembo by
Imago Publishing Ltd, Thame, Oxon

Jacket design by Leonard Williams

*Printed in Great Britain by Taylor & Francis (Printers) Ltd,
Basingstoke*

Contents

Introduction: British Public Schools

Geoffrey Walford, University of Aston

> Private schools have long been a major source of perpetuated division and the demarcation of privilege, status, esteem, power, opportunity and expectation that go with it. Private schools are not 'incidental' to the class system. They are the very cement in the wall that divides British society. The existence of private schooling with all its increments of status and complementary paraphernalia of quaint uniforms and traditions, language and accents is amongst the most effective means of perpetually imposing those divisions.
>
> (Neil Kinnock, 1981)

In comparison with most other industrialized countries, private education in Britain accounts for only a relatively small proportion of children. In 1982, for example, there were about 522,000 pupils in some 2400 private schools in England and Wales, representing about 5.9 per cent of the total school population. Small numbers, however, do not mean that fee-paying schools are unimportant or marginal to the educational system or to British society. Indeed, in some ways, it is the smallness of the numbers involved and the associated elite nature of some of the schools that is at the root of the controversy about the desirability of their continued existence. It is argued by many that private schools act as a mechanism whereby the ruling class can reproduce and legitimate class inequalities for the next generation. They are seen by Neil Kinnock as 'the very cement in the wall that divides British society'.

It is certainly true that the historic role of the private schools has been concerned with the process of reproduction of an elite. Boyd (1973), for example, documents the educational backgrounds of members of various elite groups in Britain. He shows that in 1970/71, 62 per cent of top-rank civil servants, 83 per cent of foreign ambassadors, 83 per cent of high court judges or above, 67 per cent of top-rank clergy in the Church of England and 83 per cent of directors of clearing banks had been educated at private schools. More recently Scott (1982) has reviewed evidence for army officers, the judiciary and business leaders and arrived at very similar conclusions. A count of Members of Parliament in the House of Commons for 1982 (from Dod, 1982) shows that at least 42 per cent were educated in private schools, and 20 per cent of these went to one particular school — Eton. In practice the backgrounds of members of elite groups in Britain are even more restricted than these figures suggest, for the vast majority of each elite actually attended an even smaller group of private schools — the so-called 'public schools'. Most of the controversy over private schools is, in fact, more concerned with a small group of some 200 to 300 schools rather than the whole range of 2400 schools.

The private school sector is characterized by its diversity and its terminological confusion. The range of different types of school is enormous. At one end of the spectrum are special schools for handicapped children or children with special learning difficulties. These may only cater for twenty or thirty children and many, in fact, have some of the pupils paid for by local education authorities. Preparatory schools, usually catering for the 7–13 age range, vary from the well equipped and expensive feeder schools for the prestigious public schools, to the downright cheap and shady. Private schools for the secondary age have a similar range, and at the lower end offer anything but privilege for the girls and boys who are unfortunate enough to be confined to them by their parents. Theirs is a very different experience from that of their peers at prestigious independent day schools such as Manchester Grammar School or St Paul's School, or at public boarding schools such as Eton, Winchester and Harrow.

The schools themselves, at least in open debate, now usually prefer to refer to themselves as independent schools, stressing the wide variety of provision that is available according to individual requirements. The term also has the advantage of breaking away from the extreme connotations of privilege associated with 'public schools'. Critics, on the other hand, prefer terms such as 'fee-paying' or 'commercial' (Halsey, 1981) which emphasize the market basis of these schools. In the end each author or commentator has to decide individually on the precise terminology to be used for the particular group of schools under study — an unsatisfactory but inevitable accompaniment of the ideological and rhetorical battles being waged in this area.

There is perhaps a need to justify a further book concerned with public schools, for there is no overall shortage of relevant articles and books. The vast majority of these, however, are either histories, individual reminiscences or seek to argue either for or against the existence of the schools. There is very little writing which seeks systematically to add to and clarify our knowledge of policy and practice in public schools through the results of academic research.

This is what this volume aims to do. All eight articles are previously unpublished and are firmly based on empirical research. They do not aim to argue directly 'for' or 'against' public schools, but they bring together additional information which will clarify that debate, and enable that debate to be more firmly based on fact than on opinion and speculation, as has been so often the case. This does not, of course, mean that the conclusions drawn from the data by the various authors will all necessarily agree. Data are often open to a variety of interpretations, and the conclusions drawn in the eight articles reflect these differences in interpretation. What is important is that the volume provides the opportunity for these data to be made available to a wide audience so that readers may clarify their own positions in the debate.

The Articles

The articles collected here deal with a wide range of topics concerned with public schools. Although the articles were specially commissioned for this book, the research on which they are based was not, which means that the topics are the result of authors' prior interests and activities. However, while there are several obvious gaps, for example, a political arithmetic study of girls or an ethnographic study of boys in public schools, the collection does cover in one way or another most of the important areas. Included are studies on parents, pupils and teachers, the growing emphasis on credentials, the input and output characteristics of the various types of school, the policies of the major political parties and the Assisted Places Scheme.

The spread of research methods used by the various authors is also worthy of note. By focusing on the one particular topic area of public schools, it is possible to move beyond the sterile arguments between quantitative and qualitative research which have been so much a part of the sociology of education in the last decade. The complementary nature of the various research styles is reflected in the different forms of data and information presented. Within the collection the range is from a large-scale interview survey to a small ethnographic case study. It includes structured and unstructured observation, a questionnaire survey, the secondary re-analysis of statistical survey data, oral history, in-depth interviewing and the analysis of official statistics, published documents and unpublished archive material. All have a part to play in developing our understanding of public schools, and it is possible to argue that the first steps towards bridging the gap between macro and micro research in the sociology of education might be, quite simply, to draw together the insights of both in one particular subject area.

The first chapter, by Halsey, Heath and Ridge, roots itself firmly in the political arithmetic tradition within the sociology of education. In the first section they provide a storehouse of statistical data and examine the changing fortunes of private schooling over the last century and, in particular, since the Second World War. This is then set in the context of the changing attitudes and activities of the major political parties. The authors then draw upon a more detailed, and previously unpublished, analysis of data collected in the Oxford Mobility Enquiry (Halsey *et al.*, 1980) to test the degree to which the educational system approximated to a meritocratic system during this time. First they review the evidence on entry to secondary schools and show that the private sector was far less meritocratic in its selection than were the grammar schools. This is then followed by a study of the relative academic attainment in the two sectors in terms of examination passes, where it is shown that the gap in the chance of emerging with three A-levels widened over the period under study. A process of statistical control is used which shows that the main reason why boys in the private sector were more likely to obtain A-levels was simply because they stayed on at school longer. Some differences are found between the cohorts, however, which indicate the possibility that there may be real, though small, effects due to the schools themselves. The final stage of the analysis looks at the degree to which Oxford University has acted meritocratically in its intake procedures. Halsey, Heath and Ridge use information from the Dover Report to show that progress towards meritocracy at Oxford is far from complete.

Political arithmetic gives us a picture of how, in the past, the educational system has worked on the whole. Different sorts of studies are required to bring out the details. Irene Fox's chapter deals with the question of why parents send their sons to public school. She interviewed 190 sets of parents from a sample of schools and found that more than half of the parents were themselves educated in the maintained sector. She argues that the decision to use a public school was, for the majority of both day and boarding parents, a carefully considered one, made in the light of the knowledge of schooling and the world available to them. Whilst there were differences between the two groups, the same two advantages that the public schools are believed to have over the maintained schools were mentioned most frequently by both sets of parents — the ability to produce better academic results and to develop the character through discipline. Boarding itself was not usually a main reason for choosing a public school. Fox argues that there is a crisis of confidence in the comprehensive system, where middle-class parents see themselves as being forced to use the private system in order to ensure that the advantages that were afforded them by the grammar schools are still afforded to their sons.

What life may be like for the pupils within these schools is illustrated in the chapter by Sara Delamont. Delamont's ethnographic and observational study of girls in one of the Scottish girls' public schools concentrates on classroom activity and peer groups within a single third year. Six friendship groups are distinguished, each with its own pattern of leisure interests and attitudes to school, and it is shown that these groups also have distinctive patterns of participation and interaction in the classroom. It is argued that the data can be seen as the first steps towards a much needed test of Bourdieu's (1977) theory of cultural capital. Even within a school such as this girls are not equally endowed with cultural capital, and this is reflected in the composition of the peer groups within the year. Girls exhibit different degrees of cultural competence, which is an integral part of the process of the reproduction of elites.

For the vast majority of pupils in public schools the path after school is directed towards further study at university. Greg Eglin presents data collected from sixth form pupils in four private schools in one London borough. He compares their future aspirations and expectations about higher education with those of a similarly aged sample of sixth formers in seven nearby comprehensive schools. Eglin shows that, although there were roughly equal proportions who wished to enter higher education, a far lower percentage wished to enter university, as opposed to other types of higher education. in the comprehensive schools than in the private schools. There were also major differences with regard to the subject areas that students wished to study. In the private sector there was greater emphasis on the arts and humanities, while in the comprehensives a higher proportion aimed for sciences and engineering. Information is also given on reasons for wishing to enter higher education, on sources of information used by students, and on the differences in aspirations between male and female students.

The next chapter by Geoffrey Walford returns into the public schools to look at the lives of the participants. This time the subjects are the school teachers themselves, in two prestigious HMC boarding schools. The chapter uses the framework of professionalism and proletarianization as it has been applied to teachers to trace the similarities and discontinuities of experience between public school teachers and the majority of teachers working in the maintained system. Data from an ethnographic study and from interviews with teachers are presented, and it is argued that the backgrounds and experiences of the two groups are in many ways becoming more similar.

The chapter by Christine M. Heward is an historical case study of one Woodard school from 1930 to 1950. She has been able to draw upon archive letters written by parents to the headmaster during that time, and has pieced together this evidence with oral and other written material to construct her account. Many writers have described a recent dramatic change in the academic emphasis of public schools (for example Rae, 1981; Salter and Tapper, 1981; and some articles in this collection). Heward shows that the bureaucratization of the professions occurred early, and led to increased credentialism which was beginning to be felt by middle-class parents well before the Second World War. She documents the very careful way in which some of the parents at this school planned their sons' careers, and weighed the costs of the school against the benefits to be obtained. For these parents, even then, it was very important that their son's school should provide the right academic preparation for entry into the career that they had in mind. The chapter indicates the importance of an historical dimension, for there are indications that the 'revolution' in the academic emphasis of these schools might be better seen as part of a gradual process, which may well have started in the somewhat lesser public schools many decades ago.

Edwards and Whitty's article is concerned with their current research project into the origins, operation and effects of the Assisted

Places Scheme which started in 1981. In this case they do not present 'findings' from the research, as it is too early in the lives of both the scheme and the research project to do so. Instead, they discuss the research methods that they have developed at national, local and individual school levels. They outline some of the problems that they have had to deal with so far in the evaluation of a scheme which is surrounded by political controversy. They explore the possibilities for undertaking empirical research of a sort that might be of value to the development of policy in such a politically sensitive area.

In a number of ways, the final chapter by Tapper and Salter brings together the central arguments of the book. Put starkly, private schooling in Britain only survives while sufficient numbers of parents are prepared to pay fees, and while governments permit their continued existence. The images and perceptions of private schools held by both parents and politicians are thus a key concern. Tapper and Salter review the evidence on parental perceptions provided by a previously published survey and document the images of private schooling held by politicians through an analysis of published documents. They then draw comparisons between the images and the reality of private education using results from surveys, their own research and a re-analysis of some National Child Development Study data. They use the data to argue that the independent sector and the maintained sector now offer a largely similar experience of schooling, and that parents, politicians and sociologists are largely misguided in their understanding of educational realities. In particular, they argue that British social science has been preoccupied with the class composition of private schools, that its analysis has been unsophisticated and that its observations and research base have been outdated.

It is hoped that the articles collected together in this book will go some little way to overcoming these undoubted limitations.

References

BOURDIEU, P. (1977) 'Cultural reproduction and social reproduction', in KARABEL, J. and HALSEY, A.H. (Eds) *Power and Ideology in Education*, Oxford, Oxford University Press.

BOYD, D. (1973) *Elites and Their Education*, Slough, NFER.

DOD (1982) *Dod's Parliamentary Companion 1982*, London, Dod's Parliamentary Companion Ltd.

HALSEY, A.H. (1981) 'Democracy in education', *New Society*, 28 May.

Geoffrey Walford

HALSEY, A.H., HEATH, A.F., and RIDGE, J.M. (1980) *Origins and Destinations*, Oxford, Oxford University Press.
KINNOCK, N. (1981) *Private Schools*, News Release, Labour Party, 31 July.
RAE, J. (1981) *The Public School Revolution*, London, Faber and Faber.
SALTER, B. and TAPPER, T. (1981) *Education, Politics and the State*, London, Grant McIntyre.
SCOTT, J. (1982) *The Upper Class*, London, Macmillan.

The Political Arithmetic of Public Schools

A.H. Halsey, A.F. Heath, and J.M. Ridge, University of Oxford*

The English public schools question is a debate about how small numbers exercise large influence over British life. It never goes away because crucial interests of class and status, power and advantage, familial continuity and social integration are at stake. The dispute, which has deposited a voluminous literature on the British reproduction of generations, is predominantly ideological. Our intention is not primarily to contribute to it from an ideological standpoint as adversaries, though we do in fact believe that the public schools have been an instrument of social injustice and educational narrowness from the time when the Victorians invented them. Our task rather is to analyze the phenomenon sociologically, including the ideological debate surrounding it, and with special reference to that particular set of methods which are known as political arithmetic — essentially the use of survey and headcounting to throw empirical light on value-laden social issues. Our first contention, in other words, is that the political arithmetic or sociological method can be used to test empirical claims while remaining independent of the value position we hold.

But what is the phenomenon? Perhaps because the literature has been so overwhelmingly ideological there is not and never has been a precise sociological definition of public and private schools. Ideological interest has spawned a loaded vocabulary, including such terms as 'independent' (favoured by contemporary advocates of these schools who are embarrassed by the 'image' of the public school as socially divisive and inegalitarian,[1] or 'commercial' (favoured by the critics to emphasize the essential market basis of these schools).[2] Sociologically the issues are a special facet of the analysis of class

* We are indebted to Monica Dowley of Nuffield College, Oxford, for her labours on the DES statistics used in this chapter.

formation and reproduction; organizationally the debate is about political as distinct from market supply of scarce goods; ideologically it is a dispute about the balance between liberty, equality and fraternity. All the issues have been sharpened by the resurgence of market liberalism associated with the 1979 and 1983 Conservative governments.

As political arithmeticians we shall begin with the arithmetic of the balance between the public and the private sectors of education. Then, sketching the background of attempts at reform in the twentieth century, we shall analyze the numbers sociologically. Finally, we shall draw some conclusions as to how far our evidence can be used to clarify the original political dispute. The evidence, we would stress in advance, cannot bear the weight of every element in the debate. Our intention, while recognizing the full range of issues, is to make clear what the evidence does and does not enable us to assert sociologically. Our contention is that what we are able to say is a firm basis for shifting the terms of political argument and bargaining.

The Arithmetic of Private Education

The shifting balance between the state and private sectors of education can be shown most simply by the historical trends in their relative shares of the country's pupils. Glennester and Wilson estimated that there were 2½ million pupils in private schools in the 1850s. A century later, in 1951, this had shrunk to 564,000 (480,000 at independent schools and a further 84,000 at the direct grant schools), representing 9.2 per cent of the school population, a share which continued to decline to 1978 when it was 5.8 per cent. But then in the following years some sign of reversal appeared raising slightly both absolute numbers and proportions. In 1981 they were 499,000 and 6.2 per cent.[3]

Overall, the historical fact is of small proportions in marketed schooling over the century following the first major intervention of the state through the 1870 Act, and of decline to 1978. But this is by no means the whole story. A full account would have to recognize that the market covers an enormous heterogeneity of activity and competitive enterprise of widely varying character and quality.

At the apex of a heterogeneous hierarchy are the great and famous public schools. Their definition has shifted as the context of state and other private provision has developed. Even the financial and legal definitions have been ambiguous because the boundary of control and financial support between the state and the market has not only shifted but has been drawn so as to allow mixed territories, notably the direct grant schools, with their funding from the fee-paying market and from governmental grants.

Sociologically we may say with E.J. Mack that the public schools are the 'non-local endowed boarding schools for the upper classes'.[4] Again, sociologically, perhaps the most important clue to the meaning of the adjective 'public' to describe these schools is that they were prototypically in the case of Westminster an alternative child-rearing device to the private tutor in the aristocratic household. The original seven studied by the Clarendon Commission of 1861 were the core of the system as it developed in the nineteenth century. They were Charterhouse, Eton, Harrow, Rugby, Shrewsbury, Westminster, and Winchester, but already the definition had to be modified so as to include the two famous upper-class day schools, St Paul's and Merchant Taylors.

Subsequent redefinitions were always in the direction of enlargement. The Taunton Commission (1864) added some newcomers and some endowed grammar schools. The compilers of the first *Public Schools' Year Book* in 1889 agreed on twenty-five. By 1962 the nuclear seven were still at the heart of the system, and T.W. Bamford was suggesting the figure of 106 boarding schools as a maximum, including fourteen of the direct grant schools.[5]

In 1968 Newsom's Public Schools' Commission[6] adopted the less stringent, if administratively more convenient definition of membership of the Headmasters' Conference, or the Governing Bodies' Association, or the Association of Governing Bodies of Girls' Public Schools, and there were 288 such schools when the Commission was appointed, including eleven in Scotland. The Commission noted, however, that there were over 1000 other independent schools for children mainly of secondary school age, and over 1800 preparatory and pre-preparatory schools. Public schools, as Newsom defined them, accounted for only 1.4 per cent of all pupils, compared with 1.5 per cent in direct grant schools, 5.5 per cent in all independent schools, and 93 per cent in maintained schools (excluding special schools).

In the 1980s the definitions shifted again. The outstanding voice of the apologists, John Rae (the Headmaster of Westminster), tells us that

in the early '70s the heads of independent schools were anxious to bury the term 'public school' as quickly and decently as possible. This was partly because, in the face of political threats the old established public schools decided to throw in their lot with all the recognized independent schools. A more important, if less publicly acknowledged, reason for a change in the nomenclature was the desire of the heads to disassociate themselves and their schools from the overtones of snobbery and exclusiveness that to the British ear were immediately audible in the words 'public schools'.[7]

Rae goes on to note that there are over 2000 independent schools in Britain, of which 1350 are recognized as efficient by the Department of Education and Science, and of these just over 1000 are members of the Independent Schools' Information Service.[8] That membership is Rae's criterion for defining the wider boundary of those public schools which had previously claimed the prestigious title 'public'.

Nevertheless, Rae acknowledges the heterogeneity of his ISIS schools. He describes the members of the Headmasters' Conference as headmasters of the 'oldest, richest and most prestigious boys' secondary schools', and these are still the 210 public schools. He also uses the term 'Great Schools' when he wants to refer to the handful of famous schools, by which he appears to mean the Clarendon Schools, 'that from the early nineteenth century have been upper-most in the minds of opponents and supporters alike when they have spoken of public schools.' He adds finally that the question of whether all 210 members of the Headmasters' Conference, including the seventy-six heads of ex-direct grant schools, should all be called public schools is a

> snobbish quibble ... a characteristic English diversion for almost a century [which] is now forgotten except by a few parents who, having paid the price, wish it to be known that their sons are attending a real public school. There is a lingering tension, however, within the Conference between the so-called Great Schools and the less well-known, smaller, and newer schools, but this tension has more to do with the suspicion that the heads of the Great Schools are calling the tune in the Conference than with envy of the Great Schools pre-eminence in the public eye.[9]

In terms of numbers and viability the twentieth-century history of the public schools has been that the more exclusive the definition, the more certain is the reference to schools which have not shared in the general contraction of the private sector as a whole. Led by the Great

Schools, the private system reached the height of its size and splendour at the end of the nineteenth century. Since then it is the tail and not the head which has withered. The Great Schools and the public schools, including the direct grant schools which went independent when the list was withdrawn in 1975, are full and flourishing, albeit partly at the expense of their weaker market competitors. But the private market as a whole shrank relative to the state sector as the twentieth century advanced, at least until the emergence of a new Conservative government in 1979.

The leading thesis of the friends of private education had been that it would flourish as the country grew richer, while the enemies believed that the market, and within it the public schools, would wither away or be abolished by democracy, or by working-class action using the state to raise the standards of maintained schools, to remove the advantages of the independent schools, and finally perhaps to outlaw fee-paying for full-time education. Neither the friends nor the enemies can invoke historical validation of their beliefs. Certainly state provision has enlarged and improved and market provision has declined in relative terms, but the central core of the market system remains strong. The state continues to support the market through tax advantages and payment of fees from the public purse, while the private demand continues to contribute the bulk of the resources on which the commercial or independent schools depend.

Our initial picture of the distribution of boys and girls in the state and private sector is also too simple in another way. It ignores one of the crucial features of the private sector — its retention of pupils beyond the minimum school leaving age and into the sixth form. The private sector is much more heavily weighted by sixth-formers, and much less by children of primary school age, than is the state sector. Nevertheless, the increase in sixth form attendance at state schools is a still more dramatic development of the school system in the past thirty years. Table 1 shows the trends over the post-war period. It shows the relative strength of the private sector among the older pupils but also the way in which the advance of the state sector has been most rapid at this level. From having nearly 40 per cent of the older pupils in 1951 the private sector has declined to less than 20 per cent in 1981. Private school pupils now have a vastly increased number of contemporaries in the state sector with whom they must compete for O-levels, A-levels and university places. They are now outnumbered four to one even in the sixth form and can no longer expect the easy path to university, and Oxbridge in

Table 1.   Full-Time Pupils by Age and Type of School (percentages)

	School	Age 5-10	Age 11-15	Age 16+	All
1951	Maintained	93.1	88.9	62.1	90.8
	Direct Grant	0.4	2.4	9.3	1.4
	Independent	6.5	8.7	28.7	7.8
	Total	100.0	100.0	100.1	100.0
	(N (000s)	3614	2404	131	6149)
1956	Maintained	94.0	89.5	67.2	91.7
	Direct Grant	0.4	2.5	10.0	1.4
	Independent	5.5	8.1	22.8	6.9
	Total	99.9	100.1	100.0	100.0
	(N (000s)	4312	2657	165	7133)
1961	Maintained	94.3	91.2	71.9	92.2
	Direct Grant	0.5	2.2	9.1	1.5
	Independent	5.2	6.5	19.0	6.2
	Total	100.0	99.9	100.0	99.9
	(N (000s)	3907	3140	253	7300)
1966	Maintained	95.1	91.2	77.7	92.7
	Direct Grant	0.5	2.6	7.6	1.6
	Independent	4.5	6.2	14.7	5.7
	Total	100.1	100.0	100.0	100.0
	(N (000s)	4204	3049	354	7607)
1971	Maintained	96.0	92.3	81.8	93.9
	Direct Grant	0.4	2.4	6.9	1.5
	Independent	3.6	5.2	11.2	4.6
	Total	100.0	99.9	99.9	100.0
	(N (000s)	4804	3300	418	8522)
1976	Maintained	96.2	93.3	86.2	94.4
	Direct Grant	0.4	2.1	5.4	1.4
	Independent	3.4	4.7	8.5	4.3
	Total	100.0	100.1	100.1	100.1
	(N (000s)	4738	3998	574	9310)
1981	Maintained	95.3	93.4	82.2	93.8
	Independent	4.6	6.6	17.8	6.2
	Total	99.9	100.0	100.0	100.0
	(N (000s)	3903	3794	383	8080)

Source: DES Statistics of Education.
Notes: For 1951 and 1956 the figures for independent schools not recognized as
efficient were estimated.

The figures for 1981 relate to England only, not England and Wales as for
earlier years.

Age is that at 1 January for the year in question except for 1981 when it is at
31 August 1980. The numbers are those attending school in January. For
1951–71 the 11–15 group thus includes some pupils over the school leaving
age; for 1976 and 1981 the 16+ group includes some pupils under the school
leaving age.

particular, that they might once have expected. We shall examine the
implications below after looking more closely at the factors that
underlie this changing balance.

At the primary stage (5–10), there was a decline in absolute
numbers attending private schools before the Second World War and
this has continued since, despite the fact that until the mid-1970s the
size of the age group was on the increase. The decline is both
absolute and relative, and it is probably not rash to infer that there
has been over this period a continued decline in the popularity of
private primary education which may have been caused by the
spread of attractive, purpose-built and educationally progressive
state primary schools. We should note, however, that this continued
decline took place largely among the schools 'not recognized as
efficient' in the formal language of the DES. It was the 'tail' of small
latter-day 'dames' schools' which specialized in coaching for the 11+
at relatively low fees which, we may guess, gradually disappeared
rather than the elite preparatory schools geared to the common
entrance examination of the major private schools.

At the secondary school stage (11–15), it has been a somewhat
different story. The absolute numbers in the private sector (including
as before the direct grant with the wholly independent schools) have
stayed relatively steady over the thirty-year period, fluctuating
slightly but beginning at 268,000 and ending at 251,000.[10] There was
no serious absolute decline. But meanwhile in the state sector there
were huge increases, first with the two 'baby booms' of 1946 and
1961, and then with the raising of the school leaving age in 1973.
From 2,136,000 in 1951 the numbers had risen to 3,047,000 in 1971
just before the school leaving age was raised, then to 3,731,000
afterwards in 1976, before declining again as the bulge passed
through the secondary schools to 3,543,000 in 1981. Thus there were
roughly stable numbers in the private sector coupled with an

enormous expansion in the absolute numbers of the state sector and a consequent increase in the latter's relative share.

There are different ways in which these figures for the secondary school stage can be interpreted. On the one hand, the decline in the private sector's share of pupils could be seen as evidence of a decline in their popularity as facilities within the state sector improved. Alternatively, it could be argued that the private sector effectively rationed its numbers during the 'bulges' in the size of the school-age population, preserving its teacher–pupil ratio, increasing the selectivity of its entry and thus raising academic standards. Rationing would be a rational strategy for educational charities whose goal is academic excellence. Some at least of these schools do not have the incentives of the whole-heartedly profit-making organization of expanding its 'production' in response to the increased 'demand' (if we can equate increased numbers in the school-age population with increased demand for places). Instead it was in the interest of the private schools to leave the state sector to cope with the increased demand, leaving themselves free to pursue their avowed goal of higher educational standards.

We must emphasize that the available evidence does not allow us to choose between these two rival explanations of the shifting balance between public and private schooling, that is, whether the underlying causes were choice (the popularity interpretation) or constraint (the rationing interpretration). Both may have operated, but we incline towards the latter interpretation because to our knowledge, though the cost of private schooling rose, there is no independent evidence that the attractiveness of the state schools increased, and may have decreased for some relevant elements of the population with comprehensive reorganization. We also refer below to evidence of significant changes in the internal life of private schools which may have attracted more applications.

Insofar as the rationing interpretation is correct, there are two interesting implications. First, greater selectivity could provide the conditions for raised academic standards. Second, it casts new light on the significance of charitable status in relation to the welfare of the educational system as a whole. A fully-fledged commercial sector which responded to market forces in pursuit of the profit motive might have taken up some of the burden of increased numbers, and might thus have given more parents the freedom to choose. Instead we may have been seeing the consequence of the curious paradox of a private sector constituted in such a way as to lack the great asset of the market place — responsiveness to consumer demand.

Finally, we turn to the trends at 16+ where there has occurred by far the most dramatic decline in the private sector's share, but where at the same time the absolute numbers increased by over one-third (from 49,500 in 1951 to 67,500 in 1981). The point again is that there was an even larger increase in the state sector of nearly 300 per cent. This was in part due, as at 11–15, to the increased birth rate and the raised school leaving age, but the major factor was a trend towards attendance beyond minimum leaving age. It was, above all, this trend towards longer school careers which swelled the state schools' sixth forms and provided the new competition for university places. In 1951 about 12 per cent of pupils in the state sector stayed on at school to the age of 16 compared with about 60 per cent in the private sector, and perhaps 6 per cent from the state sector were staying on into the sixth form (that is, on to the age of 17) compared with 40 per cent in the private sector. By 1981 all pupils, in both sectors, were obliged to stay to 16, but the proportion staying on till 17 had increased in the state sector from 6 to 20 per cent and in the private sector from 40 to 70 per cent. Both sectors, therefore, kept many more pupils for longer, but they were starting from different baselines and remained clearly differentiated even in 1981 despite the transformation of the state sector.[11] In the private sector a sixth form career has now become the norm, and while these sixth formers are vastly outnumbered by those in state sixth forms, it is still only a small minority of state school pupils who stay on to this stage of education.

The organizational implications of all this are important. Given that in the state sector the sixth form career is still only a minority expectation, educational effort must still be directed at the bulk of pupils who will leave at the minimum legal age. By contrast, in the private sector a sixth form career is a majority expectation and is more likely to be the focus of organizational effort. The educational goals and objectives of the two systems are thus likely to remain differentiated, just as they were at the beginning of the post-war period. Of course, this is a conjecture, but one which is not inconsistent with the numerical evidence we have assembled. We will return to it after looking at the politics of the period of which we have given a numerical description.

The Politics of Private Education

Both friends and enemies of the public schools were politically quiet in the earlier part of this century, though personal attacks on them as the locus of a resented and regretted upbringing were numerous. T.C. Worsley's *Barbarians and Philistines* (1940) is a title representing one kind of argument against the culture of these peculiar English schools. The private life of the boys' boarding school was passionately condemned by many of its more distinguished alumni from Robert Graves to George Orwell, who looked back in anger on a childhood vitiated by tribal philistinism.

A second kind of argument, from class inequality, came typically from socialists and statisticians sufficiently motivated by fascination or outrage to compile the arithmetic of injustice in tables showing the connection between the public schools and elevated jobs in Whitehall, Shell, Canterbury, All Souls, and so forth. There is, for example, a dramatic histogram in the first report of the Newsom Commission[12] in which the proportions of all 14-year-olds who were at Charterhouse, Eton, Harrow, Marlborough, Rugby, or Winchester, are too small to show in printer's ink, but in which the proportions from these schools in the Conservative Cabinet of 1963 are two-thirds.

Nevertheless, neither kind of argument, educational nor social, has had much of a place in political debate. It continues to be fashionable to suggest, as did the Newsom Commissioners, that the public schools question has occupied a central position on the British political stage for the last century. But in fact this view is only possible for those compulsive readers of the correspondence columns of *The Times* who manage to conceive of British society as a kind of family business in which anybody who is anybody knows everybody. What is really remarkable is that the Labour Party, the major political instrument of British twentieth-century radicalism, has never taken more than a marginal and fitful interest in educational injustice throughout its existence. Apart from Will Thorne of the Gas Workers, and R.H. Tawney of the WEA, there was no seriously argued attack on the private schools in terms of social justice until Anthony Crosland wrote *The Future of Socialism* in 1956.

By that time the Fleming Committee, which had been asked by R.A. Butler in 1942 to produce an integration plan, had been forgotten. Neither Labour nor Conservative governments wanted to spend, either directly or through the local authorities, the money which would have been required to pay for free places in the private sector. Both parties gave higher priority to the channelling of resources into an improving and expanding state system. For Crosland the public schools were 'the strongest remaining bastion of class privilege'. He described them as 'a system of superior private schools open to the wealthier classes, but out of reach of poorer children, however talented and deserving.' He saw this as 'much the most flagrant inequality of opportunity, as it is cause of class inequality generally, in our educational system.' And he had 'never been able to understand why socialists had been so obsessed with the question of the grammar schools, and so indifferent to the much more glaring injustice of the independent schools.'[13]

It was largely through Crosland and his book that the Labour Party began to see the possibility of education as one of the alternatives to nationalization in promoting a more just and efficient society. It was Crosland who set in train the comprehensive movement as Secretary of State of the Department of Education and Science, and who invented the Public Schools Commission and laid down its terms of reference in 1965. He instructed them to bring forward a plan of action to integrate the public schools with the state system, and for their part the Commissioners produced an up-to-date and more elaboratory documented version of Crosland's own analysis and conclusions.

They were not unanimous. Three of them (the former headmistress of a girls' public school, the headmaster of a boys' public school, and the Director General of the Confederation of British Industry) really rejected the terms of reference; and they claimed that the majority report had also done so in throwing out 'the possibility of outright integration'. These three persons did not attach the highest importance to the 'socially-divisive influence' of these schools, and they believed that 'both the report and its recommendations pay insufficient regard to the continuing interests of the fee payers' whom they 'do not consider a negligible or undesirable section of the community.'[14]

But the orders had been to integrate, and the Commissioners recommended accordingly with a scheme by which suitable boarding schools would give at least half of their places to assisted pupils who needed boarding education. It would be introduced gradually with an elaborate administrative mechanism. The details would be worked out school by school by a body which the Commissioners proposed to call The Boarding Schools' Corporation. Independent boarding schools considered to be suitable and willing to enter an integrated sector would have had to meet the condition that, by the end of a build-up period of about seven years, half of their intake would consist of assisted pupils from state-maintained schools. This compromise was a severe one in terms of the gap between the emerging aspirations of the independent schools towards meritocracy, and the emerging practice of comprehensive schools as institutions admitting pupils from the total normal range of ability. But it was not a total compromise in that it allowed serious departure from the comprehensive principle. The Commissioners had in mind an ability range which did not go down beyond those capable of tackling courses leading to the Certificate of Secondary Education. This would have excluded one-fifth or one-quarter of the ordinary school population. Moreover, there was even a loophole left for schools 'to cater entirely for gifted children from an early age', though the Commissioners wanted any such proposal to be viewed with considerable caution.

The market version of the 'leave-them-alone' solution remained in the arena, though few people outside the Institute of Economic Affairs entertained the belief that independent school places should be wholly and freely bought and sold. What perhaps was surprising was that the Wilson government did not immediately act on the plea that the 'public' school be made private by removing the tax advantages which enabled the well-to-do to buy educational privileges subsidized by the community. Such a reform was held by many to be a matter of common decency, and had nothing intrinsically to do with the public schools question. On the other hand, the possibility of abolition also remained in the arena, but since this logically involved proscription of the buying of education privately, it was wholly consistent with the non-revolutionary character of the Labour Party as well as with Crosland's libertarian version of socialism that, at least for the time being, this solution too was shelved.

In its second round of activity under the chairmanship of David Donnison, the Public Schools Commission recommended the ending of the direct grant list. This reform was delayed by the 1970 election, but put through by Mr Reg Prentice as Secretary of State at the Department of Education and Science when the Labour Party returned to power in 1974. Otherwise, political quiet was restored.

We shall move on to the 1980s below but first we must review the evidence with respect to class inequality and educational excellence which has emerged since the Public Schools Commission first reported in 1968.

Our first evidence (pp. 21–23) refers to access to secondary schools and is summarized from our previously published work. We would underline with respect to this analysis that fairness is conceived of here in terms of equal opportunity for those of equal merit and that the distribution of merit between social classes is imputed from what is known about the class distribution of measured intelligence. In other words, we focus here on a sub-set of the phenomenon of fairness in education, though one which captures the terms of the political and educational debate of the period.

Our second evidence (pp. 23–34) does not include measured intelligence. It focuses on academic attainment at the end of secondary schooling and compares state and private schools' O- and A-level output in terms of the causal weight to be attached to the social background of pupils as distinct from the organization and resources of the school itself. In terms of that comparison we look at the fairness of resource allocation.

Our third evidence (pp. 34–38) examines fairness from a third point of view. Measuring merit by A-level performance, we enquire whether the universities, particularly the Oxford colleges, distribute their places fairly between children from the state and the private secondary schools.

Entry to Secondary Schools: Fairness As Meritocracy

Demand for educational reform has taken its place in the larger movement towards enlarging the social rights of citizenship. In health the drive was towards the supply of clinical services on medical assessment of need rather than patients' capacity to pay: the goal was a national health service. In education the parallel movement was towards the supply of schooling on academic assessment of capacity to profit: a national educational service. In both cases the additional possibility of a market supply was permitted, and even encouraged. But just as in health the legitimation of both the public service and the market was that the standard of health care was to be the same whether or not the patient paid, so the citizenship principle dictated a parallel criterion for the education service.

The educational goal was meritocracy. But the validity of the parallel with health was always contested and the debate has ancient lineage. John Rae has reminded us of it by referring to a disagreement between Archbishop Thomas Cranmer and the Commissions investigating the future of the Grammar School at Canterbury in 1540. The Commissioners argued that only the children of gentlemen ought to be academically educated. Cranmer replied: 'Poor men's children are many times endued with more singular gifts of nature which are also gifts of God, as with eloquence, memory, apt pronunciation, sobriety, and such like, and also commonly more apt to apply their study than is the gentleman's son delicately nurtured.' But the Commissioners insisted that 'it was more meet for the ploughman's son to go to the plough ... and the gentleman's children are meet to have the knowledge of government and rule in the Commonwealth.' Cranmer was the prototypic meritocrat. The Commissioners put squarely what twentieth-century proponents of the public schools have preferred tacitly to assume.

A major source of evidence on class access to the independent schools and meritocratic inequality in the twentieth century is the Oxford Mobility Enquiry through which the familial, educational, and occupational biographies of a national sample of the adult male population of England and Wales were collected in 1972.[15] It showed that, at the primary stage, private schooling for boys was used by roughly one-quarter of the middle class and hardly at all by the working class. Within the middle class, families with an entrepreneurial background and parents who had themselves had experience of private education were even more likely to choose it for their children. At the secondary level the pattern of outflow from class origins to private schooling was similar. In consequence the social composition of the private schools was dominantly middle-class. Schools in membership of the Headmasters' Conference took two-thirds of their pupils from the upper-middle class, over one-quarter from the lower-middle class, and a tiny minority from the working class. In the direct grant schools the proportions were half for the upper-middle and one-third for the lower-middle class, with a 16 per cent contribution from working-class families. By contrast the unselected state schools were made up of two-thirds boys from working-class and one-third from middle-class families. Thus class and its conventionally associated schooling in the parental generation were confirmed as the major influences supporting entry to private education among twentieth-century British children.

But the main burden of our analysis in the Oxford study was to compare the real world of educational choice and selection with a model world conceived in terms of the idea of meritocracy. For this purpose our English and Welsh male sample was divided into three classes according to the occupation of the father. Second, the three classes so formed were translated into a supply of ranges of IQ. We accepted without argument that IQ could be the measure of merit, knowing the objections to such an assumption, but using it because these were the terms in which reformers called for progress towards educational equality, and knowing further that the IQ measure would give the smallest and lowest estimate possible of class inequality of educational opportunity. Third, following the opinions of both their friends and their enemies, we placed the HMC schools at the head of the queue, followed in order by the direct grant schools, the grammar schools, the non-HMC private schools, the technical schools, and the comprehensive or secondary modern schools.

We were then able to compare this ideal abstraction with the realities of the experience of our respondents. It turned out that the private sector was conspicuously less meritocratic in its selection than were the selective schools within the state system. Meritocracy had been contained throughout the century by class bias, and the private sector of education had played a crucial part in the main-tenance of this form of inequality.

Academic Attainment in Secondary Schools: Fairness As Resource Allocaton

The rising numbers of secondary school pupils which we described above (pp. 13–17) appear from another vantage point in the statistics of O- and A-level passes (see Table 2).[16] Over the period 1961–81 the state sector acquired a greater share of the certificates at both O- and A-levels. But there was a significant exception. Despite its falling share of successful candidates the private sector managed to hold its own in the competition for three or more A-levels — the crucial competition for university entrance. The private schools produced 29 per cent of those obtaining three or more A-levels in 1981 despite the fact that in the previous twenty years their share of pupils aged 17+ fell from 29 per cent to 19 per cent. As Table 3 makes plain, the private schools managed to extract an increasing quality of examination performance from the same number of pupils. In 1961 only two-fifths of the leavers from private schools had any A-levels, and less than one-fifth had three or more. By 1981 63 per cent left with at least one A-level, and as many as 45 per cent had three or more. A remarkable improvement in academic output had been achieved in these twenty years.

Improvement of this kind was not paralleled in the state schools. The output of A-levels increased tremendously in absolute terms and considerably in proportionate terms (from 6.1 per cent with one or more A-levels in 1961 to 13.5 per cent in 1981). But there was no matching of the private sector shift towards the achievement of three A-levels.

Table 2. *Achievements of School Leavers by Type of School (percentages)*

	School	1 or more O-levels	5 or more O-levels	1 or more A-levels	3 or more A-levels
1961	Maintained	78.1	72.9	69.0	68.7
	Direct Grant	7.5	9.6	12.4	15.9
	Independent	14.4	17.5	18.6	15.4
	Total	100.0	100.0	100.0	100.0
	(N (000s)	167.5	93.5	50.5	26.0)
1966	Maintained	81.4	76.2	73.8	72.6
	Direct Grant	6.3	8.4	10.5	12.4
	Independent	12.3	15.4	15.7	15.0
	Total	100.0	100.0	100.0	100.0
	(N (000s)	219.4	129.9	85.2	43.2)
1971	Maintained	83.6	78.0	76.3	72.5
	Direct Grant	6.3	8.8	10.1	13.0
	Independent	10.2	13.1	13.7	14.5
	Total	100.1	99.9	100.1	100.0
	(N (000s)	231.8	132.4	102.6	51.4)
1976	Maintained	86.1	78.1	76.6	72.3
	Direct Grant ⎫	13.9	22.0	9.5	12.3
	Independent ⎭			13.9	15.4
	Total	100.0	100.1	100.0	100.0
	(N (000s)	284.8	138.1	112.2	60.0)
1981	Maintained	87.6	79.5	77.0	70.9
	Direct Grant ⎫	12.4	20.5	23.0	29.1
	Independent ⎭				
	Total	100.0	100.0	100.0	100.0
	(N (000s)	333.0	161.0	120.8	68.6)

Source: DES Statistics of Education.

In consequence there was a clear sense in which inequality as between state and private secondary schooling increased over these two decades. The inequality in question is that the chances of emerging with three A-levels from a private school compared with a state school widened between 1961 and 1981. The chances were, of

Table 3.   School Leavers' Achievements at A-Level (percentages)

School	None attempted	Candidates' achievements			Total	
		0	*1,2*	*3+*	*percentage*	*number*
1961						
Maintained	93.1	0.8	3.0	3.1	100.0	(571.2)
Direct Grant	49.7	5.0	15.4	30.0	100.0	(13.8)
Independent	61.0	5.2	19.3	14.5	100.0	(27.8)
Direct Grant and Independent	57.3	5.1	18.0	19.6	100.0	(41.6)
1966						
Maintained	87.8	1.3	5.5	5.4	100.0	(578.0)
Direct Grant	35.4	4.8	24.0	35.9	100.1	(14.9)
Independent	50.1	5.7	22.8	21.4	100.0	(30.3)
Direct Grant and Independent	45.2	5.4	23.2	26.2	100.0	(45.2)
1971						
Maintained	84.3	2.0	7.2	6.5	100.0	(572.0)
Direct Grant	28.4	4.5	23.8	43.4	100.1	(15.4)
Independent	39.8	6.2	25.3	28.6	99.9	(26.0)
Direct Grant and Independent	35.6	5.6	24.7	34.1	100.0	(41.4)
1976						
Maintained	85.2	1.9	6.4	6.5	100.0	(664.5)
Direct Grant	26.9	4.8	21.1	47.1	99.9	(15.7)
Independent	38.5	4.2	23.4	33.9	100.0	(27.2)
Direct Grant and Independent	34.3	4.4	22.6	38.7	100.0	(42.9)
1981						
Maintained	84.6	1.9	6.4	7.1	100.0	(689.9)
Independent	33.0	4.0	17.7	45.3	100.0	(44.1)

Source: DES Statistics of Education.

course, unequal at the earlier date. The point is that, after two decades of clear progress in both sectors, they were more unequal.[17] The inequality in 1961 in terms of odds ratios was 7.6. The odds shortened slightly during the sixties, but by 1981 were distinctly longer than originally.

Inequality, it appears, has been changing its form. The older form was essentially inequality of chances of entry to the sixth form;

thereafter the attrition of working-class pupils was relatively minor. But by 1981 the door of the sixth form had become relatively less important — and indeed the success of the state comprehensives has largely been that of encouraging vastly greater numbers to pass through. The new inequality is that among sixth formers the private schools have forged ahead much faster in their capacity to prepare A-level candidates for high performance in their examinations. The state sector has expanded its sixth form numbers; the private sector has kept its numbers stable and dramatically improved their performance. In the process the selection procedures of the private schools have, we suspect, changed, just as the sharp increase of state school numbers will have changed the kind of children admitted to comprehensive sixth forms.

Is the new pattern of inequality unfair? We must be careful not to make inequality mechanically synonymous with injustice. The evidence we have reviewed in Tables 2, 3 and 4 on increasing inequality of outcome between state and private schools is descriptive not explanatory. It tells us what *certificates* have been acquired by the children who have passed through the two sectors. Only when we know why acquisition has been unequal can we determine whether there has been injustice.

The obvious method is to take postulated causes, control for each one statistically, and examine the reduction in inequality that results. In the present case differences between the state and the private schools in their examination successes could be attributed to background factors (social class, measured intelligence, ethnicity, etc.), to length of school career or to within-school factors (teacher quality, staff-pupil ratios, etc.). No data set exists which is wholly adequate to the purpose.[18] Our material from the Oxford Mobility

Table 4. *Chances of Obtaining Three or More A-Levels in State and Private Schools, 1961–81*

School	Percentage of leavers with three or more A-levels				
	1961	1966	1971	1976	1981
State	3.1	5.4	6.5	6.5	7.1
Private (including Direct grant)	19.6	26.2	34.1	38.7	45.3
Odds Ratios	7.6	6.2	7.4	9.1	10.8

Source: Calculated from DES statistics in Table 3 above.

Enquiry does not permit us to look at trends during the 1970s. But we can use it to compare respondents born between 1933 and 1942 (who would have been aged 18 and possibly taking A-levels from 1951 to 1960) with respondents born between 1943 and 1952.

The results shown in Table 5 duplicate the kind of information obtained in Table 3 from the DES statistics, although for somewhat different periods. However, the figures for the 1943–52 cohort, presented in Table 5, are roughly comparable with the 1966 DES statistics (the median year, so to speak, for our cohort), and there is an excellent fit between the two sources. The DES statistics in Table 3 relate to both boys and girls, but the figures for boys alone are very similar; the detailed DES tables (not shown here) show that 12.2 per cent of boys from the state sector and 59.1 per cent from the private sector obtained one or more A-levels, figures which are encouragingly close to those in Table 5 from the 1972 sample survey.

The next step is to see how far these differences between systems can be attributed to differences between pupils, and how far 'school type' actually makes a difference. The method is a series of regression equations in which A-level is regressed on different sets of independent variables. We begin with model A in which A-level is regressed on school type, treated at this stage as a simple dichotomous variable distinguishing the private from the state sector. This simply presents the information of Table 5 in a different way to give a measure of the gross difference between school systems. In model B a set of independent variables is added representing those aspects of family background which we can measure (father's occupation, father's education, housing tenure, domestic amenities, and number of siblings). Finally, in model C we add school leaving age.

Table 6 shows the regression coefficients for the school sector variable in each of these three models. The coefficient in model A shows the gross difference between sectors in their number of pupils

Table 5.   *Percentage Obtaining A-Level*

| | Birth cohort | |
School	1933–42	1943–52
Maintained	5.2	11.5
Private	29.7	52.9
Odds Ratio	7.7	8.6

Source: Oxford Social Mobility Study, 1972.

Table 6. Regression Analysis of State/Private Sector Differences

	Men born 1933–42			Men born 1943–52		
	Model A	Model B	Model C	Model A	Model B	Model C
School Coefficient	0.245	0.104	0.024	0.414	0.190	0.068
Standard Error	0.022	0.023	0.020	0.027	0.029	0.022
Variance Explained	0.064	0.150	0.412	0.094	0.199	0.530
N	1862	1862	1862	2322	2322	2322

Source: Oxford Social Mobility Study, 1972.

obtaining at least one A-level. In model B the coefficient shows the difference between sectors net of the set of background factors employed as independent variables. In other words, it shows how big the differences are controlling for the social background of the pupils in the two sectors. The coefficient in model C shows how big the difference between sectors is net of both background factors and school leaving age. It tells us whether boys of comparable background and years of schooling are more likely to obtain an A-level if they are educated within the private sector.

Beginning with the older cohort, in model A the coefficient for private schooling is 0.245, indicating that an extra 24.5 per cent of pupils in the private sector obtained at least one A-level (as can be verified from Table 5). In model B the value of the coefficient is drastically reduced to 0.104 by the introduction of social background variables into the equation. As we indicated above, there are large differences in the character of the intakes into the two sectors, and these differences account for a large proportion of the difference in examination performance. Model C shows that these remaining differences are largely accounted for by differences in length of school career in the two sectors. So once we control for both school leaving age and social background, the 'school type' coefficient becomes much reduced. Indeed, it is only slightly bigger than its standard error, and we can conclude that the difference between school types in model C is not significant.

Pupils of this 1933–42 birth cohort in the private sector stayed at school longer than those (of comparable social background) in the state sector, and it is to this (and the differences in the character of their intake) that the superior examination performance of the private sector can be ascribed. There is no need to postulate school differences in the form of superior teaching or greater resources, except insofar as these may have encouraged pupils to stay on longer. But once children of this birth cohort stayed on into the sixth form, model C suggests, there were no significant differences remaining in their performance. Within the sixth form the two sectors competed with equal success for A-levels; it was in retaining children beyond the minimum school leaving age that the private sector seems to have had an advantage. It was a crucial advantage, since without access to the sixth form there was little opportunity to obtain A-level. We must also remember that non-experimental data of the type we have used here cannot show that longer school careers of private schoolboys were caused by any particular 'retentive capacity' which the private school possessed: it could equally be due to some unmeasured attribute of the parents, such as greater wealth or educational ambition.

For the younger cohort (born 1943–52) there is a different story. The coefficients in models A, B, and C are all increased, and in model C in particular the 'school' coefficient is much larger than its standard error and cannot be dismissed as insignificant. Here again is evidence of an increasing differentiation between the sectors, and one that now seems to persist into the sixth form. In the 1960s, it appears, not only did private schools recruit children from more advantaged backgrounds and see a larger proportion of comparably advantaged children enter the sixth form, but they were also more likely to see their sixth formers obtain an A-level pass than their contemporaries in the state sector. The difference in this net success rate is, to be sure, relatively small compared with the gross difference shown in model A, but its presence does suggest that private education conferred some, albeit small, educational advantage on those fortunate enough, or affluent enough, to receive it.

We have checked these results by carrying out a somewhat more detailed analysis of differences between schools, replacing the simple private/state dichotomy by a division into each of the main school types — grammar, technical, secondary modern, comprehensive, direct grant and independent (distinguishing these into those belonging to the HMC and those excluded).[19] The point is that each of these two sectors is highly heterogeneous. For example, the highly selective direct grant schools had little in common with the minor independent schools which did not belong to the HMC. We know that pupils' characteristics and fortunes differed at these two types of school, as of course they did within the three components of the tripartite system. We need to check that differences within sectors have not confused our picture of differences between sectors.

This more refined analysis of school differences is set out in Table 7. The results confirm, and indeed strengthen, the earlier analysis of Table 6 as well as demonstrating the diversity within the two sectors. Thus within the older cohort and in terms of overall achievement (represented by model A), the grammar schools fared approximately as well as the direct grant and minor independent schools, with the major HMC independent schools in the lead, and the non-selective state schools trailing well behind. The same pattern obtains in model B when we control for social background, although the minor independent schools begin to lag behind. But when we add control for school leaving age in model C, none of the school differences that remain is really significant.

Table 7.   Regression Analysis of School Differences

| School | Men born 1933–42 Coefficients | | | | | |
	Model A		Model B		Model C	
HMC	0.430	(0.033)	0.287	(0.036)	−0.028	(0.034)
Direct Grant	0.271	(0.041)	0.193	(0.041)	−0.054	(0.037)
Non-HMC	0.183	(0.032)	0.103	(0.033)	−0.069	(0.029)
Grammar	0.218	(0.014)	0.187	(0.014)	−0.033	(0.015)
Technical	0.013	(0.018)	0.007	(0.017)	−0.062	(0.015)
Comprehensive	−0.002	(0.081)	0.002	(0.080)	−0.028	(0.069)
R^2	0.192		0.232		0.418	
N	1862		1862		1862	

| School | Men born 1943–52 Coefficients | | | | | |
	Model A		Model B		Model C	
HMC	0.645	(0.037)	0.473	(0.039)	0.162	(0.035)
Direct Grant	0.774	(0.045)	0.632	(0.046)	0.273	(0.041)
Non-HMC	0.223	(0.037)	0.090	(0.038)	−0.080	(0.033)
Grammar	0.400	(0.015)	0.347	(0.016)	0.052	(0.016)
Technical	0.130	(0.025)	0.112	(0.025)	−0.045	(0.022)
Comprehensive	0.075	(0.029)	0.065	(0.029)	−0.030	(0.024)
R^2	0.329		0.363		0.545	
N	2322		2322		2322	

Source: Oxford Social Mobility Study, 1972.
Note: Standard errors are given in brackets.

In the younger cohort, however, significant differences are present even in model C. The direct grant schools lead over the HMC schools, with the grammar and non-HMC schools performing distinctly less well. This is an important result. It suggests that the rise in the relative success of the private sector predates comprehensive reorganization. In the period which we are considering, the 1960s, it would still have been the grammar schools which catered for the growing numbers of sixth formers within the state sector, and it was against this competition from grammar schools that the private sector was already beginning to pull ahead.

It must be emphasized, however, that the data with which we have been dealing — the DES statistics and the 1972 social mobility enquiry — simply describe patterns of association. It is the sociological or political commentator who imputes the causal connections and mechanisms, and there are different hypotheses which could all fit the same pattern of association.

One hypothesis which is consistent with the known facts is that the developing superiority of the private sector was due to increasing selectivity. Private sector schools kept their numbers constant despite the overall increase in the size of the school-age population in general and of the sixth form population in particular. Increased selectivity could have enabled these schools to raise their academic entry requirements (and probably did in the case of the direct grant schools), or their fees, or both. Either way, the result may have been to increase the educational potential of their intake in ways which our measures of social background were unable to capture, for example, by increasing the average intelligence of the pupils or the educational ambition of their parents. If this story is correct, the 'school effects' which we discovered in the younger cohort are merely the product of unmeasured 'home background' or 'intake' effects. We could not conclude that private sector education was giving its children new educational advantages but that private schools were taking a somewhat different group of children who happened already to be more advantaged.

The main rival hypothesis is that genuine 'school effects' emerged. Again, as we have already suggested, the increased competition for university places posed by the enlarged number of state sixth formers may have stimulated responses within the private schools themselves, perhaps taking the form of changed priorities within the school, educational achievement acquiring greater emphasis and resources at the expense of, say, sport. This view has certainly been advanced by the advocates of private schooling. John Rae has descibed a spirited response to the threats represented by the Newsom Commission from the mid-1960s to 1980.[20] Part of the story, to be sure, belongs to social background factors and to the flow of private resources. There was a remarkable buoyancy of better-off families in their capacity and willingness to pay as the inflationary years of the 1970s tripled to an average annual fee in the major boarding schools of £2744 in 1980.[21]

But an important part of the story is of internal reform in the educational and social character of the private schools. While Rae may exaggerate in describing it as a revolution, there have certainly been changes to a remove of considerable distance from the 'muscular Christianity' of the high Victorian boys' boarding schools. John

Dancy led a sexual revolution by admitting girls to Marlborough; academic achievement gained ascendancy over athleticism and philistinism; the classics waned, science and economics waxed; and boys ceased to flog boys.

A third hypothesis is that the emerging superiority of the private sector was an unintended consequence of the enlarged sixth forms which the private schools acquired over this period. We have described how a sixth form career became the norm in independent schools. The numbers admitted remained constant, but more and more pupils stayed on beyond the minimum leaving age, producing larger sixth forms which held a larger proportion of the schools' pupils. This changed balance within the school would have led to some economies of scale in sixth form teaching (apart from any increased per capita resources), and might also have affected the attitudes and motivation of the pupils themselves. Studies of educational achievement too often concentrate on either the influence of home background or of teaching on pupil performance. But the influence of pupils on each other can be extremely important. The educational benefits of having a larger number of pupils all competing for the same goals should not be underestimated. James Coleman's famous study of educational achievement among black and white American children laid emphasis on the depressing effect of concentration of black children. Here we may be seeing the same kind of social force working in the opposite direction. In other words, we might expect a larger sixth form to get better results even if the pupils' background was unchanged and per capita resources remained the same.

These three hypotheses are not in themselves incompatible. All three might contribute to a full explanation, though we are inclined to put most weight on the unmeasured aspects of family background and least on actual school resources. This preference stems from the findings of other research such as Coleman's[22] which has managed to quantify the three possible variables in ways not open to us.

We would stress again that the school differences remaining in model C, even in the younger cohort, are very small. The large gross differences are substantially explained by measured differences in family background, and most of the remaining school differences are mediated by school leaving age. In other words, the main reason why children in the private sector are more likely to obtain A-levels is because they stay on at school longer. If there are genuine 'school effects' they appear in the lengthening of the pupils' school careers, and they consist in ability to retain children beyond the minimum leaving age rather than in improving the results of those who stay on.

The Oxbridge Connection: Fairness As Equal Qualifications

The final step in our comparison brings into view the transition from schools to universities. We first continue the regression analysis reported above (pp. 27–31) but substituting university entrance for A-level completion as the dependent variable. The A-level variable is accordingly transferred to the other side of the equation to produce an additional model — model D — in the process designed to assess school effects net of background factors (model B), length of school life (model C), and now obtained at least one A-level (model D). Table 8 shows the outcome.

The overall result is that on these definitions and for both cohorts the gross differences in chances of entering a university for children attending the various types of school are reduced to insignificant 'school effects' when the background, retention, and A-level performances are controlled. The net 'school effects' are negligible. The only exception is that of the direct grant schools in the 1960s (coefficient 0.204). These schools overtook and displaced the HMC schools in the competition for university places in the 1960s, though both these types of school stayed ahead of the grammar schools in the period covered by our two cohorts. Again we have documented inequality (the gross differences in model A), but the question of fairness remains hidden in the interpretation of the social background and longer school life characteristic of the private and state school pupils. The schools as such are largely transmitters of pre-established inequalities, and there remain the alternative hypotheses we have outlined as possible ingredients of an explanation of the different output of different types of school.

We recognize that our evidence is not definitive and that the variables in our regression formulae may be and probably are interactive rather than simply additive. Nevertheless, the interpretation to which we have inclined is supported by, or at least not inconsistent with, the evidence to which we now turn. It concerns the historically close organic connection between the Oxford and Cambridge colleges and the public schools. Earlier in the century these schools dominated admissions to the colleges. For example, of the men entering Oxford as undergraduates in 1938/39, 55.2 per cent

Table 8. Regression Analysis of School Differences in University Entrance

Men born 1933–42
Coefficients

School	Model A		Model B		Model C		Model D	
HMC	0.330	(0.032)	0.183	(0.034)	-0.039	(0.034)	-0.022	(0.028)
Direct Grant	0.178	(0.039)	0.097	(0.039)	-0.077	(0.038)	-0.046	(0.031)
Non-HMC	0.108	(0.031)	0.028	(0.031)	-0.093	(0.030)	-0.053	(0.025)
Grammar	0.187	(0.013)	0.157	(0.013)	0.003	(0.016)	0.022	(0.013)
Technical	0.026	(0.017)	0.019	(0.016)	-0.029	(0.016)	0.007	(0.013)
Comprehensive	-0.004	(0.078)	0.005	(0.076)	-0.017	(0.071)	0.000	(0.058)
R^2	0.141		0.195		0.301		0.526	

Men born 1943–52
Coefficients

School	Model A		Model B		Model C		Model D	
HMC	0.382	(0.032)	0.262	(0.035)	0.118	(0.035)	0.048	(0.032)
Direct Grant	0.587	(0.040)	0.489	(0.041)	0.323	(0.041)	0.204	(0.037)
Non-HMC	0.179	(0.032)	0.087	(0.034)	0.008	(0.033)	0.043	(0.030)
Grammar	0.222	(0.013)	0.187	(0.014)	0.049	(0.017)	0.027	(0.015)
Technical	0.062	(0.022)	0.051	(0.022)	-0.022	(0.022)	-0.002	(0.020)
Comprehensive	0.040	(0.026)	0.033	(0.025)	-0.011	(0.025)	0.002	(0.022)
R^2	0.197		0.224		0.285		0.418	

Source: Oxford Social Mobility Study, 1972
Note: Standard errors are given in brackets.

came from the HMC boarding schools. The direct grant schools contributed 12.6 per cent, and the private sector as a whole 74.6 per cent, leaving only 19.2 per cent for boys from maintained schools in the United Kingdom and a small recruitment from overseas. Among women the private sector was less closely connected but still dominant, 63.9 per cent being recruited from it, 32.6 per cent from the maintained schools, and 3.5 per cent from elsewhere.

The continuing improvement of the state secondary schools after the 1944 Act against the background of increasing pressure towards meritocratic selection led to changes in these proportions. The maintained schools had increased their share by 1965/66 to 40.2 per cent of the men's, and 42.7 per cent of the women's places.[23] The fact that the maintained schools in 1963/64 had produced 64 per cent of the men and 72 per cent of the women who intended going on to the universities in Britain[24] clearly raised the question of how far places in the Oxford and Cambridge colleges were being allocated on merit and how far particularly there was a selective bias in favour of the private sector.

Both the Robbins Committee (with respect to Oxford and Cambridge) and the Franks Commission (with respect to Oxford) concluded from the evidence that the qualifications of men entrants from the maintained schools had been better on average than those of entrants from independent boarding schools.[25] Moreover, the independent boarding schools had provided the lowest proportion of Firsts and the highest proportion of Thirds in degree classification among men entering from the different types of school. The independent day and direct grant schools had contributed the highest proportion of Firsts, and the maintained schools the lowest proportion of Thirds.[26] Thus the traditional public schools were suspect in this crucial test of meritocracy at the time of Anthony Crosland's new initiative in dealing with the public schools question.

We have referred to the response in the schools as described by John Rae. We must also note two relevant subsequent developments in Oxford admissions and degree performance. First, Oxford in the 1970s made dramatic progress towards meritocratic entry as measured by A-level performance. Oxford attracts the aspirations of less than 5 per cent of university applicants. But it admits a high and rising proportion of those with high A-level attainment. The universities collectively admitted 21.4 per cent with AAA, AAB, AAC, or ABB in 1970. The Oxford figure was 58.6 per cent. But in 1980, while the figure for all universities had hardly moved (to 22.5 per cent), the Oxford figure had shot up to 73.5 per cent. Thus

Oxford admissions progressed markedly in the 1970s towards severe selection on academic criteria. Second, in 1983 Oxford appointed a committee on admissions under the chairmanship of Sir Kenneth Dover, yielding new evidence on the relation between type of school of origin and class of degree destination.[27]

In 1982/83, 51 per cent of Oxford admissions were from the maintained schools compared with 40 per cent in the mid-sixties, and a quarter in the 1930s. Was this a trend towards meritocracy? The report of the Dover Committee makes possible some kind of answer for the present day. First, it appears that the high scoring A-level applicants to the British universities as a whole were distributed as shown in Table 9. Thus 33 per cent of the maintained school applicants for university places were 'high flyers' and 36 per cent of the independent school applicants. But if one calculates percentages for the columns instead of the rows, the same figures indicate that 62 per cent of these high flyers are from the maintained schools and as many as 38 per cent from independent schools. This pattern of university application reflects our description of the transformation of the sixth form life of private and state schools.

Nevertheless, if high flying at A-level is taken as the measure of merit then Oxford's progress towards meritocracy is incomplete. Our measure would give it 62 per cent from the maintained sector: it actually took 51 per cent in 1982–83 (and in 1981–82), that is, 11 per cent of the places, if the system were completely meritocratic, were in the event taken from the maintained school high flyers and given to independent school applicants.

Of course, we must be careful not to assume that this outcome necessarily reflects bias in the selection procedure. It could be entirely due to a preference among high flying maintained sector applicants for other universities than Oxford. The Dover figures do not permit

Table 9. *Private and State School Applicants to British Universities with High A-Level Scores, 1982*

	High scoring[1]	All
Maintained	3,610	11,060
Independent	2,260	6,210
Total	5,870	17,270

Source: Dover Report, 1983.
Note: [1]That is, with scores 13–15 at A-level (= AAC or better).

resolution of this question. They do show that in general maintained sector applicants are less likely to put Oxford and Cambridge as their first choice, and that the success rate among those who do apply is markedly less for maintained compared with independent school applicants (31 per cent compared with 42 per cent in 1982–83). But they do not specifically relate A-level scores to applications and admissions.

Without such data it is not possible to assess how much, if at all, Oxford admissions still fall short of perfect meritocracy. However, it appears from the Dover enquiry that, once within the walls of a college, the significance of school background for progress towards a degree disappears. Entrants from the two sectors are scattered in exactly the same pattern between Firsts, Seconds, Thirds or Passes. The differences found by the Franks Commission in the 1960s seem to have disappeared by the 1980s. The private schools do not, in other words, carry a distinctive academic culture into the ancient universities.

The Implications for Policy

In this last section we explore the implications of our analysis for the continuing political dispute. After Newsom, like Fleming, had failed to persuade Parliament, the less complacent and more prescient champions of the private sector recognized that the threat of further reform and possibly abolition remained. Indeed Roy Hattersley renewed it in a candid speech in 1980, Neil Kinnock reiterated it when he in turn became shadow education spokesman, and the Labour Party committed itself to removing the charitable status and tax advantages of private schools as an intermediary step towards outlawing fee paying for full-time private schooling. Meanwhile, the larger and more successful schools of the private sector consolidated their ranks under the increasingly confident banner of 'the independent schools'. There were even those who, like Rae himself, sincerely regretted the introduction of a new assisted places scheme in 1981 by the Thatcher administration. They recognized the vulnerability of the independent schools to charges of social inequality, and they appreciated the resentment likely to be aroused among teachers in the state schools who found themselves creamed of some of their most talented pupils.

What light, then, does our analysis throw on the threats and responses? Our first answer must be that we have *not* unequivocally isolated genuine school effects on A-level performance and university entrance. If we accept the first of our hypotheses, viz. that school differences are largely due to unmeasured family background effects, then school reform would be inappropriate (except in the form of positive discrimination to help children from disadvantaged backgrounds). If schools have no effect, but are merely passive transmitters of parental and individual advantage, reforming them or abolishing the private sector will have no effect apart perhaps from obscuring the true sources of inequality, namely the advantages and disadvantages conferred on children by their place in the social structure. School reform becomes a distraction from the real enemy, social class and the cultural differences which are more or less closely tied to it. This is a lesson which all potential reformers should learn thoroughly. We must be sure that there is a causal mechanism at work if reform is to be effective. Our evidence cannot conclusively demonstrate any such causal mechanism, but it does show that any such school effect, if it does exist, is certainly smaller than the home background effect. Differences between home background, not differences between types of school, are the more important source of educational inequalities whichever of our three hypotheses is preferred.

If our third hypothesis is preferred (the economies of scale of larger sixth forms and the influence which pupils have on each other), the implications for reform must surely be that similar economies of scale should be sought within the state sector, perhaps by encouraging the further growth in sixth form colleges. On grounds of efficiency and optimum use of resources it would seem inappropriate to try to equalize the two sectors by reducing economies of scale in the private sector. On this line of argument, the private sector should be left untouched and reforms, which are not hard to envisage, put in motion to increase the efficiency and hence competitiveness of the state sector. If small sixth forms are a handicap for their members in competition with the private schools, sixth forms should be amalgamated so that educational and social and not only technical economies of scale can be realized.

With respect to our second hypothesis and the resource argument, it is of course consistent with the data to postulate that the school differences shown in models B, C and D are wholly the product of the different resources available to the schools. As we have said, we do not ourselves find it plausible to contend that resources *wholly* account for the differences, but the convinced reformer need not agree with us. We are dealing in plausibilities not certainties when we talk of the causal mechanisms that generate the statistical patterns we have shown.

So let us, for the sake of argument, agree with the convinced reformer that the school differences are wholly the product of unequal resources. We would still have to point out that equalizing resources among schools would not necessarily remove the school differences shown in models B, C and D. The difficulty is that non-experimental data of our sort at best allow us to infer the causal processes that generated the existing differences *within the current system.* But if the system itself is reformed, for example, by equalizing resources, the causal processes may change too. To put the point crudely, if private schools were not allowed to use extra teaching resources to secure educational advantages for their pupils, they might devise other — non-teaching — methods to protect their position, perhaps by exploiting personal connections, voluntary staff, guest speakers and so on, to increase the educational input which their pupils received. In principle, these too could be outlawed, but we suspect that a free society which encourages personal initiative would find it difficult to close all such possible stratagems. In short, a free society is bound to leave many different devices whereby the advantaged can protect their position. If one is outlawed, another can be used in its place. And so, even if the present school differences were wholly caused by unequal resources, equalizing resources might have no effect at all: the differences might persist unaltered but now caused by different devices.

We should add that the same argument applies if the abolitionist line is taken. Even if private schools are outlawed, the privileged social classes which currently use them to give educational advantages to their children may simply use alternative educational devices to secure the same end result. Educational inequality between types of school is a product of the more fundamental inequality between social classes. School reform will be merely a cosmetic exercise if social class differences continue unchallenged.

The case for equalizing resources is more firmly based on the quite different grounds of social divisiveness or fraternity. It is here that a bridge might be built between the abolitionist and the *laissez-faire* camps. The outstanding moderate champion of the independent schools, John Rae, largely concedes the case for equality of resource and is at least sympathetic to arguments from fraternity (especially if they are phrased in the language of patriotism). As he puts it:

... In Britain, as in other countries such as Australia, a flourishing independent sector does exacerbate divisions in society and creates — or at least appears to create — inequality of access to opportunity. There are those who believe that the only solution to these problems in a democracy is for all the maintained schools to reach the high standards that some already achieve, so that parents will no longer wish to spend large sums on private education. I share that view because it seems to me the only one that reconciles the demands of equal opportunity and of liberty.[28]

The reasonable opponent of private schools may readily agree. He may do so without being impressed by any special claim to educational excellence or academic creativity or even commitment to freedom which may be put forward in defence of the independent schools. He may well, for example, view with scepticism the protestations of support for improved standards in state schools by those of whatever party political stripe who send their own children to a private education. He may note that Rae, for all his moderate reasonableness, never seriously discusses the meaning of freedom in this context. He nowhere, for example, recognizes that a socially and academically selective private sector debars the majority of parents from the freedom to bring up their children in daily consort with the full range of other children in their own country.

But none of these reservations is an insuperable barrier to a realistic bargain across the divide between abolition and *laissez-faire*. If the opponent of private education is willing, as well he might be, to concede at least some value to the freedom delivered by market and voluntary organization, the bargain still has to be struck in terms of equality.

Unequal resources is no part of Rae's case for freedom. We doubt that they have much effect on academic performance. Yet the resources *are* unequal as between the public and the private sector. The most obvious inequality in this respect is that of pupil-teacher ratios. In the maintained schools in 1980 they were 16.6 compared with 12.5 in the independent schools. Surely a bargain could be struck in which the material fortunes of the state schools were geared to equality with their private competitors. The formula could be sophisticated. LEAs already have elaborate equations to take into account sixth forms, special educational programmes, boarding and the like. All such relevant elements could be examined, agreed, and applied to yield equal material terms of competition. Few would then oppose the claims of freedom in either sector.

Accord along these lines is worth seeking, and within the horizon of the politically possible. But would it, we may finally ask, dispose definitively of the tension between citizenship and class? We think not. The social roots of inequality lie deep. The right to a fair start for all children implies equality in the conditions of educational opportunity, but while the market exists inequalities will also be generated. And if the market is outlawed, then a black market will appear, as it has in Russia and Eastern Europe, to continue a flourishing, if fugitive, existence. Nevertheless, the bargain we have outlined would crucially shift the balance between two great contending forces towards a more civilized and acceptable consensus in a society which seeks to optimize fairness with freedom.

Notes

1 The most articulate and persuasive advocate of this usage is John Rae (1981) *The Public School Revolution: Britain's Independent Schools 1964–1979*, London, Faber and Faber.

2 The term 'commercial' was suggested by one of us; see HALSEY, A.H. (1981) 'Democracy in education', in *New Society*, 28 May 1981.

3 GLENNESTER, H. and WILSON, G. (1970) *Paying for Private Schools*, London, Allen Lane, pp. 13–17. The figures for 1951, 1978 and 1981 exclude children in nursery and special schools. They are calculated from DES statistics. See also Table 1.

4 MACK, E.J. (1938) *Public Schools and British Opinion 1780–1860*, Matthew, p. xi.

5 BAMFORD, T.W. (1967) *Rise of the Public Schools: A Study of Boys' Public Boarding Schools in England and Wales from 1837 to the Present Day*, London, Nelson, pp. 268 and 269.

6 PUBLIC SCHOOLS COMMISSION (1968) *First Report*, Vol. I, London, HMSO.

7 RAE (1981) *op. cit.*, p. 16.

8 In 1983 there were actually more than 2500 independent schools in Britain with 1352 in membership of ISIS.

9 *Ibid.*, p. 18.

10 This small decline is accounted for wholly by a drop in the number of girls in the private sector; the number of boys actually increased.

11 The slight increase in the private sector's share at 16+ in 1981 may be a further consequence of the stability in their absolute numbers compared with the fall in the overall age-group. It cannot, without independent evidence, be assumed to be a consequence of Conservative policy.

12 PUBLIC SCHOOLS COMMISSION (1968) *First Report*, Vol. I, London, HMSO, p. 59.
13 CROSLAND, C.A.R. (1956) *The Future of Socialism*, London, Jonathan Cape, pp. 260 and 261.
14 PUBLIC SCHOOLS COMMISSION (1968) *First Report*, Vol. I, London, HMSO, p. 220. Mr JOHN VAIZEY, though he signed with the majority, pointed to the evidence that the number of people buying education was steadily declining, while support for maintained schools was rising. He thought that the private sector of education was 'probably less divisive than it once was; it is probably becoming less divisive.' He pointed also to a basic confusion in the thinking of the Commissioners between boarding need and boarding demand, and complained of the tenuous character of the evidence on which the Commission was proposing in effect to use the private schools as boarding institutions for children of all classes rather than for the boys and girls of the well-to-do.
15 See HALSEY, A.H. *et al.* (1980) *Origins and Destinations*, Oxford, Oxford University Press.
16 The DES statistics, in the form in which we need them, go back only to 1961. But the trend is clear. Note that, unlike Table 1, the figures refer to school leavers, not the whole school population.
17 The odds ratio measures the relative chances that pupils entering different types of school will succeed or fail in the competition to achieve three or more A-levels.
18 The National Children's Bureau data on a 1958 birth cohort could yield such an analysis for a single group which entered secondary schools in 1969, but to date they have not been used to compare state and private schools.
19 To represent these seven school types in our regression equations we need six dummy variables. The seventh school type, in our case secondary modern, is constrained to a score of zero on all six dummies. The coefficients in Table 7 thus give the difference between the named school type and the seventh, omitted, one.
20 *Op. cit.*, 1981. For a perspicacious review of the literature on educational change in the public schools see JUDGE, H.G. (1982) 'The English public school: History and society', in *History of Education Quarterly*.
21 A further part of the story was the rise in this service industry of new forms of financial management, appeals to industrial and other sponsors, and in general measures to earn for these schools the label of commercial which their critics would bestow upon them. Still less agreeable features of the same managerial reform were the deliberate employment of public relations consultants to improve their 'image', and ungentlemanly poaching by boys' schools on the sixth form market of their sister institutions.
22 COLEMAN, J.S. (1966) *Equality of Educational Opportunity*, US Government Printing Office.
23 *Report of Commission of Inquiry* (The Franks Commission) (1966) Vol. II, Oxford, Clarendon Press, Tables 31 and 32, p. 47.
24 *Ibid.*, Table 72, p. 86.

A.H. Halsey, A.F. Heath and J.M. Ridge

25 *Ibid.*, p. 88.
26 *Ibid.*, p. 89.
27 *Report of the Committee on Undergraduate Admissions* (1983) Oxford Colleges Admissions Office.
28 RAE (1981) *op. cit.*, p. 181.

The Demand for a Public School Education: A Crisis of Confidence in Comprehensive Schooling?*

Irene Fox, Polytechnic of Central London

In Britain, the private schools in general and the public schools in particular have attracted a level of public debate which is out of all proportion to their numerical significance. This debate extends well beyond educational arguments to include a consideration of the very nature of the society in which schools are to be found.

On the one hand, the private sector of education has been attacked both for creating a class divided society and for reproducing such a society by serving as a mechanism for allocating individuals to top positions within it, allowing a small and controlled amount of upward mobility of new blood which is bound into a unified class able to exercise hegemonic control. As a consequence, the maintained sector is seen to be diminished both materially and educationally. On the other hand, these self-same schools have been staunchly defended for preserving the freedom of choice which is central to the workings of a market economy; for furnishing this economy with a highly educated elite; and for both providing educational standards against which the maintained sector can be measured and upholding the cultural and moral standards of the society.

Earlier proposals to bring the two sectors of education closer together or possibly to integrate them have since yielded to a polarization of the programmes of the two main political parties. The Fleming Committee was established in 1942 by R.A. Butler in order to consider how the public schools could be brought into closer association with the maintained sector of education. It recommended that there should be an annual intake into the boarding

* This paper is based upon the book *Private Schools and Public Issues* to be published by Macmillan Press. The author is grateful to Macmillan for permission to reproduce some of the material in this paper.

schools of at least 25 per cent of assisted pupils from the elementary schools. It was over twenty years later that a Labour government set up the Public Schools Commission 'to advise on the best way of integrating the public schools with the state system to education'. Its first report in 1968 dealt solely with the boarding schools, believed to be the nub of the problem, and recommended that initially half the places in the boarding schools should be made available to assisted pupils who need a boarding education and that this proportion should be gradually increased. Whilst the members of the commission rejected any notion of the abolition or takeover of the schools by the state, they did envisage some changes would be necessary in the organization of the participating schools. The Labour Party's long-standing commitment to weaken the private sector has culminated in the publication of its programme to finally abolish it over a ten-year period.[1] This sector has not remained idle in the face of the growing threats to its very existence. In 1972 it established the Independent Schools Information Service to act as a public relations as well as an information giving body and in 1974 the Independent Schools Joint Council (ISJC), originally Committee, to coordinate the policy of the whole sector. As the Labour Party escalated its threat of abolition, the ISJC became more vigorous in its defence, establishing an action sub-committee to consider and combat these threats. In 1980 the ISJC recommended increased collaboration with the maintained sector.[2] Meanwhile the Conservative Party has remained steadfast in its support of the private sector and its return to office in 1979 succeeded in removing the immediate threat of abolition. The passing of the 1980 Education Act confirmed its belief in parental freedom of choice and the introduction in 1981 of the Assisted Places Scheme has enlarged the number of parents who are able to exercise a realistic choice between two alternative forms of provision. As a result of the establishment of 5500 assisted places annually the secondary schools within the private sector, predominantly but not exclusively the more prestigious public schools, have witnessed an increase of the order of 6 per cent in the size of their market without having to yield any of their control over selection procedures or curriculum content. The splintering of the Labour Party with the subsequent loss of part of its 'right wing' to the Social Democrats poses a continuing and more resolute threat to the private sector; the re-election in 1983 with an increased majority of the Thatcher government, clearly committed to a programme of privatization, means that this threat has receded for the immediate future but has not been totally removed.

With the battle lines clearly drawn between the opposing factions, there is one interest group whose members have used the market as a means of expressing their own views, the parents who have turned their backs on the educational provisions of the maintained sector and have chosen to buy their children's education but have largely remained silent about their reasons for doing so. This silence has not precluded claims being made on their behalf as to their motives for using the private sector. Eighteen years separate 1964 when Glennerster and Pryke, in discussing access to top positions, wrote that 'parents who pay high fees to send their children to these schools obviously believe that they are important (in obtaining top positions) or they would not waste their money'[3] and 1982 when Hoggart told the North of England Education Conference that 'this education is so expensive that parents must see it as having long term value rather than being concerned with the niceties of education'[4] and in this time the face of Britain's secondary system of education has changed greatly. The passing of these eighteen years has witnessed the transformation of the infant scheme of comprehensive schooling into a fully fledged system such that the proportion of children in England and Wales who have been educated in comprehensive schools has risen from 10 to 84 per cent. Most of the parents who were choosing private education in 1964 when Glennerster and Pryke were writing were in fact rejecting the tripartite provisions which existed at the time; today's parents are facing an ostensibly different alternative to the private educational market in the guise of the comprehensive schools. Szamuely, writing in the second set of Black Papers published in 1969,[5] predicted that with the abolition of the grammar schools all well-to-do parents would send their children to the private schools and this would in turn lead to demands for their abolition. Yet the belief that both the earlier and the current generation of parents using these schools have their sights firmly set on top positions survives both the passage of time and the transition from selective to essentially comprehensive secondary schooling.

The opportunity to discover why the earlier generation of parents made the decision to educate their children privately has been largely missed. Only Lambert's study of parents choosing a boarding education in the mid-sixties[6] and Marsden's earlier interviews with the parents of both day and boarding pupils[7] stand as testimony of the reasons why parents rejected the tripartite provisions of the state in favour of the private sector.

Education does not take place in a vacuum but is located within wider social space — a society which has a history, structures, institutions, people, classes and values. As such, the meaning that education has for those who use it (or more accurately for the parents who make choices on behalf of their children) has to be understood within the macro-context within which it is located. Whilst this context is objectively structured, it is subjectively perceived, giving rise to a variety of educational ideologies which contain ideas of the nature of the world in which people will have to live, what makes or constitutes an educated person and hence the kind of educational experience necessary to fit him or her into his world. Each ideology inevitably includes a perception of the relationship between education and work; if the relationship is seen as contiguous, the nature of work and the skills it requires education to develop will be closely defined and consequently a greater degree of emphasis will be placed upon the need for education to meet the technical requirements of work. If, however, work and education are seen as relatively autonomous spheres of life the purpose of education will be defined as the preparation of people for life and developing the powers of the mind. The work of the Oxford Social Mobility Group and of Goldthorpe and Llewellyn in particular,[8] has served to provide a graphic account of the growth of the 'service class' — the class of professional, administrative and managerial employees. This expansion of 'room at the top' has meant that there have been abundant opportunities for upward mobility with the consequent result that in Britain only about a quarter of the men in these top positions have fathers drawn from the same class, fewer in fact than men of proletarian parentage. This upward mobility is the result of the structural changes that have occurred in Britain which have not fundamentally altered the nature of its class structure in the sense that there are few signs of exchange mobility. This relative absence of any downward mobility meant that not only did those with fathers occupying top positions have a high chance of maintaining these positions but a disproportionately high chance of so doing.

In exploring the relationship between education and the macro-social structure there is the temptation which few writers on the subject have resisted, to assume that parents who choose the public schools do so predominantly to advance or to consolidate the position of their sons in a class structure which is conventionally defined in terms of the social and/or technical division of labour, namely ownership of the means of production and occupation. Even if education is not seen by all parents as an important determinant of position within the class structure defined in these terms, it is still assumed that it will be viewed as status-confering. Marsden, in his consideration of why parents paid fees at the beginning of the sixties,[9] examined their motives carefully but nevertheless concluded that 'inevitably, if not always willingly, they were drawn into a web of snobberies and social exclusiveness.' The chance to examine why today's parents are in fact rejecting, in the majority of cases, comprehensive schooling and to compare their reasons for choosing private education with those given by the earlier generation studied by Marsden is afforded by interviews with 190 sets of parents of boys choosing the traditionally independent (as opposed to the now defunct grant-aided) public schools within which to educate their sons. These parents were chosen at random from a stratified sample of these schools and, with the exception of those resident abroad, can be considered to be a random sample of all the parents using the schools. The faith in the randomness of the sample is supported by the fact that only 6 per cent of the sample were non-contactable and only 6 per cent declined to be interviewed, giving a response rate of 88 per cent. The fieldwork was carried out in 1979–80, after the announcement of the intention to introduce the Assisted Places Scheme but before these places had actually been made available and therefore, as access to the schools was largely determined by ability to pay the fees, the parents are by definition occupying positions in the higher echelons of the class structure. Though not primarily the legal owners of the means of production or even the elite as defined by the various elite studies[10] the parents are nevertheless drawn predominantly from the service class; they are the agents of capital who provide its legal owners with the professional and managerial skills necessary to formulate and implement strategic decisions. The parents are recruited from a variety of backgrounds but they share in common the fact that they are clearly beneficiaries of the system of capitalism and are therefore likely to remain loyal to its fundamental tenets which have served them so well.

The use of the ideal-typical 'prestige model' introduced by Bott[11] and developed by Goldthorpe and Lockwood[12] has served as a heuristic device to highlight the way in which essentially 'middle-class' people perceive the class structure as an extended hierarchy of relatively open strata offering ease of access to those seeking individual social mobility. Subsequent empirical attempts to confirm the use of such a model by the middle class(es), notably the study of surburban Liverpool by Roberts and his colleagues[13] and of the business elite by Fidler[14] have only partially succeeded in doing so. Both studies show the variety of models that middle-class people use to make sense of their worlds. Fidler found that only a handful of the business executives whom he interviewed failed to recognize the existence of classes or even of strata, depicting an infinite number of individual differences in terms of money, interests, attitudes, etc. which fail to add up to any recognizable collectivities. The consciousness of these men is that of total freedom of social movement giving rise to the belief in individual and, presumably, parental responsibility of human action. In this they do not differ significantly from about a quarter of those interviewed who either see the class structure in terms of the ladder described by the ideal-typical prestige model or who do recognize the existence of clear boundaries which serve to delineate one class from another but not to create insurmountable barriers which can only be breached by collective class struggle. These boundaries are defined in terms of differences in the earning power, occupations and above all attitudes and education which distinguish the members of one class from those of others, but they are boundaries which can be breached by those who have the motivation and necessary skills to do so. The majority of the remainder of the business elite who do acknowledge the difficulties of achieving individual mobility do so because they believe that there is a clearly identifiable top class, a class which is more likely to be based upon birth and breeding than upon the acquisition of power and wealth. Many believe that this class is shrinking in both size and importance, being associated with the values and style of life of another era when land was a dominant force. As a consequence there is inevitably a recognition of the possibilities, indeed dangers, of downward mobility from this class, but it is not an 'open' class in the sense that people can move into it with equal facility, membership is essentially a matter of birth. Few of those interviewed by Fidler were prepared to identify themselves as a part of this top class, seeing themselves as men who have to work for a living. The parents interviewed in this research, like the members of the business elite, believe that access to the positions which lie below this apex of inherited class position is not restrained by structural forces. Whilst members of both of the samples clearly recognize the opportunities that this openness of access presents, the parents at least believe that there are attendant dangers of downward mobilty. Whilst such a belief is not actually rooted in their experiences, there is, in theory at least, the possibility that with the recent economic changes this could be the case in the future.

In such circumstances, where class position is perceived as individually rather than structurally determined, what do parents believe the public schools can offer which the maintained sector is failing to provide? At the heart of the stereotype of the British public school lie their 'expressive goals', so labelled by Lambert.[15] These are the qualities or attributes which are seen as ends in themselves — the values of behaviour, morals, taste and expression — the goals most frequently mentioned by the headmasters of the public schools used in the research of Lambert and his colleagues. Lambert sums these up as laying stress on character training towards an ideal pattern of moral, religious and cultural ends which put a greater emphasis on serving the community than upon the pursuit of individual success. In 1968 the first report of the Public Schools Commission (the Newsom Report), devoted to a consideration of the boarding public schools, identified the manner in which these traditional values have expanded to embrace but not to be replaced by academic success. Others see the change in more radical terms and Rae has depicted it as an 'academic revolution' initially forced upon the schools by the need to respond to the success of the grammar schools in securing Oxbridge places in the fifties and reinforced by the failure of the comprehensive schools to provide the academic education that the parents require.[16] There are signs that some parents and even headmasters feel that this change has gone too far succeeding in undermining the very ethos of the schools which Lambert has described.

More recently, Scott, in discussing the upper classes in Britain today, identifies the three possible advantages that a public school education can offer to those seeking access to and acceptance by these classes.[17] Undoubtedly there is a need for academic skills, the necessary certificates to prove technical competence but, argues Scott, using data from the Oxford Social Mobility Study, the grammar schools have shown themselves to be fully competent in furnishing their pupils with such skills. Heath, a member of the Oxford Mobility Study Group, has described the grammar schools as 'escalators of upward mobility'.[18] Secondly, there is the importance of promoting cultural integration, ensuring that all those who belong to the upper classes, irrespective of their social origins, share a common set of values and beliefs which in a capitalist society is an ideological commitment to the rights of property and the value of credentials. Scott denies that the public schools do have a monopoly over this function of cultural integration and in this he is supported by an earlier paper by Smith.[19] Smith discusses the manner in which those who were sponsored into the grammar schools were set apart from the multitude and were offered a sense of cultural inclusion with the ruling elite. Thus the third and final advantage that a public school can offer to its pupils, over and above those offered by the grammar schools, is the web of social assets which are believed to be of crucial importance for membership of the upper class: a distinctive style of life and the possibility of forming useful social contacts, which comprise the 'old-boy network'. Smith continues his discussion of the role of the grammar schools by saying that whilst they do offer a sense of cultural inclusion with the ruling elite they simultaneously preserve relational segregation through spatial separation.

How useful is Scott's analysis in explaining the use of the public schools today? The parents interviewed were reluctant to specify the types of jobs that they envisaged, let alone desired, for their sons — vehemently asserting that such ambitions are both unrealistic and futile. In a world which is seen as open to individuals to succeed and to fail according to merit and ambition it is pointless and possibly dangerous to cherish dreams whose translation into reality cannot be ensured. The most that the majority of parents realistically believe they can do is to offer their sons the best opportunity to make what they can of their lives, and a public school education is a part of this offering. Given the perceptions of the nature of the class structure today, fluid in the middle with an upper class which is seen either as non-existent or as closed to upward mobility, it would in turn be unrealistic to believe that many parents are using the public schools to facilitate the entry of their sons into the very top positions in society. Whilst they may wish for such a future for their sons it is much more likely that their immediate concern is to ensure that they offer them the chance to succeed in maintaining current class position in a world which is seen as increasingly competitive and where success is believed to be dependent upon the possession not only of technical skills but also of the appropriate values — ambition, deferred gratification and above all the determination to succeed.

Even if Scott's analysis of the unique role of the public schools, initiation into the 'old-boy network', might have had some validity in the past, it is dated by the fact that the grammar schools with which he is comparing the public schools have virtually ceased to exist. Attempts to monitor the results of comprehensive reorganization are confounded by the fact that education is a service which is provided locally with a consequent lack of unity in its organizing principles and resultant forms of comprehensive school as well as varying rates and patterns of change. Consequently, whilst some local education authorities maintain an element of selection in their secondary provisions, others do not. In general, it would appear that the comprehensive schools have found favour with neither supporters nor opponents; the former are disappointed by their failure to reduce inequality, whilst the latter claim that they have succeeded in lowering the educational standards of this country. The most recent research into the effects of the reorganization of secondary schooling on educational performance is that being carried out by the National Children's Bureau which is monitoring the progress of a group of children born during one week in 1958. Its findings provide little in the way of support for either side of antagonists in the war over comprehensives; its latest report deals with the performance of the children at GCE Ordinary level.[20] Whilst this shows that the total impact of reorganizing secondary schools into comprehensives is minimal, with the possibility that the children of average ability who came from middle-class homes and went to comprehensive schools fared slightly less well than their grammar school educated peers, its value is reduced by the lack of homogeneity which characterizes comprehensive schooling.

Alterations in the institutional characteristics of schooling have undoubtedly been accompanied by more subtle changes in the actual experience of learning. Such changes are not the subject of legislation and documentation in the same way as the reorganization of secondary education, and their identification is dependent upon research, both academic and journalistic, to show the extent to which the recommendations of the Schools Council have actually been implemented. Comprehensive reorganization took many forms and was fuelled by both meritocratic and egalitarian principles, and progressive education, with its emphasis on child-centred-education, seemed to be a necessary accompaniment.[21] At the end of the 1960s what has come to be known as the 'new sociology of education' launched its critical attack upon the 'received' view of what is problematic in education and why working-class children are failing to succeed in middle-class terms. This received view is manifested in the concern to maintain the traditional goal of education, the reproduction of inequality, whilst seeking to broaden the social base of recruitment to unequal positions. By the early 1970s the new sociology was beginning to be introduced into teacher training courses and the combination of progressive methods and social radicalism undoubtedly influenced a number of socially committed teachers. The unique autonomy of Britain's teaching profession ensured that many of those trained in the seventies were able to put their ideas into practice, the most widely publicized example of these and the responses that they evoked being the William Tyndale episode. As with comprehensive reorganization, changes in teaching practice have been welcomed neither by those who support nor by those who oppose them. Members of the Centre for Contemporary Cultural Studies, in describing the failure of the teachers who were trained in the seventies in the new sociology of education to challenge the Fabianism of the reformist left, identify how the combination in their training courses of 'high abstraction and crushing detail, as well as distance from the everyday world of the schools, has served to inoculate teachers against such "experts" with the consequence that the newer forms of socio-educational analysis are no more attractive or accessible to practising teachers....'[22] At the same time the fear that there are many more William Tyndales which have never seen the light of day has provoked a backlash from the media and politicians alike. This has ensured that, unlike the low visibility of the findings of the National Children's Bureau, parents have been drawn into the moral panic about Britain's educational standards. At the same time it is evident that the present Conservative government is pursuing the policy initiated by its Labour predecessor of taking increasing control over what is happening in the classroom. Superimposed upon this essentially right-of-centre critique of the content of state educational provision is the growing uncertainty about the very future of this sector as the Thatcher government looks increasingly to the private sector for educational provision.

Although only a third of the parents interviewed actually expressed direct criticism of the provisions of the maintained sector, the use of the private alternative could be construed as a condemnation of the provisions and uncertainties which are associated with it. With so many question marks hanging over the maintained sector it would be surprising if some of the parents who can afford to do so did not play safe and purchase an education whose short-term future at least seems secure and whose methods and environment have an air of familiarity. About half of the parents were themselves educated within the maintained sector, but in the vast majority of cases they received a grammar school education whose similarity to that provided by the private schools has already been discussed. There are several flaws in the argument that parents are totally isolated from and ignorant of contemporary state provision as a result of their own educational experiences and that their rejection of state secondary education is dependent upon the media and the politicians for an account of what is actually taking place, an account which they then use to reject the provisions of the state in favour of the private alternative. The majority, if not all, of the parents share a variety of 'experiences' of state education which serve to mediate their second-hand, received knowledge of it. The most far removed of such experiences is that of being an employer of those who have been educated by the state. It is paradoxical that it is one of the few fathers who was himself educated in a secondary modern school who should have concluded, in discussing the employees in the garage that he owns, that: 'the state is a waste of time — they come out at sixteen as complete duffers.' For the majority, the experiences are more immediate than merely being the employers of state educated labour. Most of the parents have friends and relatives who have recently made use of the maintained sector for the education of their children and three-quarters of them have had direct contact, using it for the whole or part of the education of some or all of their own children. A quarter of the parents have actually had at least one child in the secondary schools which they are now rejecting, and an additional 50 per cent have made use of the primary schools, an experience which may have affected some of them in their choice of secondary school. Some parents may have used the primary school as a pre-preparatory school with their children destined for the private sector regardless, whilst others have genuinely turned to the public schools only after their disappointment with what they found in the primary school. The option of turning to the public schools at a relatively late stage without the preparation implied by the term 'preparatory school' is being made increasingly available as a result of the private sector's growing flexibility in taking children at the age of 11, either re-cruiting them into the last two years of their preparatory depart-ments or opening up such departments for this specific purpose. At the other extreme there are very few families (7 per cent) who have had no recent contact with the maintained sector either through their own children or through those of their friends and relatives and who could therefore justifiably be said to be largely ignorant of what is taking place.

The reasons that parents actually give for choosing a public school education for their sons are many and varied and are presented at different levels of abstraction which range from 'doing one's best' to the specifics of 'better facilities'. It would be wrong to assume that choosing this education necessarily involves conscious rejection of the state alternative, for there are some parents who are merely following family tradition and others who have a blind faith in the powers of the public schools. To introduce the distinction between the parents of day boys, just under half of the total interviewed, and those of boarders is both helpful and confusing. It is to the boarding schools that much of the literature on the subject has been devoted and to which the label 'public school' has been most frequently attached. Public day schools do to some extent model themselves on their boarding counterparts but it is the boarding which enables the schools to attempt a more complete control of their pupils' lives and minds in the pursuit of their ends. Although parents of boarders and of day boys are drawn from similar occupations and share the same perceptions of the class structure, there are undoubtedly differences between the two sets which are largely the result of their own different experiences. The parents of boarders are stable as opposed to mobile members of the service class and they are more likely to have spent the major part of their school lives in the private sector, to have friends and relatives who are educating their children in a like manner and, in the case of the fathers at least, to have experienced some boarding education. Therefore, they bring with them a predisposition towards boarding, a belief that it is good for the child to be away from home, which necessitates good financial or other reasons to deny. Marsden virtually discounts any other motive for using the private schools, believing that the parents who take the decision to board their sons do so early and are primarily concerned with boarding, believing in the discipline and independence (from the mothers) that this form of education has to offer.[23] The parents he interviewed gave little thought to the state alternative, and he found that less than 50 per cent of the boarders had sat the 11+ examination. Some twenty years later it is amongst the parents of the boarders that one is more likely to find the small number of those who give tradition as an important part of their reason for making this particular choice — those who have either never given a serious thought to the state alternative who Marsden believes typify the majority of boarders or who, after seriously doing so, come to the conclusion reached by this mother: 'I have no choice in the matter — I am programmed to choose private schools.' Today parents such as these are the exception; overall parents of boarders are surprisingly similar to those of day boys. Parents do not inevitably reproduce their own experiences in those of their children. Thus about a third of the fathers who have themselves boarded are not boarding their sons; nor are the boarding schools dependent upon parents who have themselves experienced boarding, or even a private education, to supply their future generations of pupils, for 43 per cent of the boarders have parents who jointly have no experience of boarding. A few of both sets of parents display what can best be described as a blind faith in the schools, believing that they are doing what is best for their sons by sending them to schools which offer every single advantage: 'Why use furnished digs if you can afford a five star hotel' is how one father explained his decision. But for the majority of day and boarding parents alike the decision to use a public school is a carefully considered one — carefully considered in the light of how the world looks to them. The two sets of parents differ in as much as the boarding parents are clearer about what they believe to be the specific advantages of a public school education, giving on average fewer reasons than their day counterparts for choosing it. This is partially reflected in the difference between their main reasons for doing so, but they display a remarkable similarity in the qualities that they seek, manifesting their common class position and shared view of the world and largely obscuring the variation in their social and educational origins. For parents of boarders, boarding is not a primary consideration, fewer than 10 per cent of them give the need or desire for a boarding education as the sole or even main reason for choosing a public school; the majority believe that there are benefits to be gained from boarding but these are in addition to the other benefits listed by the day parents and not an alternative to them. If for some reason a boarding education were not available, most of these parents would substitute a day education, as indeed is already the case amongst some of the day parents who would have preferred a boarding school. It is thus that the same two advantages that the public schools are believed to have over the state secondary schools are mentioned most frequently by both sets of parents — the ability to produce better academic results and to develop the character by instilling discipline.

Academic results are essentially about examination perform-ance, doing well at GCE O-levels and A-levels and above all gaining entrance to the universities and the professions. It is in this sense that the 'academic revolution' referred to by Rae[24] is fuelled by parents who can no longer turn to the grammar schools to ensure that such results are achieved. Marsden may well have been correct when he concluded at the beginning of the sixties that whilst academic results were important to the parents using the day schools they were not the exclusive or the main reason for their use, but by the eighties the situation has changed dramatically.

The search for development of character through discipline bears little resemblance, in the majority of cases, to the service to the community that Lambert sees as central to the public school ethos.[25] What parents require of the schools is that they impose discipline upon the children, teaching them what is right and wrong, to dress properly and ultimately to develop a tidy mind and self-discipline in order that they can learn to live in a world which has rules. Preparation for leadership and the development of a sense of responsibility are mentioned by very few of the parents. Significantly more of the day parents mentioned the importance of academic results and an equal proportion of both, that of character and discipline, but it is in the attempt to determine the predominant motives for using the schools that the two sets of parents are found to differ slightly. In addition to those who use the boarding schools primarily for their boarding facility, and those who see private education in general and boarding in particular as a part of their own sub-culture (the traditionalists), more of the boarding than the day parents do stress the importance of character and discipline as a single advantage without adding it to the other benefits to be derived from a public school education. Nevertheless, many parents, day and boarders alike, see academic success and a disciplined person as complementary rather than as alternatives. These are the qualities that parents believe their sons need to possess if they are to succeed in a world hallmarked by economic recession and a corresponding contraction in employment opportunities. It is in this sense that both can be understood as important determinants of individual success, getting on in the world, the single most important motive of both sets of parents for rejecting the maintained sector and its provisions. As one father (himself educated at a well-known boarding school and now the financial director of a multinational company having had to liquidate the family business that he inherited and only able to afford a day education for his children) put it: 'We are all anxious about our children and ninety-nine per cent of us do not have a business to pass on.'

Looking to the schools to provide their children with these qualities is not an abdication of responsibility on the part of the parents but is viewed by them as entering into a partnership between home and school where the values of the two institutions can be assumed to be in harmony rather than in competition. Even the parents using the boarding schools stressed the importance of, and succeed in maintaining, a high level of regular contact with their sons. The choice of a particular school was primarily determined by its ease of access in order to facilitate the frequent visits to the school that the parents make as well as the possibility of bringing the boys home as frequently as possible.

Allied to the qualities of academic success and the ability to accept discipline, necessitated by occupational success, is the importance of confidence and independence; some parents believe that in addition to the possession of the necessary qualities and skills to compete in the market place it is important to believe in oneself and to have the ability to convince others of one's worth. It is the parents who are not members of the service class, the petit bourgeoisie, who are the most likely to be looking to the schools to provide this self-confidence. It is interesting to note that those who have been mobile into the service class are hardly more likely than its stable members to look to the schools for this — success, however it is achieved, appears to breed its own confidence.

Some parents provide more details than others of how they believe the schools come to achieve the desired results. In particular, many emphasize the attention that is given to the individual child not only as a result of smaller classes but because of the deliberate policy to treat the child as an individual, paying specific attention to his own needs and encouraging him to progress at his own pace rather than at that of the group. Composed of a higher proportion of those who have been state educated, parents of day boys concern themselves to a greater extent with how the desired results are achieved and in particular they attach more importance to actual teaching methods; the parents of boarders are more likely, probably as a result of their greater familiarity with this form of education, to put their trust in the schools and not to concern themselves to such an extent with the detail of their day-to-day organization.

Few parents directly mention the importance of the social contacts which Scott identifies as the crucial element of a public school education.[26] Such concern as is expressed about the social characteristics of the boys whom their sons are likely to meet at the schools is more to do with allaying fears of them being pulled down than with ambition for them to climb up. The day parents, in particular those living in or near the 'inner-city', are worried about bullying and about the possibility of their sons getting in with a 'bad crowd'. (It is difficult to ignore the father who sent his son away to board for fear that he should become part of the local 'ear-ring wearing crowd' and not to associate him with the father whose son had been expelled for taking drugs.)

The overriding concern of these parents to secure their sons' positions in the world must not be allowed to obscure the fact that education and work are not always viewed as intimately bound together. Even some of the parents who stress the importance of academic results do not believe that they are all that matters in life; the opportunity of a fuller and broader education that these schools are believed to offer is valued by day and boarding parents alike. Many view the maintained schools as nine-to-five institutions, leaving the pupils to pursue their own interests outside this period. The public schools, by contrast, are seen as providing their pupils with the opportunity to sample many different activities, an opportunity which can only be gained with great difficulty elsewhere. The experiences gained as a result can be interpreted as having both intrinsic and instrumental qualities, for whilst they are undoubtedly seen by a few parents as an early socialization into the lifestyle of the upper classes, for the majority this fuller education is a concern with the quality and enjoyment of life that is far removed from the issue of social class and social control.

If the parents' motives for using a public school are to be construed as an initiation into the old-boy network this will have to be done out of their desire to prepare them for a lifestyle which can more appropriately be described as bourgeois than upper-class, for the majority of parents who are paying for their sons to be public school educated are paying to keep them in an environment which they can themselves recognize and whose main tenets — discipline, academic standards and indeed what actually counts as educational knowledge — they value and believe that future employers still count as important.

An examination of the crisis of confidence in the comprehensive schools cannot be confined to an analysis of parents' concern and ambition for their own children. No doubt many parents would be surprised to learn of the translation of their seemingly legitimate desire to do their best for their children into procuring advantage for them at the expense of others, but it is the extent to which parents are seen as attempting and succeeding in doing just this that has informed much of the debate about the role of the public schools. But the social and political significance of the schools runs deeper than their use as a tool in the competitive struggle between classes or class factions. The real significance of the public schools to non-Marxists and Marxists alike lies in the manner in which they allegedly play a major role in keeping alive and legitimating the ideology of class. Rubenstein has claimed that 'to take a small group of the wealthy and to educate them separately from the rest of society is to assure the continuation of a class-ridden society such as Britain.'[27] Hoare highlights the manner in which the schools are 'the key element in the formation and continued pre-eminence of the hegemonic class ... and infect the maintained sector with their values.'[28] It is in this sense that the crisis of confidence in the comprehensives can be understood as a concern about the challenge that they represent to the dominant values reproduced by the public schools and the now virtually extinct grammar schools.

The disappearance of the grammar schools and the continued existence of a private sector alongside a maintained sector which is organized on non-selective principles serves to polarize the experiences of those who use the two sectors of education. Abolition of the private sector, in line with the intentions of the Labour Party, would largely succeed in eliminating the fount of hegemonic control but would also serve as an incentive for the parents to increase their commitment to state provision and to act as a powerful pressure group; it has always been the case that those who design and administer the public system of education rarely use it. The parents interviewed in this research are overwhelmingly against abolition, denying their ability to exercise the degree of control over the maintained sector necessitated by their desire to preserve the core values of its private counterpart. They believe that to remove the alternative provided by the private sector would both be a denial of the freedom that is central to capitalism and succeed in finally removing the high academic standards that began with the disappearance of the grammar schools. Thus they feel that it is only through institutional segregation that they can continue to exert any control over the education that their children receive, and they appear to have largely abdicated their collective responsibility for the maintained sector. Even the minority who recognize the inequities of two separate systems of education and the denial of freedom of choice to the majority believe that the elimination of the private sector should come about as the result of market rather than political forces.

It is in this context that the provision of assisted places and the possible introduction of the voucher scheme should be welcomed by parents. In addition to ensuring the short-term political future of the private sector, such schemes help it to overcome the financial and demographic threats that it faces and thereby contribute to the survival of a form of education whose core values the parents have wholeheartedly endorsed. Simultaneously, however, by extending the opportunities and advantages offered by a private education to those who could not otherwise afford it, the Assisted Places Scheme effectively increases competition for access to privilege; if the number of places in the schools remains the same, the competition is over access to such an education; if they are increased, the arena of competition shifts to access to jobs. Any plans to introduce a system of vouchers which could be used partly to meet the cost of a private education would only magnify the scale of the competition. The contradiction, between extending opportunities and restricting privilege to a few, that is inherent in the Assisted Places Scheme is reflected in parents' collective ambivalence towards its introduction. Whilst the majority of parents are in favour of the scheme, believing that the extension of the educational benefits offered by the schools will help more children to take advantage of the opportunities to be upwardly mobile that society offers, the scheme did not find the wholehearted, unequivocal support that one would expect from parents who are concerned about standards in the maintained sector. Having already expressed their views about the need to prevent abolition and the difficulties of exercising control over standards in a collectively provided service, many of the parents who opposed or were ambivalent towards the Assisted Places Scheme felt that the extra resources would be better spent on improving the provisions of the maintained sector. Similarly, some of the parents feared that, despite their avowed belief in the openness of our society, the discontinuities between the culture of the schools and of the home would be too great for those children who are intended to benefit from the scheme.

Thus the crisis of confidence in the comprehensive system of education has to be understood primarily as a crisis of confidence in its ability to ensure that in a world which is seen as increasingly competitive the advantages afforded to middle-class children by the grammar schools can continue in a system of education which has changed in terms of both organization and content. But above all the use of the public schools is a crisis of confidence in the parents' own ability to secure control over a system of education which is governed by political rather than market forces.

Notes

1 LABOUR PARTY (1981) *A Plan for Private Schools*, London TUC-Labour Party Liaison Committee.
2 INDEPENDENT SCHOOLS JOINT COUNCIL (1980) *The Case for Collaboration*, London, Independent Schools Information Service.
3 GLENNERSTER, H. and PRYKE, R. (1964) *The Public Schools*, London, Fabian Society.
4 HOGGART, R. (1982) Address to the North of England Education Conference, 5 January.
5 SZAMUELY, T. (1969) 'Russia and Britain comprehensive inequality', in

Cox, C.B. and Dyson, A. (Eds) *The Black Papers on Education 1–3*, London Davis-Poynter.

6 Lambert, R. (1975) *The Chance of a Lifetime? A Study of Boarding Education*, London, Weidenfeld and Nicolson.

7 Marsden, D. (1962) 'Why do parents pay fees?', *Where?* 10, pp. 19–21.

8 Goldthorpe, J. and Llewellyn, C. (1977) 'Trends in class mobility' in Goldthorpe, J. *Social Mobility and Class Structure in Modern Britain*, Oxford, Clarendon Press.

9 Marsden (1962) *op. cit.*

10 For example, Boyd, D. (1973) *Elites and Their Education*, Windsor, National Foundation for Educational Research; Giddens, A. and Stanworth, P. (Eds) (1974) *Elites and Power in British Society*, Cambridge, Cambridge University Press.

11 Bott, E. (1957) *Family and Social Network*, London, Tavistock.

12 Goldthorpe, J. and Lockwood, D. (1963) 'Affluence and the British class structure', *Sociological Review*, 11, pp. 133–63.

13 Roberts, K. *et al.* (1977) *The Fragmentary Class Structure*, London, Heinemann.

14 Fidler, J. (1981) *The British Business Elite: Its Attitudes to Class, Status and Power*, London, Routledge and Kegan Paul.

15 Lambert (1975) *op. cit.*

16 Rae, J. (1981) *The Public School Revolution: Britain's Independent Schools 1964–1979*, London, Faber and Faber.

17 Scott, J. (1982) *The Upper Classes: Property and Privilege in Britain*, London, Macmillan Press.

18 Heath, A. (1981) 'What difference does the old school tie make now?', *New Society*, 56, 970, pp. 472–4.

19 Smith, D. (1976) 'Codes, paradigms and folk norms: An approach to educational change with particular reference to the work of Basil Bernstein', *Sociology*, 10, 1, pp. 1–9.

20 Steedman, J. (1983) *Examination Results in Selective and Nonselective Schools*, London, National Children's Bureau.

21 See Jones, K. (1983) *Beyond Progressive Education*, London, Macmillan Press for a fuller account.

22 Centre for Contemporary Cultural Studies (1981) *Unpopular Education: Schooling and Social Democracy since 1944*, London, Hutchinson.

23 Marsden (1962) *op. cit.*

24 Rae (1981) *op. cit.*

25 Lambert (1975) *op. cit.* A fuller account of the variety of motives that parents have for using public schools is contained in Chapter 6 of the author's book *Private Schools and Public Issues* to be published by Macmillan, in 1984.

26 Scott (1982) *op. cit.*

27 Rubenstein, D. (1970) 'The public schools', in Rubenstein, D. and Stoneman, C. (Eds), *Education for Democracy*, Harmondsworth, Penguin.

28 Hoare, Q. (1975) 'Education: Programme v. men', *New Left Review*, 32, pp. 32.

Debs, Dollies, Swots and Weeds: Classroom Styles at St Luke's

Sara Delamont, University College, Cardiff

Mrs Milton: While we are on the subject, we might just discuss what makes a novel, a great novel?

Jill: I think it's about people with emotional feelings — about human emotion.

Alexandra: I don't think a novel needs to be emotional, it's just a story.

Mrs M: Mmmmmm ... What do you think, Rosalind?

Rosalind: I agree with Alexandra. It's just a story.

Mrs M: How about you, Jackie?

Jackie: A novel is fiction which I read in my spare time.

Barbara: It's a sloppy, wishy-washy thing.

Mrs M: What makes a great novel?

Penny: A classic story.

Evelyn: There are two sorts of novel — classic ones and popular ones, the ... modern ones ... the ones people read to relax, that won't last.

Henrietta: Like detective stories or James Bond.

Mrs M: What separates the two?

Evelyn: I think it's a matter of who wrote them — how well written they are.

Mrs M: Anything else? Yes Selina?

Selina: A classic novel is old, it's lasted ... the sort of book that everyone reads.

Henrietta: It's a book which is timeless ... it goes on and on.

Mrs M: Can you have a modern classic?

Charmian: (very languidly) No you can't — it's got to last before it can be a classic.

Evelyn: That's not true — all the classics were modern in their day.

Henrietta: I think it depends how memorable the book is.

This discussion took place between a class of 15-year-old girls and their English teacher at St Luke's School for Girls.[1] Mrs Milton had stopped the previous discussion of *Pride and Prejudice* and moved on to the wider question of 'the novel'. Most of the pupils who contribute to the discussion come from one friendship group which is a central focus of this paper. The rest of the third year girls[2] were divided into five groups, and these are also described. The aim of the paper is to show how peer groups, with different leisure interests and attitudes to school, have distinctive patterns of participation in classroom discourse. These patterns are demonstrated and analyzed, using data from both ethnographic field-notes and a pre-specified coding schedule.[3] It is argued that these data on classroom participation provide insight into the role played by 'cultural capital' (Bourdieu, 1977) in the reproduction of Scottish elites.

The paper opens with a brief account of the school, St Luke's, where the research was conducted. The cliques which existed in the third year are described, and their classroom behaviour differentiated. Finally, the implications of these data for testing Bourdieu's ideas on cultural capital are examined.

St Luke's School

St Luke's is a public school for girls situated in a Scottish city.[4] It takes day girls from kindergarten to sixth year, and some boarders from the age of 9. It was founded in 1888 by a group of feminist educational pioneers (Delamont, 1978). The establishment of St Luke's was part of a wider campaign to improve women's education in Scotland. Since the 1880s it has been both academically and socially exclusive, while today the school prospectus announces that the school's aims are 'providing a liberal education and maintaining the pioneering spirit of its founders'. The links with the nineteenth-century feminists were still visible in 1973, when the school magazine carried the obituary of one of the first pupils to enrol at St Luke's in 1888. She had just died at the age of 95, after graduating in medicine at the turn of the century and spending a lifetime practising *zenana* medicine in India (Scharlieb, 1924).

The socially exclusive nature of St Luke's is exemplified by my particular study population: the forty-three girls who made up the third year in 1970 all had fathers with occupations in Social Class 1. The school is popular with senior staff at the local university, with professional families, and with business men. The social exclusiveness is related to the costs of St Luke's. In 1971 it cost £95 a term for a day girl in the secondary school and £52 in the kindergarten. Boarding fees were an additional £100 per term. These fees included the loan of textbooks, but not stationery or 'extras'. The fees for extras are shown in Table 1, and their nature is, in itself, revealing about the school. Table 1 shows a great deal of musical activity, and that while needlework is available, cookery is not. Unlike many girls' public schools (Dyhouse, 1977) St Luke's has never given in to pressure to train 'good wives and little mothers'. The high academic standards are maintained by admitting only girls who pass a difficult entrance exam. All but one of my study group had IQs of over 110. The public examination results discussed below show the standards obtained by St Luke's.

There are 450 girls in the secondary school, arranged in parallel classes. That is, each year is divided into two or three forms of mixed ability, and subjects are taught in sets. My sample year had two sets ('A' and 'B') for maths, English, French, biology, Latin, history and geography (the core curriculum of the third year) and one group for physics, chemistry, Greek, German, Spanish and needlework. Other subjects, such as PE and RE, are taught in mixed ability groups. Pupils are steered by the school towards their subject choices, with strong encouragement for taking sciences and Latin at least to O-grade. All pupils are expected to sit at least six subjects at O-grade, and the majority stay on to 17 and take Highers.[5]

The school buildings represent various architectural styles from 1914 onwards, and are set on a bleak hilltop in a suburb which

Table 1.   *Fees per Term for Extras*

	£
Piano (lower school)	8.40
(upper school)	11.55
Recorder	.50
Other Instruments	7.35
Orchestra Training	.50
Fencing	2.10
Riding	7.35
Speech Training	3.15
Swimming	1.05
Fabric Fee	3.15

contains several other fee-paying schools, including 'Dr Knox's Academy for Boys', the school regarded as its 'brother' establishment. There is a House system, of five houses called after famous Scottish castles: Traquair, Craigievar, Bothwell, Tantallon and Dunvegan. All boarders are part of Tantallon, which wins all the inter-house sports trophies due to the boarders being keener on athletics and having longer to practise together. The school plays lacrosse and hockey in the winter, tennis in the summer, and fencing, squash and badminton. St Luke's girls are a source of recruitment for the Scottish girls' fencing team, one of my sample captaining it in her sixth year.

The staff of St Luke's is divided into primary and secondary teachers. There are thirty-one full- and part-time academic secondary staff plus the headmistress, Mrs Michaels. Ten further teachers teach the 'non-academic' subjects, such as PE, art and music. All these permanent teachers are women. Thirteen peripatetic music teachers visit St Luke's, covering all the brass and woodwind instruments as well as strings and piano. Some of these peripatetics are men; all are marginal to the everyday life of the place. Of the thirty-one academic staff all but one have honours degrees and three (including Mrs Michaels) have doctorates. Seventeen of the academic staff are, or have been, married. The longest serving secondary teacher has been there twenty-four years, while three of the staff joined in the 1969/70 session. The average length of service for academic teachers was 7.8 years and for non-graduates 5.6. Single teachers have a longer average record of employment (9.9 years) than the married (5.6). These findings are similar to those of Wober (1971) in English girls' boarding schools. Thirty-one women taught my sample, and twenty-three of them were observed. This covered all the major subjects except the 'A' French set, whose teacher (Miss Paris) refused me access. Further details of the precise numbers of lessons observed and so forth are given below. Teaching at St Luke's presented few discipline problems and, like the other fee-paying girls' schools I have studied, was more concerned with imparting knowledge than keeping order. This contrasts with both fee-paying boys' schools and LEA schools in which I have done observation.

The Girls of St Luke's

My detailed study focused on the 1969–70 third formers. There were forty-three girls in two parallel forms, one-quarter of whom boarded at St Luke's. Twenty-five per cent of these girls had been at the school since the age of 5, and the average length of time there was 6.2 years. Seven of my sample eventually received the Gold Badge awarded to girls whose whole school career has been at St Luke's.

The third year of St Luke's contained six friendship groups which existed inside classrooms, in the school, and in some cases outside it as well. The full data on the discovery and investigation of these groups derived from a triangulated enquiry (Denzin, 1970) which used interviews, an unobtrusive measure (Webb *et al.*, 1966) and observation, and are presented in Delamont (1973). Although there were forty-three girls in the third year, only forty-one were observed. One girl, Una, was away on a skiing course designed to produce the future British women's ski-team, and another, Isabelle, was ill. (Her illness was described to me variously as a 'breakdown' and as *anorexia nervosa*.) Isabelle returned to complete her school career and was a member of a peer group discussed in the paper. Two girls had left the cohort in the previous six months, one (Mandy) to an English girls' boarding school, one kept back to repeat the second year. Two new girls had joined the cohort in 1969/70 — Wendy and Michelle. Forty-four girls appear in the sociometry of the third year, for Mandy was still claimed as a friend by several pupils. There are six cliques, and three relatively isolated individuals. Table 2 shows the members of the six cliques with nicknames as mnemonics. The formation of friendship patterns was partly as a result of school organization, especially the existence of the boarding house and partly voluntary associations among pupils with shared interests and abilities.

Group 1 — The Boarders — consisted of the ten third year girls who lived together in the boarding house. It was relatively self-contained with only four choices crossing its boundary. The boarders were relatively successful academically, and many of them were active in school sports, providing the backbone of several teams. The members of Group 1 were: Janice, Fleur, Eleanor, Jackie, Alexandra, Karen, Mary, Barbara, Esther and Hazel. All were boarders, and all the third year boarders were included in the clique. The internal structure was complex, with many choices inside the boundary.

Three choices which went outside the boarding house were to Group 2. This was the largest group with twelve members and had a clearly distinguishable lifestyle. They called themselves 'grown-up' and were self-consciously involved in an adolescent lifestyle. They dressed fashionably, drank coffee (and perhaps alcohol), smoked cigarettes (and perhaps pot), wore make-up and went around with a

Table 2.   The Friendship Groups at St Luke's

Group 1 — The Boarders	Group 2 — 'Debs and Dollies'
Alexandra	Vanessa
Jackie	Nancy
Barbara	Katherine
Fleur	Lorraine
Eleanor	Yvonne
Janice	Gale
Esther	Louise
Hazel	Tessa
Mary	Zoe
	Monica
	Caitlin
	Olivia

Group 3 — 'Little Women'	Group 4 — 'Proud Riders'
Belinda	Rosalind
Cheryl	Sharon
Lorna	Frances
Geraldine	(Isabelle)

Group 5 — 'Swots and Weeds'	Group 6 — 'Intermediates'
Jill	Angela
Charmian	Selina
Philippa	Clare
Evelyn	
Henrietta	
Penny	
Michelle	
(Mandy)	
	Isolates
	Wendy
	Una
	Deborah

crowd of boys. This was demonstrated during the research when a
large number of this group arrived for their interviews (which were
taking place in the school holidays in a flat in the city centre) with a
group of boys from Dr Knox's. They had all been thrown out of a
coffee bar. Some of the girls in this group used a coffee bar which
was later raided by the drug squad, and Vanessa was eventually
expelled from the school. However, many of the group were
academically ambitious, and were doing well at schoolwork. The
twelve girls in this group were: Tessa, Monica, Caitlin, Katherine,

Olivia, Lorraine, Gale, Yvonne, Louise, Nancy, Vanessa and Zoë. Apart from the links with the boarding house no choices were made to other pupils in the third year. This group, along with the boarders, was the mainstay of the sports team.

Cliques 3 and 4 were both small. Belinda, Geraldine, Cheryl and Lorna made up Group 3. These girls were keen on the Guides, doing relatively poorly at schoolwork; they spent their leisure time in family and church-based activities. Group 4 — Rosalind, Frances, Sharon and Isabelle (the 'anorexic' absentee) — were similar, but could be distinguished by a love of riding. These two groups were not involved in school sport, were doing relatively poorly at their schoolwork, and were not academically ambitious. However, they were not badly behaved and worked hard, so were no trouble to staff.

Group 5 had seven members: Charmian, Jill, Philippa, Penny, Henrietta and Michelle and had included Mandy. This group called themselves 'the clever ones', and Henrietta even said, 'We're the academic set — the intellectuals.' They were all hostile to school games, and had more intellectual leisure pursuits than any other group. Group 5, though regarding themselves as the cleverest pupils were called by Group 2 'the swots and the weeds'. This, though rude, does capture two of their main characteristics — hatred of team games and a devotion to reading and other solitary, intellectual pastimes — archaeology, computing, origami, *petit point*, psychology and music. Equally apt was Henrietta's nickname for Group 2, 'the debs and the dollies'. Group 2 girls were either involved in the lifestyle chronicled in the Scottish *Tatler* (hunt balls and grouse shooting) or in a more teenage lifestyle centred on disco dancing. Very few of the Group 2 girls enjoyed reading, few played an instrument and none belonged to the Guides.

Finally, Group 6 had only three girls — Clare, Selina and Angela, who scored higher academically than any group but 5. These girls were relatively colourless, and had no distinguishing hobbies or lifestyle. Additionally, there were three relatively isolated pupils — Wendy, Una and Deborah — who receive attention later in the paper.

The relative academic standing of each of the six groups is shown in Table 3.[6] A large score is indicative of poor school achievement, and the table shows that Groups 5 and 6 were the most academically successful. The same pattern is apparent from a questionnaire administered about leisure reading. This included a question on how much leisure reading each girl did on a scale from '1'

Table 3.   Academic Scores of Cliques in Descending Order

Cliques	Average score
5	6.7
6	7.6
1	8.8
2	10.6
4	12.3
3	13.0

(considerably more than the average person in my form) to '5' (considerably less than the average person in my form). A mean score was calculated for each group, which gave the results shown in Table 4.

The different lifestyles of the six groups which were apparent at 14 were maintained throughout the rest of their school careers. The girls who stayed at school until 18/19 (predominantly from Groups 1, 2 and 5) showed the same divergence in school involvements as they had in the third year. This can be seen from the school awards, offices and distinctions achieved by the girls. School awards and distinctions can be divided into school offices (prefect, house captain, head girl, etc.); sporting honours (captains and vice-captains of school teams); intellectual offices (president of the school history society, captain of the choir); and awards for social responsibility (running charities, the Duke of Edinburgh's Gold Award). The number of each type of award or office held by girls in each clique is shown in Table 5. This reveals that Group 5 dominated the intellectual activities, while Groups 1 and 2 divided the sporting ones. The Boarders (Group 1) held many school offices, but all groups were involved in that sphere. The predominance of girls from Groups 1 and 2 in sport is evident from team membership as well as captaincy. The sixth year girls who were members of St Luke's first teams are shown in Table 6 with their group membership. (The rest of the team members were in the fifth year in 1973.) Responsibility as house captains and vice-captains was equally divided among the groups.[7]

Academic success was achieved by girls from all groups. To understand the context in which my sample achieved examination success, it is necessary to look at the overall exam results at St Luke's. Girls in my sample were in their sixth year in 1973 and the results obtained by fourth, fifth and sixth year girls that year are presented.

Table 4.   Mean Amount of Reading by Clique

Cliques	Mean reading score
5	1.4
4	2.0
3	2.25
1	2.6
2	2.8
6	No data

Table 5.   Table of School Honours

	Group 5	Group 2	The Rest	Group 1
School Officers (e.g., House Captain)	5	3	3	12
Sports Honours (e.g., Squash Captain)	0	4	0	6
Intellectual Officers (e.g., President of the School History Society)	7	0	2	2
Social Responsibility Awards (e.g., Duke of Edinburgh Award)	2	5	5	1

Table 6.   Membership of School First Teams by Clique, 1973

Girls' names by cliques	Sports				
	Lacrosse (1st XII)	Hockey (1st XI)	Tennis (1st VI)	Badminton and Squash	Fencing
Group 1	Hazel Fleur Mary Jackie Alexandra	Fleur Mary Jackie Alexandra	Fleur Mary Alexandra	Mary Esther	
Group 2	Tessa Monica	Tessa Monica	Tessa		Monica Gale Lorraine

Examination Results, 1973

In the fourth year forty-seven girls took 381 subjects at O-grade and only in ten cases did any mark gained fall below 'C'. In addition, girls in the fifth form and sixth years added twenty-eight more O-grades in sixteen different subjects. The O-grade pass rate was 97 per cent. In the fifth and sixth year there were 234 H-grade passes in seventeen subjects among eighty girls, ninety-one of which were in the 'A' band. This was an H-grade pass rate of 91 per cent. In the sixth year there were thirteen A-level subjects available. Eight girls took three A-levels, eight took two and seven took one. Forty passes were obtained.

The results obtained by my sample, who had taken O-grades in 1971, H-grade in 1972 and further H-grades and/or A-levels in 1973, are shown, by clique, in Table 8. Only Belinda from Group 3, and Frances and Isabelle from Group 4 were still at school after Highers, and all Group 6 had left. Most of the Boarders, all Group 5 and about half of Group 2 were still in school at 18/19. The average number of passes at O-grade, H-grade and at A-level obtained by girls remaining from the three cliques and from the rest, are shown in Table 7. As expected, Group 5 obtained the most exam passes at all levels, but the other girls achieved considerable success.

Thus while the groups differed in their involvement with school activities, they had successful academic careers. The ways in which they participated in classroom learning to achieve these successes are the main focus of this paper. Members of different cliques actually had contrasting styles of classroom participation, related to their perspectives on schoolwork. Before these are presented, a brief

Table 7.   Public Examination Results by Clique (of girls staying till age 18)

	(1971) O-grades	(1972) Highers	(1973) A-levels
Group 5 (swots and weeds)	9.3	5.4	2.6
Group 1 (boarders)	8.6	5.2	1.6
Group 2 (debs and dollies)	8.4	5.1	1
Rest of sixth year	8.4	5.0	1

description of the isolates and the light they throw on the common value system of all the sample is given.

The Isolates

There were three isolates, Wendy, Una and Deborah. Wendy had only been at the school for two terms. She had previously been at another school with Hazel and was still friendly with her in class. However, as a day girl, Wendy was also making friends in Groups 3 and 6. Her isolation was probably temporary. Una — away skiing — was also socially absent. Henrietta said she was a friend but no-one else in thirty-eight interviews mentioned her at all. In contrast, Mandy and Isabelle were mentioned to me, although Mandy had left and Isabelle was away ill. Deborah was actively disliked by everyone in the sample, and indeed served as a *negative* reference point for most pupils. She was stigmatized for two main reasons — over-protective parents and an exaggerated sense of family pride. St Luke's was a school where boasting about one's family's wealth or status was *not* acceptable. Penny summarized the first complaint: 'Mummy won't let her go swimming unless she's there to watch her. . . . I once went to stay with them at their summer house in _____ and she wasn't allowed in the sea. They've got a pool, the sea's too dangerous for darling little Doodles.' (This last comment was uttered in a parody of Deborah's mother's voice.) Jill told me how Deborah was unpopular because: 'She's always going on about the McNamara heritage, and the oar Daddy won at Cambridge.' While Penny and Jilly were both from Group 5, girls in other groups were equally disparaging about Deborah. Sharon (Group 4) said: 'Deborah is completely spoiled — she's not allowed to go out and she doesn't wear make-up. She thinks anyone who wears make-up is stupid. They won't let her ride . . . frightened she'll fall off.' Sharon made this last comment with withering scorn, for she regarded everyone who did not ride as odd, but someone whose parents did not let them experience riding as beyond redemption. Monica (Group 2) told me how Deborah's father had come to collect her from a badminton match and insisted on taking her home even thought it was still in progress. St Luke's had lost and this was blamed on Deborah's leaving. By allowing her father to prevail, she had violated another school norm. Deborah's isolation throws light on the common culture of the other girls, and was linked to a unique pattern of study habits and classroom behaviour (Delamont, 1973). Deborah's parents were the only ones to forbid me to interview their daughter, so that I am unable to present her views on St Luke's, her peers and her ambitions.

Thus in 1970 there were six groups of girls experiencing different academic success, having different leisure activities, and participating diffentially in the sporting, musical and cultural life of the school. The most involved in 'adolescent' lifestyles (Group 2) were *not*, however, failing in their work or lacking in scholastic ambition. The next part of the paper looks at classroom participation.

At Classroom Level

A major part of the research at St Luke's was focused upon teacher-pupil interaction in the classroom, and especially on a search for differences in pupils' patterns of verbal contributions to classroom discourse. The hypothesis was that individual differences in attitudes to schoolwork, and in study habits, would be reflected in their contributions to classroom talk: and that there might be sub-groups of pupils who shared common attitudes of schooling and common patterns of contribution. The academic lessons were therefore observed with this in mind, and, as soon as I had learnt all the girls' names, their classroom contributions were recorded with a coding scheme of my own invention, shown in Table 8 and Figure 1. Where possible a *verbatim* record was also kept, so that some extracts of natural language are available, such as that at the opening of the paper. Table 8 shows all the codings used, and Figure 1 shows them arranged according to their logical structure. The basic distinction operated was between pupil contributions central to the lesson content *as defined by the teacher*, and those tangential to it. Thus if the teacher asked, 'What is the date of the Battle of Waterloo?' a pupil who volunteered the answer '1815' would be coded 'VR', one who said '1814' would be coded 'VW', but one who said 'Mrs Flodden, why did Napoleon decide to fight in Belgium?' would be coded 'QE1'. A girl who asked 'Mrs Flodden, should we be making notes?' would be coded 'QDS(P)'.

Such a coding scheme is open to all the criticisms made of such schedules by Delamont and Hamilton (1984) and others (Walker and Adelman, 1975; Coulthard, 1974; Mehan, 1981; Edwards and Furlong, 1978). However, the data, though rough and ready, are interesting and unique. No other author has presented evidence of

Table 8. Pupil Talk Categories

Code	Explanation
VR	A correct, or at least acceptable answer, produced by a volunteer
VW	An incorrect, or unacceptable answer, produced by a volunteer
VT	A volunteered translation
AR	A correct answer, produced on demand
AW	An incorrect answer, produced on demand
AT	A translation, produced on demand
HUNA	A pupil raises her hand, but is not asked by the teacher
QDSP	A dependence-seeking question, concerning procedure
QDSF	A dependence-seeking question, concerning facts
RNA	A question revealing that a pupil has not been paying attention
QEI	A question asking for extra information
QUIB	A quibble with the teachers' explanations, etc.
VPO	A volunteered personal experience or opinion
APO	A personal experience or opinion produced on demand
ST	A pupil doing seat work indicates that she is stuck
HELP	A teacher gives a pupil doing seat work some individual help
T	Pupil talk taking place, illegally, during lessons
REP	A reprimand (received)

different pupil contribution patterns across the secondary curriculum which can be related to pupils' accounts of how they relate to their schoolwork. Additionally, these data show how Scottish elites are reproduced (Delamont, 1976), throw light on Bernstein's (1975) theories about the 'new middle class', and are relevant to debates about what Bourdieu (1977) means by 'cultural capital'.

Exhaustive detail on classroom life at St Luke's is available in Delamont (1973), The reader sceptical of the approach, or the argument which follows, is referred to that volume. Here the focus is on the sociological importance of the findings.

Classrooms at St Luke's were quiet, orderly and academic places. Most lessons were teacher dominated. The typical forty-minute lesson at St Luke's contains twenty-five minutes of teacher talk and eight of pupil talk. Very little silence occurs, and little time is lost in confusion (about four minutes in forty). The data from the pupil talk system were, effectively, a detailed breakdown of the eight minutes in each lesson when a girl was talking. In an average lesson,

Sara Delamont

Figure 1. *Logical Structure Underlying Pupil Talk Categories*

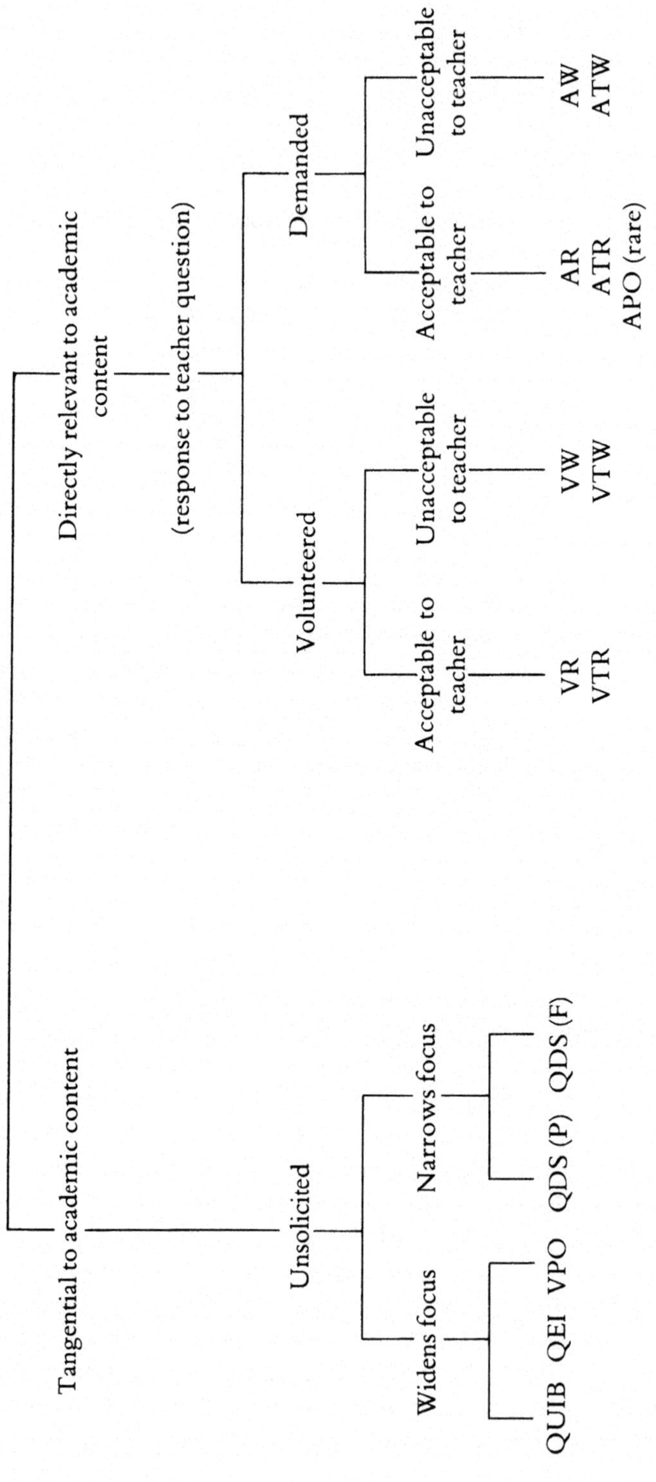

there were twenty-four pupil contributions, approximately fifteen content-oriented and nine tangential. (These findings accord well with other research done in academic secondary classrooms, such as Barnes (1971), Bellack *et al.* (1966) and Smith and Meux (1970).) Teachers varied in the number and type of pupil contributions they received, and pupils varied in the amount and type of contributions offered. For example, the senior classics teacher, Miss Iliad (see Delamont, 1973) received hardly any tangential contributions, while Mrs Milton (quoted at the head of the paper) received many. Similarly, some girls (such as Wendy and Geraldine) hardly ever spoke in class, while others (such as Henrietta and Cheryl) took an active role in the discourse. There are no published studies of this type on pupil contributions, so it is not possible to relate the St Luke's girls to other pupils. It would be interesting to know if the boys studied by Bullivant (1978) in a very academic Jewish school, and the students observed by Larkin (1979) in an elite American high school had similarly varied contribution patterns.

Nearly all pupils made more content-oriented contributions than tangential ones, but there were large differences between the nature of different girls' contributions as well as their volume. There are relationships between the amount of speaking each girl did and her perceptions of what school is for, as well as between the nature of her speech and these perceptions. For example, Hazel (a boarder) saw learning as an essentially passive process. Teachers have knowledge, and the pupil's task is to listen to them. Hazel therefore spoke very little in class, and made few contributions in any category. Another boarder, Alexandra, described her outlook as follows: 'I mean, I'm quite content to take facts', and she too spoke very little. In contrast, most of the girls in Group 5 had an active view of schooling in response to my enquiry about what type of pupil teachers like:

Chairman: 'Popular with teachers? — well — the bright ones to start with — it's awfully difficult to think of what a teacher would like — they're always telling you not to quibble. It depends on the teacher — Mrs. Flodden likes it. If you can produce things about the period you're in — like I once took something in Greek that I wanted translated to Miss Iliad and she — positively *beamed* at me. A great occasion. It depends — I think perhaps enthusiasm's probably the most important thing'.

SD: 'And girls who are unpopular?'

C: 'People who never put up their hands and even try to answer a question.'

This active orientation is carried over into behaviour. The girls in Group 5 spoke more than their classmates, and made more independent contributions than pupils in any other group. My argument is that they saw the creation of school knowledge as a shared activity, in which they had a role to play, and not as a fixed body of material which they merely had to learn, passively. One or two other pupils had similar contribution patterns, but no other group consisted entirely of pupils with a high participation level and many independent contributions. These differences in classroom style at 14 clearly paid off in terms of public exam success, in that Group 5 girls were the outstanding performers in their cohort.

Any explanation of this success is inevitably somewhat speculative. However I wish to argue that Group 5 contained those girls who came from the intelligentsia rather than the entrepreneurial upper-middle class, and that they were the possessors of what Bourdieu has called 'cultural capital'. As I have argued elsewhere (Delamont, 1976), Group 2 girls — the debs and dollies — were from entrepreneurial homes (the old middle class in Bernstein's (1975) terms), and St Luke's was preparing them to take their places in that sector of the Scottish elite. The swots and weeds (Group 5) were representatives of Bernstein's 'new' middle class, and were preparing to enter the intellectual elite of the country. Evidence from the girls' family backgrounds supports this. Girls in Group 5 had parents in higher education or the 'liberal' professions or the civil service; both mothers and fathers were graduates, and all the mothers had careers. Group 2 had no graduate mothers, no parents in higher education or the liberal professions, and most fathers were in industry or were self-employed. For example, both Michelle's parents were university lecturers, while Monica's father manufactured sports equipment and her mother was not employed. Group 1 (the boarders) was an intermediate clique, in that many of the fathers were in 'the professions', but the mothers were not employed. The 'typical' boarder was Barbara, whose father was a doctor in a rural area of Scotland.

The three large groups of girls could be seen to bring differing amounts of cultural capital to the school. St Luke's can be used as a test of the sociology of Pierre Bourdieu. Such a test is badly needed in Britain. Halsey *et al.* (1980) attempted to test some of Bourdieu's ideas on their sample of 10,000 adult males in England and Wales. Hammersley (1981) criticized this attempt, and a debate ensued (Heath *et al.*, 1982; Hammersley, 1982). All parties appear to agree that

> A sensitive ethnographer might well get a much better sense of a family's cultural capital than we [Halsey, Heath and Ridge] could ever get from out survey research. But even the ethnographer has to know what to look for. (Heath *et al.*, 1982, p. 88)

The difficulties arise because 'Bourdieu's theory is couched in obscure, ill-defined language. He does not specify what would constitute an acceptable operationalisation of his concepts' (Heath *et al.*, 1982, p. 88). Halsey *et al.* (1980) were concerned with gross differences between sectors of male secondary education (secondary modern, grammar, direct grant, and 'public' schools) and argued that differences in cultural capital between families did not seem to have much importance once selection for male secondary education has taken place. For these authors, economic capital — wealth — was more significant in enabling school fees to be paid. Their conclusion rests on a crude operationalization of cultural capital (parental education), and has been attacked by Hammersley (1981).

My own position is that, just as Atkinson (1983) has argued against the application of Bourdieu's work 'in any simple all-embracing sense for any given educational setting', it is too simple to see St Luke's girls as being equally endowed with cultural capital. Rather the Group 5 girls have a much larger cultural legacy than their peers, deriving from *both* parents. Nowhere in the debates has the issue of girls' education been examined, but my contention is that the professional careers of the Group 5 *mothers* meant that they saw *women* as active negotiators of knowledge in a different way from other pupils. Unfortunately I did not arrange to interview the girls' mothers, nor did I gather sufficient data on their perceptions of sex roles (see Delamont, 1984b), so this has to remain a speculation. It is, however, a speculation supported by the 'swots and weeds', as the following material on Charmian shows. Typical of the 'academic set', Charmian wants to be both intellectual and original in all spheres of her life, including her hobbies. These are predominantly musical — playing two instruments and singing — but she also belongs to the Girl Guide movement, where her attitude is intellectual and idiosyncratic: 'I don't like doing things like Child Nurse and Homemaker — far more interesting to do the interesting things like Speaker, and Singer — Local History.' (These are also, of course, the awards which have no particular feminine or domestic qualities.) These qualities come through particularly in science lessons, where Charmian and her friends in Group 5 adapted better than any other pupils to the discovery-based learning. The girls' physics teacher, Dr Cavendish, had the most pupil-centred regime, which Charmian characterized as follows:

> C: 'Mrs Cavendish — I think she makes simple things complicated — you have to — oh — I think — I don't know — you do things — I think if you're given enough things to do for yourself you'll learn Physics quite well that way — but oh it's more Teach Yourself Physics — with the experiments — and you explain how to do the experiments — and — have to — the book's a jolly good one, and you have to understand from that.'
>
> SD: 'Do you usually understand things?'
>
> C: I've worked out how, why a thing is what it is, then I'm alright.'

Lesson notes show this process in action:

> *Physics 4 and 5/Tu/5.*
> A lesson on acceleration, mass and force. Mrs Cavendish announces 'Last week you discovered a very important relationship' — greeted by ironic laughs — Mrs C. gets out Newton Balances (all stored in chocolate boxes) ... I sneeze, am asked if I'd like a window closed ... Mrs C. leading class step by step to the number of Newtons in a kilogramme — passes balances around. Charmian asks for more information (QEI), has picked out a flaw in the argument ... class all playing with balances ... (Later) ... Mrs C. gets out another bit of apparatus, has Henrietta and Charmian holding springs as part of demonstration ... Charmian makes music whenever nothing else is going on — flipping the spring and a board ... (Later) sends Charmian to get out equipment for a third experiment ... this experiment done by groups of girls ... Henrietta, Michelle and Charmian are a group — they are 'with-it' have actually got some figures out of it — then as second part doesn't work they all argue furiously.

Similar behaviour from Group 5 girls in science is apparent from the biology lesson (discussed in detail in Atkinson and Delamont, 1976, and reproduced in Delamont, 1983, pp. 131–2) where Michelle unmasked the stage management of Mrs Linnaeus' guided discovery. These girls, using resources from outside school, challenge the teacher's control over knowledge, and see lessons as arenas for negotiation, discussion and controversy. Hence their large number of independent contributions, their commitment to schooling, and their eventual academic achievement. The 'swots and weeds' valued St Luke's for its academic standards, and its music. They actively disliked the sport and the religion, but did not mind the uniform or rules.

In contrast, the 'debs and dollies' hated the uniform, complained of 'petty' rules about behaviour and deportment, but were (mostly) happy with the sporting programme. They saw schooling as about facts, and objected when teachers tried to monitor other aspects of their lives. Olivia summarized this view of staff: 'They don't like to think that we're old enough to dispute what they say.... You can't obviously disagree with facts, but disapproving of [their] rules, petty, stupid, unnecessary rules.' For Olivia and her friends, sensible pupils 'always agree' with teachers *in public*, and keep quiet when they disagree, because teachers are not worth arguing with. Pupils always lose, and the consequences are serious. Vanessa's expulsion was seen as a consequence of her failure to suppress her 'real' self and keep it safely from the staff. No girl in this group saw academic knowledge as negotiable, and all found the 'swots and weeds' annoying, because they interrupted the lessons with 'irrelevancies'.

The staffroom saw this divide rather differently. Group 5 girls were seen as coming from the 'right' kinds of family — one with books, and one which supported the school. Henrietta, for example, explained how both Dr Michaels and Mrs Flodden were family friends, as one of her parents is an historian, and they 'came to our bonfire party, and all knew each other at Oxford and Cambridge.' In contrast, many of the families of girls in Group 2 were seen as 'inadequate' — plenty of material goods, but uncultured. One teacher summarized this view by dismissing a Group 2 father with: 'he made all his money in scrap metal.' This type of judgement is a perfect example of what Bourdieu (1977) terms *habitus*. As Atkinson (1983) puts it:

> In the world of education the habitus which defines successful schooling remains implicit.... The education system assumes that its pupils are possessed of the necessary cultural competence, the character of which is never made manifest.... In this way the essentially social distribution of cultural capital appears to be a natural distribution of personal qualities.

At St Luke's the 'debs and dollies' lacked some element of cultural competence, which prevented them becoming active manipulators of knowledge.[8] Compared with most Scottish adolescents, of course, they were enormously privileged and achieved academic success. However, in the context of St Luke's, they had failed to grasp the opportunity to become active manipulators, users and eventually producers of knowledge, and remained mere consumers of it.

Notes

1 St Luke's is a pseudonym, as are all the names of pupils and teachers used in this paper. The school was studied in 1970 as part of my PhD research (Delamont, 1973) at Edinburgh University. I am grateful to the SSRC and to SCRE for financing me while I did the research and while I wrote the thesis. I also wish to thank Paul Atkinson for his criticisms of the early drafts of this paper, and Val Dobie who typed the final version for me.
2 Scottish pupils transfer to secondary education at 12. Therefore the first public examinations (SCE Ordinary Grade) are taken in the *fourth year* at 16. My sample were aged 14 and 15, and one year away from O-grades.
3 The reader unfamiliar with classroom research is referred to Delamont (1983 and 1984a). Readers unfamiliar with St Luke's are also advised to consult Delamont (1976) for an argument parallel to this one.
4 This article is largely written in the ethnographic present. While the data refer to the period 1970–74, the author feels that their flavour is better captured by the same style of presentation used in Delamont (1973).
5 In Scotland O-grades at 16 are followed by 'Highers' at 17. Pupils heading for higher education may then take the Certificate of Sixth Year Studies (CSYS) at 18. In the private sector, however, English A-levels are taken at 18, and in the most elite schools 'Highers' are bypassed altogether by brighter pupils. At St Luke's girls took O-grades, 'Highers' and those planning on university took some A-levels.
6 An academic score for each girl was calculated by giving her one point for being in an 'A' set, two points for a 'B' set and three for a 'C' set in the six core school subjects. A girl with a score of six was therefore in top sets for all her work. Each clique could be given an average academic score on the basis of the achievement of its members.
7 In 1973 Traquair House was captained by Belinda (Group 3) with Jill (5) as Vice Captain (she was also Head Girl). Frances (3) and Yvonne (2) were Captain and Vice-Captain of Craigievar; Philippa (5) Captain of Bothwell; and Tessa (2) Captain of Dunvegan. Tantallon, the Boarders' House, had Fleur and Esther as its officers.
8 This may have been a 'progressive' infant/junior schooling characterized by what Bernstein (1975) calls the 'invisible' pedagogy. Group 5 girls were much more likely to have attended some form of 'open' schooling in early childhood (Delamont, 1976).

References

ATKINSON, P. (1983) 'The reproduction of the professional community', in DINGWALL, R. and LEWIS, P. (Eds) *The Sociology of the Professions*, London, Macmillan.

ATKINSON, P. and DELAMONT, S. (1976) 'Mock-ups and cock-ups', in HAMMERSLEY, M. and WOODS, P. (Eds) *The Process of Schooling*, London, Routledge and Kegan Paul.

BARNES, D. (1971) *Language, the Learner and the School*, Harmondsworth, Penguin.

BELLACK, A.A. et al. (1966) *The Language of the Classroom*, New York, Teachers College Press.

BERNSTEIN, B. (1975) 'Class and pedagogies: Visible and invisible', in BERNSTEIN, B. (Ed.) *Class, Codes and Control Vol. 3*, London, Routledge and Kegan Paul.

BOURDIEU, P. (1977) 'Cultural reproduction and social reproduction', reprinted in KARABEL, J. and HALSEY, A.H. (Eds) *Power and Ideology in Education*, New York, Oxford University Press.

BULLIVANT, B. (1978) *The Way of Tradition*, Victoria, ACER.

COULTHARD, M. (1974) 'Approaches to the analysis of classroom interaction', *Educational Review*, 22, pp. 38–50.

DELAMONT, S. (1973) *Academic Conformity Observed*, unpublished PhD thesis, University of Edinburgh.

DELAMONT, S. (1976) 'The girls most likely to: Cultural reproduction and Scottish elites', *Scottish Journal of Sociology*, 1, 1, pp. 29–43, (reprinted in PARSLER, R. (Ed.) *Capitalism, Class and Politics in Scotland*, Farnborough, Gower, 1981.

DELAMONT, S. (1978) 'The contradictions in ladies' education', in DELAMONT, S. and DUFFIN, L. (Eds) *The Nineteenth Century Woman*, London, Croom Helm.

DELAMONT, S. (1983) *Interaction in the Classroom*, 2nd ed., London. Methuen.

DELAMONT, S. (1984a) (Ed.) *Readings on Interaction in the Classroom*, London, Methuen.

DELAMONT, S. (1984b) 'The old-girl network: Reflections on the fieldwork at St Luke's', in BURGESS, R. (Ed.) *The Research Process in Educational Settings*, Lewes, Falmer Press.

DELAMONT, S. and HAMILTON, D. (1984) 'Revisiting classroom research: A continuing cautionary tale', in DELAMONT, S. (Ed.) *Readings on Interaction in the Classroom*, London, Methuen.

DENZIN, N. (1970) *The Research Act in Sociology*, Chicago, Aldine.

DYHOUSE, C. (1977) 'Good wives and little mothers', *Oxford Review of Education*, 3, 1, pp. 21–35.

EDWARDS, A.D. and FURLONG, V.J. (1978) 'Language in classroom interaction', *Educational Research*, 19, 2.

HALSEY, A.H. et al. (1980) *Origins and Destinations*, Oxford, Clarendon Press.

HAMMERSLEY, M. (1981) Review symposium on Origins and Destinations, *British Journal of Sociology of Education*, 2, 1, pp. 93–5.

HAMMERSLEY, M. (1982) 'Rejoinder to Heath, Halsey and Ridge', *British Journal of Sociology of Education*, 3, 1, pp. 91–2.

HEATH, A.F. *et al.* (1982) 'Cultural capital and political arithmetic', *British Journal of Sociology of Education*, 3, 1, pp. 87–91.

LARKIN, R.W. (1979) *Suburban Youth in Cultural Crisis*, New York, Oxford University Press.

MEHAN, H. (1979) *Learning Lessons*, Harvard, The University Press.

SCHARLIEB, M. (1924) *Reminiscences*, London, Williams and Norgate.

SMITH, B.O. and MEUX, J. (1970) *A Study of the Logic of Teaching*, Urbana, Ill., The University of Illinois Press.

WALKER, R. and ADELMAN, C. (1975) 'Interaction analysis in informal classrooms: A critical comment on the Flanders system', *British Journal of Educational Psychology*, 45, 1, pp. 73–6.

WEBB, E.T. *et al.* (1966) *Unobtrusive Measures*, Chicago, Rand McNally.

WOBER, M. (1971) *English Girls' Boarding Schools*, London, Allen Lane.

Public Schools and the Choice at 18+

Greg Eglin, North East London Polytechnic

Education and Occupation

The relationship between education and the entry of individuals into particular occupations is both complex and problematic. However, within this complexity two distinct but interrelated trends may be discerned. Increasingly, the point of entry into the occupational hierarchy is determined by the length of time spent in the formal institutions of education, while the position of an occupation within the hierarchy is determined more and more by the level of education required for entry.

Ashton and Field (1976) have identified three main types of occupational category: careerless work; short-term career work; and extended career work. These three groupings have different educational requirements for entry, the first requiring little or no formal qualifications, the short-term category requiring Certificate of Secondary Education/General Certificate of Education, ordinary level qualifications, while the latter group normally requires an education beyond post-compulsory level. It is with entry to this last group that this study is concerned.

The extended career work group of occupations has been expanding relative to other groups. The reasons for this development, according to Levitas (1974), are: increasing applications of specialized knowledge, resulting in training for many occupations being concentrated on systematic education over long periods of time; an increasing number of occupations requiring high academic attainment for entry as a means of maintaining occupational prestige; and a general increase in the educational threshold. This technical division of labour, however, also has a social element. The three groupings have variable levels of job security and current and future financial rewards. In particular the extended career types of occupation carry with them considerable power, wealth and privilege at the expense of other types, making them more desirable.

This could cause social control problems as not all can achieve the desirable occupations. Therefore, some mechanism is necessary whereby occupational aspirations can be matched with ability and selection for the more desirable occupations can take place. Furthermore, this mechanism must meet with general acceptance by society. Arguably, this mechanism is education, as recruitment to high-status occupations is increasingly by the possession of degrees, diplomas and certificates. Husen (1975) claims that

> the expedience value of educational credentials to employees also refers to the need for a device that objectively justifies the selection that is made. Selection according to credentials is regarded as a fair system with wide acceptance among both employers and employees.

Husen continues that 'the credentials determine the level of employment and this, in turn, the salary', while studies by Berg (1970) show that those individuals who possess degrees, diplomas and the like can command additional income and status in the labour market.

Consequent upon the above there has been pressure to expand post-compulsory education. This has been caused partly by the needs of the economy for a highly skilled section of the workforce, and partly by the demands of pupils and parents for access to higher education as a means of entry into the higher-status occupations. As Wilby (1977) points out, 'in spite of the recent need of successive governments to cut public expenditure, the mighty apparatus of education is one of the most striking creations of the twentieth century.' For example, the period between 1960 and 1975 saw the proportion of Gross National Product devoted to education double, with the main reason for the increase being a rising demand for access to post-compulsory education. Furthermore, while the impetus for this increase is often attributed to Robbins (1963), as Bell *et al.* (1973) point out, Robbins accelerated rather than instigated the expansion.

It should be noted that since 1975 the main direction of government funding policy for education has been to curtail expenditure. Undoubtedly, some policy decisions have been the result of non-educational factors. For example, the mid-seventies oil crisis had an important bearing on the fall in public spending between 1975/76 and 1977/78. Demographic factors have also been of some influence. However, justification of decisions to reduce expenditure on post-compulsory education is more problematic. The demand for post-compulsory education is dependent on factors other than the total numbers of 16-year-olds in any one year, and, while there was a fall in demand for places after 1975, this could largely be accounted for by changes in teacher training, and the current trend is upwards.

Cutting expenditure on post-compulsory education during a time of increasing demand for places requires some explanation. The answer lies partly in the economic philosophy of monetarism, partly in shifts of priorities within government expenditure, and partly in the ideological role of education. As well as being the means whereby individuals are placed within the technical division of labour, education can also be used to reinforce the social relationships consequent on the labour process. As Worsley (1974) states:

> the growth of education is linked, not only to economic rationality, but also to the way power is distributed in society. Education becomes increasingly important for determining entrance into occupation.... This being the case, those that enjoy a favourable position in society are likely to maintain it for their children through securing them a privilege education.

Swift (1969) would agree with this argument. He points out that one important aspect of maintaining the established order is the preservation of social stratification and that one of the major ways in which education plays a part in this process is by particular kinds of schools being reserved for particular sectors of the population who are then given access to higher-status occupations on the basis of having attended these schools. Swift continues that the training of a selected few for leadership and authority in state and civil society is, in the main, the prerogative of the public schools, while both Bottomore (1964) and Barron (1966) have cited the historical link between the public schools and the occupational structure. As evidence provided by Glennester and Pryke (1964) and Wakeford (1979), amongst others, shows, public schools can be seen as preparing their pupils for expected positions of dominance in the economic, political and legal power structure of capitalist society.

It could be argued that the existence of a category of schools conferring an advantage on their pupils in the pursuit of desired occupations would cause social unrest. However, as Bowles and Gintis (1980) point out, the formal institutions of education not only meet the needs of capitalist society in terms of manpower, they also have an ideological role. Thus, formal education transmits a general

ruling-class ideology which justifies the capitalist system and repro-
duces the attitudes and behaviour required by the ruling and
subordinate groups within the division of labour. In this respect the
attendance at different schools by different groups assists in the
process of assimilating the ideology of the dominant group; and the
social composition of the school reflects the wider social experiences
of the pupils, and conditions the expectations that pupils have of the
school and vice versa.

Therefore, occupational 'choice' is governed by what Gramsci
(1972) terms cultural hegemony, the process of ensuring that individuals assimilate the values and norms of their class, thereby
providing a framework in which individuals can construct their
idea of reality and can also form a bond with those similarly raised.
Having gained this consciousness, Willis (1977) argues, working-
class boys demonstrate a 'realistic understanding' of their likely
future position in the labour market, and therefore make realistic
occupational choices.

However, while there may be considerable evidence for the
Bowles and Gintis and Willis argument, it can be claimed that their
view is too deterministic. For example, it could be argued that since
the Second World War increasing political power for the working
class has enabled them, in alliance with progressive educationalists,
to obtain concessions from the ruling elite, normally in the form of
expansion of provision. This has led to an absolute increase in the
number of children of manual working-class origins achieving
higher education places, although, on the evidence of Halsey *et al.*
(1980), the proportion of such children in universities has hardly
changed.

It should be noted that reforms such as the expansion of the
higher education system in the sixties and the raising of the school
leaving age to 16 were supported by all parties. However, the major
reform of the sixties, the introduction of comprehensive secondary
education, was not. The Labour Party policy of comprehensivization
was, amongst other things, an attempt to answer the argument,
articulated by Bowles and Gintis, that a differentiated school structure results in a reinforcing of class structure. Indeed, the numbers
staying on at school after 16 increased between 1965 and 1970, the
time of major reorganization, but the numbers staying on past 16
increased at a slower rate after 1970 and by 1975 had levelled off.

A number of explanations have been posited as to why comprehensive schools failed to achieve all that was expected of them in
respect of giving larger numbers of previously educationally dis-

advantaged groups the opportunity to achieve higher education places. Young (1971) and other exponents of the 'new' sociology of education have put forward the argument that the internal operation of the school is important, and Levitas (1974) pointed out that reorganization on comprehensive lines will not result (necessarily) in comprehensive education. Furthermore, Ford (1969) has demonstrated the fallacy of concluding that changing from tripartism to a comprehensive form of secondary education would necessarily mean a fundamental change in the relationship between the education structure and the occupational structure. However, as a Labour Party discussion document (1980) makes clear, the real barrier to comprehensive education is the existence of a private sector of education.

> Private schools ensure that economic status, social position and influence are transferred from generation to generation. The ending of private education is therefore an important part of a democratic socialist assault on privilege, wealth, power and influence in our society.

The emergence of radical right-wing theories, epitomized by the Cox and Dyson (1971) *Black Papers*, has countered this call from the left for the abolition of the private sector of education, and, given the radical right-wing government of Thatcher and the general disarray of the left in the late seventies/early eighties, such theories are having an increasing influence on policy. At its harshest this policy advocates education for an elite and training for the rest. Thus, as Bourdieu (1972) points out, cultural capital will be the preserve of the few. Indeed, Roger Scruton (1980), a leading Conservative academic, claims it is the nature of educational institutions 'to create privileges and determine their distribution'. In this atmosphere public schools, very much on the defensive in the seventies, have begun to prosper, helped by a market philosophy and practical aid such as the Assisted Places Scheme.

Nonetheless, both private schools and local authority comprehensives produce sixth formers who are capable of passing A-level GCEs and obtaining a higher education place. Furthermore, the Employment Training Act of 1973 imposed a mandatory duty on every local education authority to provide vocational guidance for those in schools. One of the main aims of this service, the Careers Service, is to ensure that every child reaches his or her potential. Thus, once in the sixth form there should be no differences between the aspirations of public school and local authority comprehensive school students. This study looks at sixth formers in private sector schools and local authority comprehensive schools, and compares and contrasts their backgrounds and aspirations. It also looks at the extent that careers officers and others influence their decisions.

Research Methods

This study forms part of a larger study into the background and aspirations of students in 16–19 education (Eglin, 1982). The population of the study were those students in the final year of a course, the successful completion of which would enable entry into higher education, and who were resident in three adjacent local authority areas (metropolitan districts). The students concerned were studying at private sector schools, local authority comprehensive schools and further education colleges.

Information was obtained by interviews and questionnaires. The purpose of the interviews was to obtain the perceptions of the various providers and recipients of 16–19 education in the three boroughs as to that provision, and to ascertain any underlying value assumptions of significant individuals, groups of individuals, professional associations and others. These qualitative data were also used to place in context and tentatively advance explanations of the quantitative data obtained from the questionnaire.

Interviews took place during 1980 and some 100 people were interviewed. The interviews (unstructured) were held with various individuals involved in the provision of 16–19 education in the three boroughs, namely: politicans; local education authority (LEA) administrators; LEA advisors/inspectors; careers officers; teachers at LEA schools; teachers at independent schools; teachers at the further education colleges; students at LEA schools; students at private sector schools; and students at further education colleges. At no time was I refused an interview and all respondents were extremely cooperative.

The questionnaire was designed for the purpose of obtaining both quantitative and qualitative data from the recipients of 16–19 education. During the eighteen months the questionnaire was being designed, four pilot surveys were undertaken, two at comprehensive schools and two at further education colleges, and discussions were held with academics and practitioners in the area of study.

Some information was pre-coded on the questionnaires, for example, LEA, type of school and gender. Questions were of two types. The first requested demographic details such as type and tenure of dwelling, father's and mother's occupation and position in, and size of, family. For the purpose of this study fathers' occupations were used to indicate the occupational status of the families of respondents and occupations were aggregated into extended careers, short-term careers and the careerless. The second requested information as to student's aspirations for, and knowledge of, higher education. There was a total of 115 information variables. with each variable having a number of pre-coded values.

The questionnaires were distributed and collected during January–June 1980, in one of three ways. The most common pattern of distribution and collection was my explaining to a group of students at their school or college the purpose of the research and the completion of the questionnaires at that time which were then returned to me. The second method consisted of an interview with a sixth form tutor, or course tutor at a college, after which the tutor took away the questionnaires together with envelopes addressed to me (to preserve confidentiality). The tutor explained the purpose of my research to his or her students and organized the completion of the questionnaires which I collected at a later date. The third method followed the same pattern as the second, but, instead of my collecting the completed questionnaire, students were given a stamped-addressed envelope by the sixth form tutor, with the request to complete it in their own time and post it on to me.

The type of distribution and collection pattern adopted in the schools depended entirely on the requirements of particular school heads and/or sixth form tutors, although the first pattern was preferred. When I spoke to groups of students it was pointed out that the completion of the questionnaire was not compulsory, but not one school student that I spoke to refused to complete. A total of 950 questionnaires was completed and returned, and in order to process and analyze the large amount of information obtained on the questionnaires a computer programme involving application package SPSS was used.

The questionnaire also contained one open-ended question: 'If there is anything you think is missing in career guidance at any stage in your progress so far, please state it here.' Over half the respondents replied to this question, some at great length.

For the purpose of this study the data are limited to one of the three boroughs. The main reason is that this particular borough contained 100 of the 101 private sector school respondents; 170 pupils from comprehensive schools in the borough had also responded. This represents a response rate of 89 per cent for the public schools and 79 per cent for the comprehensive schools. It should be noted in this respect that, while it was necessary to obtain an adequate representative sample of students in the various groups being analyzed, it was not necessary for these groups to be in proportion to their size in the population as analysis is by a comparison of the internal distribution of answers within each group, not by any comparison of absolute numbers. In comparing the sets of data the chi-squared test was used to determine whether or not there were any statistically significant differences. It should also be pointed out that the comprehensive group was adjusted so that the male:female ratio was the same as the private sector group 57:43. This point is taken up later in the study.

The Schools

Information is drawn from four private sector and seven local authority comprehensive schools. While all seven local authority schools are located inside the authority's boundary, two of the private sector schools lie just outside. However, these schools take a large number of pupils from the borough. One of the private sector schools is all girls, the other three being all boys, although two of the latter have recently become co-educational at sixth form level. Two of the boys' schools take boarders but in both cases the proportion of boarders to day pupils is decreasing. All the students in the survey are day pupils.

All four private sector schools are selective. As one of the headteachers stated, 'this organization has to be understood in terms of pupils selected from the top twenty to twenty five percent of the ability range.' Another headteacher pointed out that the school took pupils capable of five or more O-levels and 'does not cater for anything else'. All four schools offer scholarships and there are some places paid for by the armed forces and local education authorities. There are some direct entrants to the sixth forms in the three boys' schools and one headteacher stated that his school also got 'refugees from the state system'. This, he claimed, is because:

A very intelligent boy can underachieve if peer group pressure is anti-work. Underachievement will occur. The tradition here is for boys to go as far as they can in the education system. That road is natural to the school so pupils follow it. This is a place where a sensitive boy can flourish. A boy can walk here carrying a violin without ridicule.

All four headteachers claimed that comprehensivization by the local education authority had provided their school with a boost in recruitment. The history of the girls' school is particularly interesting in this respect. Originally a direct grant grammar, the school put forward a plan to go comprehensive but this was not accepted by the local education authority. The governors then decided to close the school, but parental pressure, allied to local pressure, prevailed upon them to keep the school open. The demand for places now greatly exceeds provision. The headteacher of one of the boys' schools added that it was not necessarily comprehensive education *per se* that worried the middle class but rather an irrational fear of it. 'Two local schools are claimed by locals to have gone "down-hill". This is nonsense, of course, but it is believed.'

The social mix claimed of their students by the heads was particularly interesting. The head of girls' school claimed that the school had a good social mix, with daughters of 'doctors, accountants, dentists, but also tailors and manual workers — a complete range'. Another head conceded that the social background of pupils was middle-class although this 'reflected the geographical area', and while there were few working-class pupils, 'on the other hand there are few upper class ones either'. A third head pointed out that the background of his pupils was mainly professional, although pupil backgrounds 'are increasingly trade; taxi drivers, publicans and others'.

All four schools reported that a small number of pupils qualified for sixth form entry had left at 16. However, the majority of pupils enter the sixth form and, as one headteacher stated, the role of the school is seen by both parents and pupils as 'maintaining standards and producing the goods, as kids are not sent here for foolishness nor an accent but to get a clutch of 'O's and 'A's and university entrance.' This opinion was reinforced by another head, who, after pointing out that his school was 'not your Radley', stated that 'people realise education matters. In the end a materialistic money-making approach is the one adopted by most parents.'

The historical background of the comprehensives is varied, some having been formed from grammar schools, some from amalgamations of grammar and secondary modern schools, and others from secondary modern schools. All are co-educational.

One of the comprehensive schools involved in the research was formed from a single grammar school. The headteacher did not think that comprehensivization had resulted in many changes. 'There have been no major differences in staying on at sixteen. There have been minimal changes in the curriculum.' Furthermore, he considered that the position of the sixth form had even improved as the school used to have well-qualified pupils who left school at 16 for financial reasons but this was no longer the case.

> We used to cater for disadvantaged social groupings from poorer areas who won scholarships to the grammar school. We don't any more because our catchment area is predominantly middle class. Parental motivation is strong. Staying on into the sixth form is considered an achievement. . . . Falling rolls should not affect us because of our popularity. Parental choice ensures we will remain our current size.

Another comprehensive school in the research was the product of a merger between a grammar school and a secondary modern school. It is situated in the most affluent part of the borough. Comprehensivization in the view of the sixth form tutor has been a success.

The other five comprehensive schools involved were all formed from either single secondary modern schools, or amalgamations of secondary modern schools. All the upper sixths were relatively small but in all cases the staff interviewed were optimistic. One headteacher claimed that 'the brighter children we have received as a result of comprehensivization have had a beneficial effect on the school as a whole', while a sixth form tutor of another school stated that 'the sixth form is increasing in terms of numbers and ability.' However, various problems were noted, although these varied from school to school, and staff at a school in the poorest part of the borough reported that 'pupils from some areas have a tendency to move to get a job as soon as possible. Others leave in the sixth form.'

The Students' Background and Aspirations

Family size saw an almost exact match between the two groups of students, as did the pattern of house tenure. However, there was a difference between occupational backgrounds. While very few of either group came from careerless backgrounds, the ratio of private sector school students to comprehensive school students with an extended career background was almost 2:1 while the corresponding ratio for short-term careers was almost 2:5.

With regard to educational background the private sector students tended to have more qualifications than the comprehensive school students, 66 per cent of the former having nine or more O-levels compared with 41 per cent of the latter. Furthermore, a higher percentage had obtained O/CSE 1 in both English and maths (95 per cent compared with 77 per cent). All respondents had English and/or maths passes at O/CSE 1 and all had four or more O-levels.

Students were asked whether they intended to apply for a university place. Those who replied in the negative were asked for their alternative plans — either some other form of higher education or employment. In this respect Ashton and Field (1976) point out that there are two main types of entry pattern into occupations which provide extended careers, each of which is related to differences within these occupations. One group consists of those who leave full-time education at 18 with A-levels as the immediate qualification aim, although they may continue their education on a part-time basis, and enter managerial, administrative and certain commercial operations. The second group contains those who continue with some form of full-time higher education before entering the higher professions or managerial and administrative positions at a higher level than the former group. Given the evidence of Roweth (1981), that a considerable proportion of these qualified for higher education at 18 do not avail themselves of the opportunity, the importance of the questions for this study is apparent.

The response to the above mentioned questions is contained in Table 1. There was no statistical significance between the private sector students and comprehensive students in relation to aspirations for higher education. However, there was a significant difference as to choice of higher education institutions.

The ratio of private sector school students to comprehensive school students aspiring to university was approximately 3:2 whereas the ratio for other higher education was 1:3. One possible explanation for this phenomenon is that the aspirations of comprehensive school students are conditioned by what Willis (1977) refers

Table 1. Preferred Destination of Respondents at 18+ (percentages)

	Private sector	Comprehensives
University	73	47
Other Higher Education	10	30
Work	17	23
(Total Numbers	100	100)

to, albeit in another context, as 'a realistic understanding of their position'. Indeed, I found that a number of students in the comprehensive schools were aiming, not just at polytechnics, but at higher diplomas rather than degrees on the understanding that they had a 'realistic chance of entry'. Those that did aim high, however, faced problems, as one student found concerning his attempt to gain entry to Oxbridge.

> When one comes up against the public school set and the old establishment the lack of preparation is highlighted and can be a serious problem. Even at other universities the confidence which shines through the crest and tie of the public school boy cannot be met by a comprehensive student who has not had such advantage.

However, another explanation can be offered, that of a lack of knowledge by private school students as to what is on offer in the local authority sector of higher education. For example, the Director of Studies at one of the private sector schools admitted 'we have not been very good at polytechnics', while the headteacher of another private sector school claimed that an important factor was parental pressure 'for pupils to strive for university'. Both, on the other hand, claimed that this situation was changing. The Director of Studies claimed that the number of students at his school applying for polytechnic places, while small, was growing, while the headteacher stated that more students were going to polytechnics once these were explained to them and their parents.

It should be noted at this point that some care has to be exercised in the interpretation of these comments, as the interviewees were aware that the interviewer was a polytechnic lecturer and may have slanted their answers to take account of this fact. For example, some students at the private sector schools put forward the view that polytechnics and other non-university education institutions were not considered to have a high enough status for them to apply. One student claimed that 'school is too snobby and only plugs universities while polytechnics are hardly ever mentioned: perhaps they are socially unacceptable at public schools', while another stated that 'advice on colleges and polys rather than universities is only reluctantly given.'

The next question asked was designed to throw some light on this issue. All the students who indicated that they wished to go to university were asked whether or not they would be prepared to study for a polytechnic degree should they fail to obtain a university place. Seventy-two per cent of comprehensive school students and 51 per cent of private sector students answered in the affirmative.

Should those who wished to achieve higher education do so, there was an interesting difference in the subjects that the two groups aspired to study. As can be seen from Table 2 the emphasis in the private sector schools was on arts/humanities, whereas in the comprehensive it was on science and engineering. Furthermore, a higher proportion of private school students tended to aim to study the more prestigious subject areas of law and medicine, while the comprehensive school students aimed to study paramedical subjects. This choice would appear to be reflected in, and thus reinforced by, the curricula of the different schools.

The Reasons for the Students' Choice

As Raby and Walford (1981) point out, 'as a research area the transition from school to work has moved from the fringes of educational research to bcoming a central topic of enquiry.' Accompanying this move has been the development of a number of theories of occupational 'choice'.

The first group of theories, known collectively as developmental, stresses the way in which various agencies, particularly education, help individual children gain experiences enabling them to become aware of their abilities. As children pass through education

Table 2. Subjects to Be Studied by Respondents in Higher Education (percentages)

	Private sector	Comprehensives
Arts/Humanities	30	12
Law	12	7
Science	12	19
Engineering	11	18
Social Science	10	4
Medicine	8	3
Paramedical	5	11
Teaching	4	5
Business Studies	4	7
Other	4	14
(Total Numbers	83	77)

their role perspective can be revised with regard to occupational choice to take account of these experiences. Newman (1968), for example, claims that since changes in the labour market have resulted in more white collar occupations social mobility was evident and could be achieved by 'individual ambition'. However, although the relationship between educational qualifications and occupations is apparent, it cannot be claimed to be the solitary factor governing the process; Ginzberg as early as 1951 outlined the roles played by 'key persons' such as the family, teachers and peer groups. Other theorists such as Super (1971) place stress on the individual's own social environment, and Musgrave (1974), in a British context, has developed the theory of anticipatory socialization.

However, these theories have been challenged. Coulson *et al.* (1967), for example, take Musgrave to task for attempting to explain occupational choice in terms of an over-simplified functionalist theory while Ford and Box (1967) claim that in most cases the transition from school to work cannot be described as choice at all. Roberts (1975), writing on this point, states:

> The notion that young people possess freedom of occupational choice and that they can select careers for themselves upon the basis of their own preferences is a pure myth. It is not choice but opportunity that governs the manner in which many young people make their entry into employment.

Roberts posits a structure-opportunity model as an alternative to the individual-ambition model claiming that careers opportunities are determined by the opportunity structures to which individuals are exposed, 'first in education and subsequently in employment'. Roberts considers that developmental theories ignore factors such as social class, type of neighbourhood and family, each of which has an extensive literature demonstrating the link between that factor and lack of success both within the formal institutions of education and later on in the occupational structure.

A more fundamental criticism of the developmental theorists has come from the cultural reproduction theorists who claim that in practice the system operates as a selective winnowing device, distributing life chances, allowing a strictly controlled degree of mobility. This is argued by Willis (1977) and Bourdieu (1977) amongst others. However, the degree for manoeuverability for individuals within this framework is disputed, with Bowles and Gintis (1980) being at the more determinist end of the spectrum and Young and Whitty (1977) being at the other.

The questionnaire was designed partly to ascertain the degree of influence of various agencies on the students' choice. The first question of relevance for this study concerning choice was the reasons why respondents decided to enter the sixth form. From Table 3 it can be seen that a higher proportion of private sector school students entered sixth forms aspiring to higher education (79 per cent compared with 59 per cent). Interestingly, a higher proportion of comprehensive school students gave parental advice as a reason for entering the sixth form.

Students were also asked for the reasons for their proposed choice at 18+. It is interesting to note in this respect that there were no identifiable factors, either demographic or academic, in the backgrounds of those opting for work compared with those aiming at continuing their full-time education. Neither were there any significant differences between private sector school students and comprehensive school students in this respect. However, it can be seen from Table 4 that the reasons for choice of destination after 18 varied between the two groups. While the majority in each group gave employment prospects as a reason for wanting higher education, the second most mentioned reason (over half) by the private sector students was social life. This was not the case for the local authority students. Careers officers' advice was quoted by over one-third of each group. It is also interesting to note that peer group pressure, while appearing to be a marginal factor, operated to keep private sector students in the full-time education system, whereas it operated to take local authority students out of it.

Table 3.   *Reasons for Respondents Deciding to Enter the Sixth Form (percentages*)*

	Private sector	*Comprehensives*
Aspired to Higher Education	79	59
Parents' Advice	31	46
Careers Service Advice	15	23
Teachers' Advice	13	16
Peer Group	12	10
Unable to Obtain Work	3	5
No Response	7	12
(Total Numbers	100	100)

Note: * As respondents could give more than one answer the total percentage is greater than 100.

Greg Eglin

Table 4.   Reasons for Choice of Destination at 18+ (percentages)

	Private sector	Comprehensives
(1) *Higher Education*		
Employment Prospects	79	76
Social Life	56	32
Careers Service Advice	35	39
Parents' Advice	27	34
Peer Group	8	2
Teachers' Advice	3	—
(Total Numbers	83	77)
(2) *Work*		
Obtained Work	71	91
Wanted a Break from Education	59	83
Parents' Advice	12	4
Peer Group	—	17
(Total Numbers	17	23)

The final question of relevance to this section of the study asked if they had received information on universities, other higher education and/or work, and, if so, from whom? Knowledge of the higher education system is an important factor in choice, and Table 5 shows the extent of this knowledge and its source. A larger number of the private sector school students had obtained information on universities than comprehensive school students, while the reverse is true of other higher education. Indeed, more comprehensive school students had obtained information on local authority sector higher education than on universities. It is interesting that a higher number of private sector school students obtained information direct from universities, polytechnics or colleges of education, whereas the comprehensive school students relied more heavily on careers officers.

The LEA's older leaver specialist in the Careers Office claimed that the above trends were occasioned by some parents' knowledge base of the professions being greater. However, she pointed out that parents from all social backgrounds had a lack of knowledge of career requirements. Many gave advice based on the circumstances of twenty to thirty years ago and this could be quite harmful: 'It is a totally new world for the sixth formers compared with their parents' time. Many children have to correct their parents' fantasies before making a decision as to their future career.' She was of the opinion

Table 5.   Extent of Knowledge of Higher Education (percentages)

	Private sector	Comprehensives
(1) *Information Received*		
on the Following		
Universities	92	71
Other Higher Education	54	75
Work	35	49
(Total Numbers	100	100)
(2) *Information Received*		
from the Following		
School	74	79
Higher Education Establishments	48	31
Careers Officers	34	52
Parents	15	14
Other Relatives	11	14
Total Numbers	100	100

that parents were the biggest influence on career choice, and a pupil's choice was normally set in the context of parental expectation. In this respect the careers service role was seen as encouraging parents who had not thought of further and higher education for their sons and daughters to do so. It would appear from Table 5 (2) that they were meeting with some limited success in this instance. However, a number of pupils claimed some difficulty with the careers officers. One student claimed that they were 'too keen to tell you that you are not capable of doing what you want', while another claimed that they (careers officers) 'tend to discourage ambitious careers.'

Gender

As Acker (1982) points out, 'gender has been at best a peripheral concern' for educational studies, but, she continues, 'there are sex differences in educational experiences and outcomes as striking as the class differences which preoccupied sociologists for years. With reference to occupational choice women comprise a significant proportion of the working population and, as Reid and Wormald (1982) point out, the proportion of women to men in the workforce increased steadily during the fifties, sixties and seventies. It would also appear, according to the latest census, that more and more families are dependent on the earnings of women and the phenomenon of the mother as a major or sole breadwinner of the family is no longer an isolated one.

However, as Reid and Wormald (1982) also point out, while girls obtain more passes than boys at GCE O/CSE 1 this position is reversed at GCE A. Furthermore, despite an increase in the proportion of women students in higher education over the last decade, the ratio of male to female undergraduates is still 3:2, and Roweth (1981) points out that more women qualified for higher education entry leave full-time education at 18 than men.

The problem, according to Wolpe (1978), lies in the relationship between the type of education and the level of attainment on the one hand and position in the occupational structure on the other. Recently an attempt has been made to redress the omission outlined above by Acker and a series of studies on the role of education in reinforcing women's occupational position has been undertaken. Some of these studies, for example Deem (1978) and Wolpe (1978), have looked at the role of education in the reproduction of the sexual division of labour, while others, such as Stanworth (1981), have looked at the process of sexual divisions within the classroom and how these discriminate against women.

It is partly because of the differences in educational experiences and outcomes between male and female students, mentioned above by Acker (1982), that this study uses an equal proportion of male and female students in each group. If one group in the study contained a higher proportion of one sex than the other, this may well cause distortions in some of the answers, for example, the choice of subject to be studied. The 100 private sector school respondents included fifty-seven boys and forty-three girls. The 170 comprehensive school students were stratified by gender and respondents chosen at random on a ratio of fifty-seven to forty-three.

Another reason for balancing the male and female students in each group is that one of the purposes of this study is to look at the differences between the sexes in relation to aspirations on leaving school at 18. The first stage in this process was to test for any significant differences, either demographic or in terms of qualifications, between the sexes. It was found that when tests were carried out within the respective group of students, private sector and comprehensives, there were no statistically significant differences between the sexes.

The next stage was to test for differences in respect of preferred destination on leaving school. As can be seen from Table 6 (1), some differences emerged. While there was no significance in the differences between male and female in either group with regard to higher education aspirations, there were significant differences as to choice of higher education establishments. In both groups more male students aspired to a university place than female students, although it should be noted that the proportion of male university aspirants from comprehensive schools was lower than that of female aspirants from the private sector.

More pronounced than differences in choice of higher education establishments was choice of subject area. This followed a typical pattern, with male students tending to opt for the 'masculine' subjects such as science and engineering; conversely women students opted for arts, teaching and paramedical subjects. The only exception to this tendency was the high proportion of male students in the private sector studying for arts/humanities.

The replies to the questions asking respondents the reasons for particular choices were also analyzed by gender. The reasons given for deciding to continue education into the sixth form demonstrated a remarkable degree of similarity between boys and girls within the different school groups. For example, the percentages giving the

Table 6.   Preferred Destination of, and Knowledge of Choices Available to, Respondents at 18+ by Gender (percentages)

| | Private sector | | Comprehensives | | All schools | |
	Male	Female	Male	Female	Male	Female
(1) Preferred Destination						
University	81	63	51	42	66	52
Other Higher Education	5	16	23	37	14	26
Work	14	21	25	21	19	21
(Total Numbers	57	43	57	43	114	86)
(2) Information Received on the Following						
University	94	88	83	56	89	72
Other Higher Education	50	56	77	72	63	66
Work	20	54	33	70	26	62
(Total Numbers	57	43	57	43	114	86)

answer 'aspiring to higher education' were: private sector schools, male students, 85, female students, 84; comprehensive schools, male students, 69, female students, 66. There was one exception to this conformity. Amongst comprehensive school students there was a significantly higher percentage of male students (37) compared with female students (12) giving the answer 'careers service advice'.

The answers concerning the extent of knowledge of higher education yielded some interesting data. As can be seen from Table 6 (2) two major phenomena concerning gender differentiation can be observed. The first is that a statistically significant percentage of female students (compared with male students) had received advice on seeking employment. This was true for both the private sector and the comprehensive schools. The second phenomenon is the relative lack of knowledge of the university sector of higher education by female students at comprehensives.

Summary and Conclusions

A number of conclusions can be drawn from the evidence of this study. The first is that aspirations to higher education are similar between private sector and comprehensive school sixth form students drawn from the same local authority area. This appears to be the case regardless of the occupational background of the students concerned. It may be suggested that once in the sixth form an ethos is created which is higher education-oriented. This process was described by a number of the comprehensive school students, one comment being: 'There was a lot of jealousy. My old friends felt really out of it and eventually I stopped going out with them. I have made new friends in the sixth and completely rearranged my social life.' However, the evidence also shows that aspirations to particular types of higher education are differentially distributed between private sector school students and comprehensive school students, with private sector school students having a higher propensity to aspire to university than comprehensive school students. The converse is true for non-university higher education. It should also be noted that while female students had lower aspirations to university than male students within each group, female students at private sector schools had a higher aspiration rate than male students at comprehensive schools.

Both the quantitative and qualitative data of this study would appear to support Glennester's and Pryke's (1964) assertion that attendance at a private sector school is part of an elite socialization process that includes a university education and that a university place is an expectation of independent school students. Certainly, knowledge of the non-university sector was lower amongst private sector school students and one such student remarked, 'I have no idea what happens if I don't get into university.' On the other hand, knowledge of the non-university sector was higher amongst comprehensive school students than knowledge of universities. This particular finding was unexpected and so no questions were asked on the questionnaire concerning the type of higher education chosen, all questions relating to higher education in general. This is obviously an area for further research.

In many respects the evidence would also support the work of Bowles and Gintis (1980) who claim that different schools produce different aspirations in their pupils. It has been argued, for example by Bennett and Eglin (1982), that the current direction of educational policy is to have a small academic sector of secondary education based on private schools, with assisted places for the bright state pupils and the possible reintroduction of grammar schools. The expectation here is for pupils from these schools to go on to university. The other pupils will be educated in the vocational sector, which will encompass the comprehensives. These comprehensives will contain a wide range of abilities from those taking Youth. Training Scheme (YTS) type courses to those capable of GCE O- and GCE A-levels who will then obtain vocational training to degree or diploma level at a polytechnic. We may well be seeing the first evidence of this development from this study.

However, it is difficult to put the findings of this study into total context without knowing what the full implications of the binary system of higher education mean in terms of success or otherwise of polytechnic and other non-university graduates in the professions, management and similar occupations. Certainly, those students taking Technician Education Council and Business Education Council higher diplomas are being educated, or is it trained, for senior technician posts. The position of Council for National Academic Awards degree holders is less certain. Perhaps this is another area for further study.

It is now nearly twenty years since the Secretary of State for Education and Science announced the 'dual' system of higher education which eventually became known as the 'binary' system. The policy envisaged different but equal institutions with the polytechnics making a distinctive contribution in the field of technology. Whether or not the polytechnics, and the colleges and institutes of higher education which followed them, were, at any time, considered equal is debatable. Their current position is clear. In terms of government funding and client choice they are very much second-class institutions.

In this respect the attitude of the teachers and students in the study is interesting. Private sector schooling is concentrated on university entrance, the comprehensive schools less so. This is reflected in the differential knowledge that students had of the various forms of higher education. However, the fact that there is an orientation to higher education within comprehensive sixth forms, despite the fact that less than half of their students come from extended career families, is important, and can, therefore, be regarded as a success. This success, on the evidence of this study, can partly be attributed to the careers service, certainly in respect of the provision of information.

However, what has emerged from this study is that the attitude to institutions on either side of the binary divide differs between private sector school staff and students and comprehensive school staff and students. The binary divide in higher education may well be a binary divide from 11 onwards.

References

ACKER, S. (1982) 'Women in education', in HARTNETT, A. (Ed.) *The Social Sciences in Educational Studies*, London. Heinemann, pp. 144–5.

ASHTON, D.N. and FIELD, D. (1976) *Young Workers*, London, Hutchinson.

BARRON, G. (1966) *Society, Schools and Progress in England*, Oxford, Pergamon, pp. 139–40.

BELL, R. *et al.* (1973) *Education in Great Britain and Ireland*, Milton Keynes, Open University Press.

BENNETT, N.D. and EGLIN, G.J. (1982) 'Structural unemployment, education and training', *PRISE*, 82, pp. 10–15.

BERG, I. (1970) *Education and Jobs! The Great Training Robbery*, New York, Praeger.

BOTTOMORE, T.B. (1964) *Elites and Society*, Harmondsworth, Pelican, p. 30.

BOURDIEU, P. (1977) 'Cultural reproduction and social reproduction', in KARABEL, J. and HALSEY, A.H. (Eds) *Power and Ideology in Education*, New York, Oxford University Press.

BOWLES, S. and GINTIS, H. (1980) 'Education and the long shadow of work', in NICHOLS, T. (Ed.) *Capital and Labour*, London, Fontana.

COULSON, M.A. *et al.* (1967) 'Towards a sociological theory of occupational choice — a critique', *Sociological Review*, 15, pp. 301–9.

COX, C.B. and DYSON, A.E. (1970) *Black Paper Three*, London, The

Critical Quarterly Society.

DEEM, R. (1978) *Women and Schooling*, London, Routledge and Kegan Paul.

EGLIN, G.J. (1982) *Aspirations for Higher Education amongst Students in Sixteen to Nineteen Education in Three London Boroughs*, unpublished PhD thesis, Brunel University.

FORD, J. (1969) *Social Class and the Comprehensive School*, London, Routledge and Kegan Paul.

FORD, J. and BOX, S. (1967) 'Sociological theory and occupational choice,' *Sociological Review*, 15, pp. 287–99.

GINZBERG, E. (1972) 'Towards a theory of occupational choice: A restatement', *Vocational Guidance Quarterly*, 20, pp. 169–76.

GINZBERG, E. *et al.* (1951) *Occupational Choice*, New York, Columbia University Press.

GLENNESTER, H. and PRYKE, R. (1964) 'Born to rule', in *The Public Schools*, London, Fabian Society.

GRAMSCI, A. (1972) *The Modern Prince and Other Writings*, New York, International Publishers.

HALSEY, A.H. *et al.* (1980) *Origins and Destinations: Family, Class and Education in Modern Britain*, Oxford, Clarendon Press.

HUSEN, T. (1975) *Social Influences on Educational Attainment*, Paris, Organization for Economic Cooperation and Development.

LABOUR PARTY (1980) *Private Schools*, London, College Hill Press.

LEVITAS, M. (1974) *Marxist Perspective in the Sociology of Education*, London, Routledge and Kegan Paul.

MUSGRAVE, P.W. (1974) 'A sociological theory of occupational choice', in WILLIAMS, W.M. (Ed.) *Occupational Choice*, London, George Allen and Unwin.

NEWMAN, B. (1968) 'Occupational choice', unpublished paper quoted in SPEAKMAN, M.A. 'Occupational choice and placement', in ESLAND, G. and SALAMAN, G. (Eds) *The Politics of Work and Occupations*, Milton Keynes, Open University Press, pp. 121.

RABY, L. and WALFORD, G. (1981) 'Career related attitudes and their determinants for middle- and low-stream pupils in an urban, multiracial comprehensive school', *Research in Education*, 25, p. 19.

REID, I. and WORMALD, E. (Eds) (1982) *Sex Differences in Britain*, London, Grant McIntyre.

ROBBINS REPORT (1963) *Higher Education*, London, Central Advisory Council for Education (England).

ROBERTS, K. (1975) 'The developmental theory of occupational choice: A critique and an alternative', in ESLAND, G.M. *et al.* (Eds) *People and Work*, Edinburgh, Holmes-McDougall/The Open University Press.

ROWETH, B. (1981) 'The Enigma of APR=QLR×QPR', *The Guardian*, 11 September.

SCRUTON, R. (1980) *The Meaning of Conservatism*, Hamondsworth, Penguin, p. 157.

STANWORTH, M. (1981) *Gender and Schooling*, London, Hutchinson.

SUPER, D.E. and BOHN, M.J. (1971) *Occupational Psychology*, London, Tavistock.

SWIFT, A.F. (1969) *The Sociology of Education*, London, Routledge and

Greg Eglin

Kegan Paul.
WAKEFORD, J. (1979) *The Cloistered Elite*, London, Macmillan.
WILBY, (1977) 'The diploma disease', *New Statesman*, 17 June, p. 804.
WILLIS, P. (1977) *Learning to Labour*, Farnborough, Saxon House.
WOLPE, A.M. (1978) *Some Processes in Sexist Eduction*, Women's Research and Resources Centre.
WORSLEY, P. (1974) *Introducing Sociology*, Harmondsworth, Penguin.
YOUNG, M.F.D. (Ed.) (1971) *Knowledge and Control: New Directions for the Sociology of Education*, London, Collier-Macmillan.
YOUNG, M.F.D. and WHITTY, G. (1977) *Society, State and Schooling*, Lewes, Falmer Press.

The Changing Professionalism of Public School Teachers

Geoffrey Walford, University of Aston

This chapter is concerned with a small group of teachers and the ways in which their working lives are changing. It draws upon the debate over professionalism and proletarianization as it has been applied to teachers and traces the discontinuities and similarities of experience between public school masters and the majority of teachers who work in the state system. After a brief review of the literature on professionalism, new empirical data about present-day school masters are presented and it is argued that the discontinuities between the two types are becoming less sharp.

The Study of Professionalism in the Literature

The junk room of educational studies is littered with discarded theoretical and empirical works concerned with the professionalization of school teachers. The professions, whatever they may be, have frequently been seen by teachers as being associated with higher status and salary levels, better working conditions, security of tenure and greater autonomy over everyday activities. Professionalization and professional development have thus been used as rallying cries by teachers in their attempts to improve their position by arguing that teaching should have similar status and conditions to the more widely recognized professional occupations.

Many early studies of professionalism within the sociology of education thus exploited a trait model of the professions with which teaching could be compared. A limited range of occupations with high status such as lawyers, doctors and priests was taken by various sociologists as being indicative of the 'true' and generally accepted professions. Their common attributes were then isolated, and used as criteria against which further occupations could be judged, to assess the extent to which they approximated to the 'true' professions. The result is many different, although partly overlapping, lists (for example, Flexner, 1915; Goode, 1969) which range in the number and applicability of the criteria selected according to the polemical or theoretical aims of the study. Leggatt (1970) summarizes the most commonly appearing characteristics:

(a) Practice is founded upon a base of theoretical, esoteric knowledge.
(b) The acquisition of knowledge requires a long period of education and socialization.
(c) Practitioners are motivated by an ideal of altruistic service rather than the pursuit of material and economic gains.
(d) Careful control is exercised over recruitment, training, certification and standards of practice.
(e) The colleague group is well organized and has disciplinary powers to enforce a code of ethical practice.

It can be seen that the nature of the traits selected for inclusion and comparison in these early studies tended to emphasize the rather more positive aspects of professionalism from the point of view of the client. The altruistic nature of the relationship, in particular, received great stress and has a distinguished parentage. Marshall (1965), for example, believed that altruism was the fundamental distinction between professional and other occupations, and proposed that: 'Service depends on individual qualities and individual judgement supported by individual responsibility. That, I believe, is the essence of professionalism and it is not concerned with self-interest, but with the welfare of the client.' A similar emphasis can be found in the work of Parsons (1954) who also saw the professions as being distinguished by their orientation towards the rest of the community rather than towards self-interest.

Such idealism is now, however, generally regarded with some scepticism. This model of professionalism has been strongly questioned for its largely uncritical, ahistorical and conservative bias, and for its failure to question differences in power between client and practitioner. (See, for example, Dingwall, 1976; Johnson, 1972; Johnson, 1977; Illich, 1973.) Many radical writers would now claim that the major distinguishing characteristic of a profession is the power and control that it maintains for its members against its clients. Professions, it is argued, generate and maintain inequality and privilege, and use the rhetoric of altruistic service as a legitimating mask.

Both views of professionalism are extreme, and it is reasonable to suggest that elements of both self-interest and altruism can be found within teachers and the more widely recognized professions. It is likely that most teachers would hold with a rather more temperate definition. Gosden (1972), in his study of the 'contribution of teachers' associations to the development of school teaching as a professional occupation', states:

> Any professional occupation is generally held to possess certain attributes including a reasonable level of salaries, pensions, security of tenure, sound training and qualifications and some recognition by the community of the professional's right to influence the way in which the service it offers is administered. (Gosden, 1972, p. 111)

In making this definition Gosden calls attention to a set of rather less publicly admirable traits of professionalism. Clearly he is correct in assuming that they are not just accidental accompaniments of being a doctor or a lawyer, and it would not seem unreasonable to see this second set of traits as additional to, and sometimes in conflict with, the first set.

While some authors have argued that all occupations are gradually becoming professionalized (for example, Bucher and Strauss, 1961; Wilensky, 1964), the evidence is against this interpretation, and there remains a stubborn barrier to the general acceptance of teaching as a full profession. Etzioni (1969) has coined the term 'semi-profession' to describe teaching and a family of similar bureaucratically organized occupations. The occupations in this group, which includes teachers, nurses and social workers in particular, have much in common with each other. The size of the occupational group is large, there is a high proportion of female members, the members are predominantly from low social class backgrounds, there is a low level of autonomy as a group and the membership is segmented. All of these characteristics are clearly in contrast to the characteristics of groups such as doctors and lawyers, and separate them from full equality with these elite professions.

In another attempt to clear the fog of confusion Leggatt (1970) suggested that progress could be made by the accumulation and systematic comparison of further data about individual occupational groups. He suggested that the questions of greatest sociological interest in relation to each professional or semi-professional field were:

> What are the characteristics of (a) the particular group, (b) the group's clientele, (c) practitioner-client relations, (d) the organisational context, and (e) the environmental setting? What are the characteristic acts of professional practice? And what are the effects of these upon the quality of professional experience and the status of the occupational group? (Leggatt, 1970, p. 161)

These were indeed new and worthwhile questions but, in practice, the answers to the questions lead directly to further additions to the list of traits of 'true' professions. For if a semi-profession is where the occupational group is large, there is a high proportion of female members, the members are predominantly from low social class backgrounds, there is a low level of autonomy as a group and the membership is segmented; then a traditional profession is characteristically a small, male, upper-class, highly autonomous elite.

In a similar way the more recent work of Ozga and Lawn (1981), while very suggestive of new directions for research, still includes the implication of a basic trait model. They argue (p. 147): 'Teachers are workers, who have used professionalism strategically and had it used against them, that they have allied with organised labour in the past, and, as a consequence of pressure for proletarianisation, may develop such alliances and strategies again.' While this is clearly true, professionalism can only be used as a strategy if it carries with it the implications of a whole set of characteristics of what constitutes professionalism. The inclusion of specific elements will be argued over, but the use of professionalism as a strategy implies the construction of an ideal type.

The 'Traditional' Public School Master

In his discussion of the occupational characteristics of teachers Leggatt (1970) states:

> The outstanding characteristics of teachers as an occupational group are the large size of the group, its high proportion of female members, its lowly social class composition, its small measure of autonomy as group and its segmentation. These features, although bearing on each other, have independent

effects upon the nature of the occupation and its status. Others, such as the high rate of turnover of teachers, their low degree of commitment to their work, and the low prestige and disadvantageous stereotype of the group and its members are more consequences and reinforcements of these primary characteristics than of primary significance in themselves.

Disregarding the question of the accuracy of these remarks for the majority of teachers and the implications for their professional status, it is clear that for the traditional public school master *none* of these characteristics applies. The majority of work about teaching as a profession excludes from consideration the very group of teachers who would be regarded by many as having the greatest claim to the use of that title. It can be claimed that public school masters have occupational status and conditions in closer approximation to the acknowledged professionals than any other group of teachers.

The aim of this paper is to examine the limits of this claim which resides in the many peculiar characteristics of public school masters as compared with the majority of teachers. It will thus be necessary to examine the extent to which the group exhibits the various implicitly and explicitly derived traits that have been discussed.

It will be shown later, however, that the situation is a changing one, so it is necessary to first outline the characteristics of what might be termed 'the traditional public school master' before dealing with the rather more complicated empirical reality.

Traditionally, the public school master is part of an all-male, high-status, academic elite. While in 1980 there were some 500,000 school teachers in Great Britain, there were only about 10,000 school masters in the 200-odd HMC schools. Just as the HMC schools emphasize their superiority, so the use of the term 'school master' emphasizes the differences between teachers in these schools and other teachers. The challenge to their elite status which used to come from grammar school teachers has subsided as comprehensivization of the state sector has taken place and these schools have disappeared. As great emphasis is given to the 'formation of character' in the pupils it was necessary for school masters to be the social equals of the parents, and, characteristically, these schoolmasters have high and uniform social class backgrounds. In the tradition of Mr Chips (Hilton, 1934), school masters are themselves public school products, boarding from age 7 in a preparatory school, then at 13 moving to one of the HMC schools. After three years at Oxford or

Cambridge for a degree, they return, fairly swiftly, to their haven of intellectual endeavour.

Again, traditionally they have a high degree of commitment to their work and there has been a low turnover of masters in the schools. Long service at a particular school is the essence of the system, for housemasters are appointed from within the school, often in strict order of appointment to the school. If a master wishes to take advantage of the comforts, prestige and power of being a housemaster, he is usually required to wait some ten to fifteen years in the same school before being given the chance, and then holds office for twelve to fifteen years. During the long wait he not only has to show himself to be 'suitable' but he also has time to devote himself to furthering his academic subject. Public school masters have been, in fact, very influential in the development of school subjects, working within national and local subject associations, and on examination boards, and writing school textbooks. For example, public school masters had a very important role in promoting and defining the structure of school science through their involvement in the Association for Science Education and textbook writing (Walford, 1982).

This sort of activity clearly links with Gosden's (1972) definition of professionalism, too. Parents of boys in public school have, traditionally, had the attitude that the school master knows his job, and that school masters have the right to specify and implement the services which they wish to offer. The respect that they received from parents is accompanied by more solid rewards. Salaries are traditionally higher than those for teachers in state schools and there is often the further perk of heavily subsidized housing. Security of tenure is also reasonably strong.

The traditional public school master can also make claims to professional status through the traits characteristic of full professionalism summarized by Leggatt (1970) into five main points:

1 Practice is founded on a base of theoretical and esoteric knowledge within a specific subject area. School masters do not necessarily claim to be teachers as such; their legitimation lies in their specialized subject knowledge, which is sanctified by an Oxbridge MA rather than a teaching certificate.

2 This subject knowledge requires a long period of education, but the socialization process needed to become the 'right sort of person' to become a school master starts at 7.

3 Contracts between the schools and school masters rarely

specify explicitly more than the academic teaching requirements, yet school masters spent perhaps more of their time
involved in sports, clubs, organizations, drama, music and
pastoral activities. Altruism is a not unreasonable description
of much of this work.

4   Traditionally it is the headmaster rather than the school
    masters who exercises control over recruitment, yet the
    colleague group is tight enough to ensure that the head-
    master does not appoint anyone too at variance with their
    wishes.

5   And, again, while a code of ethics is not written, an informal
    code certainly exists, which can be enforced informally by
    the colleague group.

It would seem that the 'ideal type' traditional public school
master has numerous claims to professional status. How close are
present-day public school masters to this caricature?

The Modern Public School Master

The empirical data presented in the following sections are based
upon research that has been conducted over the last three years in
two major British Headmasters' Conference boarding schools. Both
of the schools are clearly in the top third of HMC schools, each
having about 600 pupils, a teaching staff of roughly sixty, and fees of
around £4500 per year in 1982.

I spent a four-week period at one school in 1981 and a whole
term in the second during 1982. During that time I talked with boys,
girls, masters, wives, secretaries, other staff and headmasters. Further information was gained from eighty taped semi-structured interviews with academic staff who were part of a stratified, pseudo-
random sample. I only had one outright refusal to be interviewed,
but two more 'never had time' on several askings. Eight of the eighty
'masters' interviewed were actually women, but to avoid possible
identification the masculine pronoun is used throughout. The term
'master' is often used by the schools themselves to include both male
and female staff.

Tables 1–3 show the educational backgrounds of the sample of
masters. The exact numbers in the tables are, of course, dependent
on the particular sample interviewed, but wider study of other
sources suggests that they are reasonably representative of not only

Table 1. Educational Background: School

	Secondary modern or comprehensive	State grammar	Old direct grant	Private	Other HMC	Same school
N = 80	2	23	18	5	23	9
Percentage	3	29	22	6	29	11

Table 2. Educational Background: Day or Boarding

	Boarding	Day
N = 80	36	44
Percentage	45	55

Table 3. Educational Background: Higher Education

	Oxford	Cambridge	Non-Oxbridge	Higher degree	Teaching qualification
N = 80	25	21	34	10	44
Percentage	31	26	43	13	55

the two schools involved, but also the full range of major public boarding schools. It can be seen that they no longer form on elite with regard to social background, and that there is considerable diversity of educational histories. There was a small core of 11 per cent who were teaching in the school where they had been pupils themselves. This lack of movement was not something they were usually proud of, and there was often a note of defensiveness in discussion of this aspect. For example:

67: Well in that case, I'm a bad example, because I was educated here, and I suppose I always wanted to teach.

69: I was, in fact, a boy here ... I had no intention of coming here to teach at all. Quite the reverse. I thought that it was a bad thing to come back to your own school. I thought that people were blimps who went back to their own schools.

A further 29 per cent had been educated at other HMC schools and, while many of these had an upper-class background and saw public school teaching as a natural progression in their lives, not every HMC boy was like this.

60: Well, my own background is not typically public school, let me say that. I came from a sort of ... I suppose it would be called lower middle class background, certainly not more than that and I went to a village school myself. I never went to a prep school or even knew what a prep school was until much later. So I went to a village school, then I went to a grammar school and from grammar school I was one of the very early people to get the benefit of the 1944 Act, because I took a scholarship to go from grammar school to public school. My parents didn't pay a penny for my education — they couldn't afford it.

Strangely, only a minority of the masters in the sample had experienced boarding themselves as boys. Masters were attracted to public schools as much for academic emphasis as for their desire to be involved in the total boarding community. Practically all of the masters from what used to be direct grant schools had been 'scholarship boys' rather than fee payers, and had been day pupils rather than boarders. One of the early 'scholarship boys' explained:

64: I was asked to take the job from my teaching practice school. I intended to stay for a couple of years, because I ... because I was curious. I liked what I thought the life might be. As a sort of extension to Oxford in the way of a community and academic/social/sporting thing. I had a sort of image of the public schools — I suppose based on comics and films — a sort of guilded image. But I didn't think that I really belonged to the public school group. I very definitely wasn't like the rest of the staff — most of the staff then had been at public schools — boarding schools.

A common pattern amongst those from the state sector who had moved into public schools was a desire to be able to teach their subject away from what they saw as a less academic and more trouble-ridden state sector. Some had taught in the state sector for many years before moving into the public school sector. Untypically, one had made a startling move:

88: I knew nothing about public schools when I went there. It was quite a shock, moving from a secondary modern school to a public school.

More usually, people had moved partly as a result of the closure of grammar schools during comprehensive reorganization. Typical of this group were comments concerning their desire to teach able children, for example:

84: Well, I went to a grammar school and I must say that I enjoyed it there and, as a teacher, probably if grammar schools had continued I'd be teaching in one of those.

68: So, by that time, I'd said that I liked the independent sector. I dare say I would have been looking for a grammar school job, and still might be, were there any grammar schools. Because there weren't, the independent sector — public schools — seemed to be the nearest approximation. And that's why I ended up in them — although I'm not in entire agreement with everything about them!

A surprising number of masters had tried teaching in public schools not because they had any great commitment to the idea of private education, but because they felt that the teaching there might be more convivial.

The closure of the grammar schools was not the only macro-social pressure. Thirteen per cent of these teachers had a higher degree and a decade earlier might have expected to gain a lectureship at a university. The stagnation and recent retrenchment within the universities had, especially in the sciences, forced university research workers of many years' standing to take jobs in teaching. These potential academics had little desire to teach in comprehensives. One explained:

12: I suppose I'm guilty of caricaturing some state schools now, when I say that I know so many people who are almost distracted by the difficulties of just keeping discipline. It prevents them from teaching.

A further 10 per cent of the masters had chosen to become school masters only after extended periods of quite unconnected work. The range here included international marketing, accountancy, banking, business promotion and restaurantering. For the sample of masters as a whole the universities attended also often differed from the traditional Oxbridge choice, so that, in total, 43 per cent had no connection with Oxbridge. A fair sprinkling of first-class honours degrees was more than counteracted by thirds and fourths, the majority achieving second-class degrees.

A further challenge to the traditional caricature of an all-male, high-status, academic elite is the fact that eight of the 'masters' I interviewed were actually female. Over the last few years many HMC schools have admitted girls, either at sixth form level only or throughout the school (Walford, 1983a). Some 9 per cent of full-time teaching staff in these schools are now women (Walford, 1983b), and women outnumber men as part-time staff.

From the evidence presented so far it can be seen that, in fact, there is now no clear discontinuity between the characteristics of this sample of public school teachers and the majority of teachers in state schools. The two groups overlap rather than being distinct. This does not mean that the 'traditional public school master' never existed, for historically it is clear that the discontinuities were very much greater than they are today. Lists of past members of staff, for example, show that the Oxbridge background was much more important prior to about 1970. Before that time it is only very occasionally that a non-Oxbridge degree occurs on the lists, yet now they are common. In a similar way the introduction of girls and female staff in substantial numbers can be dated to the mid-1970s in many cases.

One of the anomalies with regard to the professional status of public school masters is that teachers in independent schools are not required to have a teaching qualification. The traditional image of the public school master includes the idea of 'natural' teachers. Masters were, after all, gentlemen whose general academic and moral culture was the product of a decade of socialization in prep and public schools. The period of 'training' required to enter public school mastering was thus not a mere year or three of teacher training, but a decade or more of highly structured building of cultural capital. Yet things have changed, for in the sample, 55 per cent did in fact possess a teaching qualification, usually a one-year postgraduate teaching certificate. Again, a clear difference could be made between the older and the younger staff who were much more likely to have undertaken training. At the lowest level this was insurance: 'What else would I do if they closed the public schools?', but many had thought that it would be a useful year. Again the distinction between public school teachers and other teachers would appear to be declining.

Long service is still on important part of public schoolmastering, but with the shrinking size of the state sector and the lack of career mobility in that system, this is also less distinctive. During the 1960s and early 1970s a popular career path for the public school master who did not wish to become a housemaster was to enter the state sector at a senior level. This might be head of department, deputy headmaster or even headmaster. The movement in this direction has almost completely ceased and has been replaced by a reverse flow of highly academic teachers from the state system moving into the public school system. According to the various trait models, professionals are given great autonomy as a group and individually to influence the way in which their service is offered. Many of the masters volunteered this sort of information in answer to questions about the advantages of the job from their point of view. One housemaster explained:

> 7: You're given great freedom. Let me give you an example of the freedom you get. As a Housemaster you're given a job to do and you're allowed to get on with it. The Headmaster doesn't interfere in any way with the running of the Houses and all the Houses are different from that point of view. You'll find a different flavour in every House. He likes to know what's going on, but in a way it's like being in charge of a little school yourself. What you do in your own House is your own concern. You could be very idle and get away with it.

Another master stated:

> 45: I was thinking the other night, in one's teaching and with everything here, you know, you just are yourself and you can take a completely free line. It's not a school where everyone asks permissions of anyone else — you just get on with it.

Many of the masters were keen to point out that not only was there a fair degree of autonomy, but that the schools actively and financially encouraged staff to develop their interests. These teachers were encouraged to take an active part in the development of their subject and finance was usually provided for them to attend relevant conferences and meetings. Several had spent a term's sabbatical as a Schoolmaster Fellow at one of the Oxford or Cambridge colleges, and far more people than would be expected had been involved in the writing of school textbooks and in curriculum development.

However, not all of the staff felt quite as independent as this. Several complained about restrictions in their teaching, others complained about the heavy demands that the school made on their time both in the classroom and out. With reference to out-of-classroom activities one of the older masters explained: 'People are tending to be increasingly elbowed into doing things. But, more or less, if you decide that you're fed up with doing something then that's all right.' Quite clearly, if the school organization is to function in a reasonably efficient manner, any degree of autonomy has to be associated with a degree of altruism. It requires that the individual master takes note of the needs and demands of the community and is prepared to do a reasonable share of these tasks. Living in or near a boarding school means that masters are available to pupils for a much greater part of the week than are teachers at day schools. And most of the masters at these schools *are* prepared to give up their time to help pupils, and do not try to restrict their help to timetabled lessons. Housemasters and assistant housemasters are usually even more altruistic in the use of their time. Pupils' problems and pupils' joys for that matter, cannot be contained within a regular routine, and masters spend a very great deal of their time involved in school-related activities. Their altruism does not stop there either, for many, especially the younger staff, give up part of their holidays to treck the Scottish mountains, sail round the Isle of Wight, or explore South America. These activities, although obviously enjoyed by the masters concerned, have at least some altruistic element in them.

In summary, it has been shown that while the occupation of a public school master has many traits congruent with the professions, it also has many traits in conflict. The image of the traditional public school master is in many ways closer to the ideal of professionalism than the present-day reality, and, although the process is complex, it would seem that numerous changes are occurring in the occupation.

I wish to argue that many of these changes can be seen as elements in a process of proletarianization — a process which is occurring for teachers in the state as well as the public sector of schooling. Before doing this, however, it is necessary to discuss the somewhat different question of the class position of these two groups of teachers. For in some ways here public school teachers are further from the ideal of professionalism than their state school colleagues.

The Class Position of Teachers

Recently there has been a renewed interest in the relationships between teachers, professionalism and social class (for example, Ozga and Lawn, 1981; Harris, 1982), especially from various neo-Marxist perspectives. The key distinction to be made is between productive and unproductive labour. Productive labour, according to Marx, is labour exchanged with capital to produce surplus value, while unproductive labour is exchanged with revenue. Marx recognized that an increasingly industrialized society would involve more and more people in collective labour and he argued that it was not necessary for labour to be directly adding to use value for it to be productive.

> The product ceases to be the direct product of the individual, and becomes a social product, produced in common by a collective labourer. . . . In order to labour productively, it is no longer necessary for you to do manual work yourself; enough, if you are an organ of the collective labourer and perform one of its subordinate functions. (Marx, 1974, p. 476)

In particular, for teachers, Marx argues:

> . . . a schoolmaster is a productive labourer, when, in addition to belabouring the heads of his scholars, he works like a horse to enrich the school proprietor. That the latter has laid out his capital in teaching factory, instead of a sausage factory, does not alter the relation. (Marx, 1974, p. 477)

Harris (1982) argues that, while this may have been true at the time Marx wrote, it is now more complicated.

> Conditions have changed since Marx wrote, and now with the capitalist mode of production the vast majority of teachers . . . are no longer employed by individual capitalist proprietors. They are employed by the state and they are paid

out of revenue — they are therefore unproductive labourers.
(Harris, 1982, p. 57)

This claim, which is not original to Harris, leads directly to an area of fierce controversy amongst Marxists for many would argue that only productive labourers can be included in the working class. Some development of class theory is thus required to ensure that the majority of teachers are not thus excluded. Strangely enough, there are fewer problems with the social class location of teachers in independent schools.

Teachers is HMC boarding schools are not, of course, employed directly by capitalist school proprietors (although some of the less prestigious independent schools are still privately owned), but neither are they employed by the state and paid out of revenue. These schools are now registered non-profit-making charities, but charities largely devoted to the education of a select group of children of affluent parents.

Teachers are usually employed by the Board of Governors who delegate day-to-day responsibility to the headmaster, and they are paid, in the main, by parents or guardians of the pupils through termly fees to the school. The teachers may not 'work like a horse to enrich the school proprietors' but increasingly they do work like a horse to try to ensure that pupils obtain the necessary qualifications to enable them to get well-paid jobs.

The discussion is not merely academic. The various pressures on the schools during the 1970s have made masters much more aware of their contractual relationship. In less worried times the ideology of 'the gentleman professional' had obscured this relationship, but now through the gradual process of proletarianization, it is being revealed. One master analyzed the situation as follows:

8: Any transaction involves client, executant and product,
    In a state school the client may be said to be the child
    himself because he is a taxpayer and the state choses to
    educate him. The money comes from somewhere —
    there's no moral problem about where the money comes
    from. To that extent you are the executant and he is the
    product, but you collaborate — it's a social interaction
    which is worthy. But it gets very heavy in a public
    school. The client is the parent and the tendency is such
    that a transaction is to turn the teacher into a proletariate.
    And this school used *not* to work on this model, but it

has worked very much on this model for the last five
years.

This master then drew comparisons between the situation he
was in and E.P. Thompson's description of the changes in the position of university academics in the early 1970s (Thompson, 1980).
He continued by giving an example:

> 8: We were addressed by the treasurer on the matter of
>   money and he offered a model of how he saw the school
>   as working, which was a management structured analy-
>   sis. The Governing Body were the managers, and we
>   were on the shop floor, and the boys were the products.
>   And therefore, we had no place in the planning of policy
>   and decisions about the directions of the institution.
>   They wanted absolute loyalty.

This description, given with little prompting during an interview, emphasizes the changes in the relationship between teachers
and employers that are occurring within public schools. It is a description that makes clear that the era of the gentleman professional
school master is drawing to a close, and a process of proletarianization has begun.

Proletarianization

During the last decade or so the process of proletarianization has
begun in very many white collar occupations. Ozga and Lawn (1981)
describe the process as:

> Proletarianisation is the process whereby the worker is forced
> into a closer relationship with capital which removes the skill
> (the conception and execution of work) and therefore the
> relative autonomy of the worker. The constant drive towards
> the accumulation of capital extends the process to more and
> more workers. (p. 124)

As Ozga and Lawn explain, the somewhat analogous job to
teaching of an office clerk has changed rapidly with the increase of
mechanization, specialization and size. Office work now requires
little, if any, discretion or skill and the worker is not expected to
understand more than a small part of the whole enterprise. There is a
growing lack of autonomy and ability to initiate as tasks become
more prescribed, set and standardized. The office worker has

increasingly become a manual worker where, according to Braverman: 'The work is still performed in the brain, but the brain is used as the equivalent of the hand of the detail worker in production, grasping and releasing a single piece of "data" over and over again' (Braverman, 1974, p. 319). Ozga and Lawn summarize the process as follows:

> The process of proletarianisation is the result of the expansion of capitalist production and the concentration and centralisation of capital. This process de-personalises employer/worker relations, breaks down 'craft' skills, increases technological investment (fixed to valuable capital ratio), automates and de-skills, separates conception from the execution of work and increases management control over workers, their skills and the pace of their work. It continues the division of employees and workers, eliminating contradictory class locations in so doing. (Ozga and Lawn, 1981, p. 131)

They go on to suggest that the process of proletarianization is not confined to the industrial and commercial worker, but can be seen to be occurring to teachers in the state system as well.

We have seen that the class position of teachers in public schools is, in some ways, less contradictory than that of teachers in the state system. Their employers have always been, fairly directly, the parents or guardians of the pupils. Yet the nature of this worker/employer relationship has in the past been largely obscured by the ideology of the gentleman professional and it is only recently that public school masters have begun to experience its full force. What changes have occurred to increase its visibility?

Although we do not necessarily wish to give supremacy to the purely economic factors, it is clear that public schools were far from insulated from the recent effects of inflation, recession and unemployment and that these have been of major importance. The early 1970s, for example, saw a rate of inflation which was unprecedented. Only a few public schools have foundation income, so there was a direct need to either pass on increases in terms of fees to parents or become more efficient and cost conscious. One result was that in the year from September 1974 to September 1975 fees at major HMC boarding schools rose by 33 per cent. I have argued elsewhere (Walford, 1983a) that cost consciousness and economic stringency were part of the reason for the introduction of girls into many of these schools, but answers to questions about what changes masters had seen occur revealed that the type of pupil had changed considerably in a number of other ways as well. A very typical response from the elder masters was:

> 12: I regret that we teach such a narrow range, although that's not quite as simple as it looks. I do regret that it costs so much to send a boy to the school that it limits the field from which we draw. I've seen whole groups of people drop out from the running — schoolmasters no longer send their sons here, GPs dropped out quite a lot of years ago, Army officers, clergymen — whole groups of very interesting and worthy people, professional people, can no longer afford to do it. And I've seen the social change and the increase in the number of ex-patriots, sweating away in the Middle East because they think that this is the best way of giving their children a chance.... The 'newly' rich, the contractors and garage owners, and some business men who are sending first generation boys. Again I welcome them because they bring a breath of fresh air and sometimes an awkwardness and questioning of what we're doing — both the parents and the boys. But really what I suppose I'm saying is that I'm sorry we don't get a wider range of intake.

This changing clientele has brought with it new demands. Although most of these parents wish to enjoy the kudos of having a son at a public school, they wish their boy to acquire rather more tangible benefits too. The schools are seen as a way by which sons can be given a good chance in particular with regard to examinations. Time after time masters talked of the increased emphasis on examinations within the schools.

> 47: I think that we are too examination ridden — it's difficult to get away from it but we're now an examination mill. And parents' expectations when the boy gets accepted by the school are often quite unreasonable. Sometimes, when a new boy arrives in the House you get 'Now would you suggest Oxford or Cambridge and which College?' And I say 'I'll tell you when he's done his 'O' levels and whether we should even be considering it.'

> But, I think it's quite understandable when the parents
> are paying our high fees. If the father's a businessman,
> he regards it as an investment and he wants the dividend
> in success for his boy.

Increasingly parents are sending their sons to public schools to
ensure that they have the best chance of getting vital examination
successes and university entry. As the recession continues and
unemployment even amongst graduates increases, so do the pressures on the schools from parents. Parents are no longer prepared to
spend £4500 for their sons to 'run round fields half the time', but
want as good teaching and facilities as their money can buy.

Almost without exception, masters resent this increased examination pressure. It severely restricts their autonomy by forcing
them to neglect wider educational issues and only teach material on
examination syllabuses, and this forces them away from the gentlemen professional ideology. Pressure comes from parents and from
boys, and the emphasis on examinations is very much a contested
area. For example, at one sixth form parents' meeting I attended the
headmaster was strongly criticized for his policy of forcing every
student to take some general studies. 'Why', asked one parent, 'can't
they take an extra A-level?' 'Why', asked another, 'can't the school
offer a wider choice of A-level?' Pupils, when they complained about
masters to me, practically always did so on the basis of their not
teaching the syllabus. Even the 13-year-olds, who I watched exploiting one teacher's weaknesses in class, complained to me later that
they would prefer someone who could keep them better in order and
teach them more work for the examination. Indeed, there was very
little indiscipline in classes, and most pupils seemed fully aware of
the awesome investment that had been made for them, and their
need to succeed.

With the changing clientele and increasing academic pressures,
the underlying worker/employee relationship has been more clearly
revealed to masters. Parents are now less likely to accept that the
school always knows best, and less likely to acquiesce to the
schoolmasters' demands for treatment as professionals.

Part of the change in the backgrounds of masters can also be
explained by this increased academic emphasis. Teachers are now
much more often appointed for their academic excellence — the
'blue' at Cambridge is less important than the first-class or higher
degree. Although there are considerable tensions between the needs

of a boarding school as such and the needs of an academic institution, masters are not so expected to be 'all-round' men. Their tasks have become more narrow, more prescribed, set and standardized.

Similar changes in the nature of teachers' tasks have been noted in an important article on curriculum form by Michael Apple (1982). He argues that, in America at least, teachers are gradually losing control over their work at the level of day-to-day practice. He argues that the growth of pre-packaged, centrally produced curriculum materials is leading to deskilling of the teaching workforce in a similar way as for industrial workers. The construction and details of the curriculum are seen to be the province of experts, who produce not only the physical pre-packaged materials, but also detailed instructions for the teacher as to how to use the materials and evaluate students' performance. The teacher thus becomes an operative, conforming to standardized instructions and having very little control over day-to-day activity in the classroom.

Apple's argument concentrates on curriculum form and, while this element of control is increasing, the main factor for teachers in British public schools is curriculum content. The ever-increasing pressure on examinations from parents forces school masters to concentrate more and more on examination syllabuses. The decreasing choice and control that school masters can exercise in this area forcefully emphasizes the changing worker/employer relationship.

Such loss of control over curriculum is only one of a number of changes in these schools which have emphasized the new worker/ employer relationship. Salaries, for example, are now sometimes fiercely fought over. Within public schools there is no standard salary structure and yearly increases for staff in each school have to be agreed separately. The increasing needs for economy and financial stringency have meant that 'gentlemen's agreements' between headmasters and masters have often been under strain. Most schools advertize salaries which are 'above Burnham' but the scales are not, in fact, easily comparable. For while the Burnham Scale is a series of scales which allow for rank and responsibility as well as age, the scale in most public schools is a single age-related scale, with separate additional payments for special responsibilities. The lack of direct comparability gives schools room to manoeuvre, and several teachers complained to me about the cartel way in which headmasters in these schools had, in the recent past, tried to restrict pay rises. Most masters that I spoke to considered that their pay was not necessarily any greater than they would receive in the state system, although they were expected to work longer hours for it. The 'perk' of rented accommodation provided by the school was also not necessarily seen as an advantage. Younger masters certainly found it convenient to have accommodation provided for them in the early years after university, but as they got older the disadvantages of the 'tied cottage' system became more apparent. Schools are often in areas with little reasonable accommodation available at a price school masters can afford, so they find themselves still living in school-owned accommodation and paying rent, at a time when they would prefer to be buying their own homes. A surprising number of older masters actually owned houses in cheaper areas where they spent their vacations and would eventually retire.

The headmaster's role is also one which seems to have changed as a result of economic and parental pressures. Increasingly, it would seem, the headmaster sees himself as part of a 'management team' and uses techniques of management akin to those of corporate industry. Public boarding schools are complex institutions, providing not only teaching for about 600 pupils but also accommodation, food, entertainment and so on. As the scale of the operation has increased and the need for a tight financial grip has hardened. Headmasters have found themselves drawn away from the classroom and teaching concerns and towards the fundraising, marketing and promotional activities which have become vital for the survival of the school as an organization.

This change of emphasis shows itself in many ways, one of which is job security. Surprisingly, tenure of appointment now seems to be less secure in these schools than in state schools. In state schools it is very difficult indeed to sack any teacher, but it is not quite so difficult in the public schools. Several of the staff I talked to were genuinely concerned that their contracts might be terminated by the school. In other cases masters had, over a time, clearly been 'eased out' of their jobs. Very rarely would it come to an outright sacking for teachers know that, within the tightly restricted world of public schools, a reasonable reference from their current headmaster is vital if they are to secure future employment elsewhere. The pressures on headmasters are now such that any form of inefficiency within the staff cannot be allowed to continue for very long. Unpleasant decisions have to be made.

Another key member of the 'management team' is the bursar. It used to be fairly common for a retired army or airforce officer to occupy this post, but as one bursar explained:

36: It's getting a lot less common. It's now very much an accountant orientated game . . . I think most schools are now looking much more for the direct business management/accountant bloke than they are the retired service man. . . . In a lot of cases schools are going for straight business management. They're going for the chap out of Marks and Sparks or something like that.

Such management control on the financial side influences the more academic decisions too. Masters feel these new pressures on them in their daily working lives.

There are many indications then, that the process of proletarianization is occurring in these public school. The working conditions and degree of autonomy that masters have over their work are changing. In this way the masters find themselves in a possibly more visible worker/employer relationship than do state school teachers.

Another interesting point is that, again probably to a greater extent than state schools, these public schools are moving into a closer relationship with the needs of capital and industry. In some ways it is possible to date this movement from as long ago as the mid-1950s when an Industrial Fund was set up whereby eventually some £3¼ million was given by industry to public and direct grant schools to enable them to build and equip science laboratories. But at that time the predominant interest was with the pure sciences; it is only more recently that business and industry as such have been brought into the curriculum.

As Salter and Tapper (1981) have pointed out, public schools are no longer bastions of classical education, but have swung towards science, design and technology. They have been at the forefront of developments in O-and A-level business studies, economics and business with modern language courses. They have played a major part in Young Enterprise schemes, helped develop Science in Society courses (Walford, 1982) and have invested massively in technology within the schools in the form of computer laboratories and engineering and technology centres.

In the days of full employment and 'special relationships' between public schools and Oxbridge, few schools worried about the eventual careers of their pupils. Increasing unemployment and Oxbridge's more open admissions schemes have changed all that, so that now all the major schools are members of ISCO (Independent Schools Careers Organisation) and run substantial careers development programmes. Boys now visit industry, and industrialists and businessmen now visit schools to give talks. Malvern College is so keen to improve links with industry that one master now has a half-time teaching load and a special three-year fellowship which enables him to spend the rest of his time developing industrial contacts (Jenkins, 1982). Increasingly these public schools see themselves as serving the needs of industry, business and thus capital.

Conclusion

It has been shown that the traditional image of public schoolmasters as a distinct all-male elite group is no longer appropriate. Although there are still elements of gentlemanly professionalism, it would appear that a process of proletarianization has begun and the ideology of professionalism is becoming insufficient to mask the objective class position of these schoolmasters through their worker/employee relationship.

The pressures of inflation, recession and unemployment have had major influences on the working conditions and nature of the work experience of these masters and have in many ways brought them closer to teachers in the state sector. For teachers in the state sector Ozga and Lawn (1981) conclude: 'Our position is that teachers are workers, who have used professionalism strategically and had it used against them, that they have allied with organised labour in the past and in consequence of pressure for proletarianisation may develop such alliances and strategies again' (p. 147). Public school masters in the past have had little to do with organized labour or trade union activity. They have not seen the activities of the teaching unions as having a great deal to do with them, and few public school masters are members. It may well be that a membership drive by these unions could reap large rewards for, in their struggle against proletarianization, these school masters may well find that there is much to be gained by a collective strategy.

References

APPLE, M.W. (1982) 'Curriculum form and the logic of technical control: Building the possessive individual', in APPLE M.W. (Ed.) *Cultural and Economic Reproduction in Education,* London, Routledge and Kegan Paul.

BOYD, D. (1973) *Elites and Their Education,* Slough, NFER.

BRAVERMAN, H. (1974) *Labour and Monopoly Capital,* London, Monthly Review Press.

Geoffrey Walford

BUCHER R. and STRAUSS, A. (1961) 'Professions in process', *American Journal of Sociology*, 66, pp. 325–34.
BURNET, J.F. (Ed.) (1981) *The Public and Preparatory Schools Year Book 1981*, London, Adam and Charles Black.
DANCY, J.C. (1963) *The Public Schools and the Future*, London, Faber and Faber.
DINGWALL, R. (1976) 'Accomplishing profession', *Sociological Review*, 24, pp. 331–49.
DOD (1982) *Dod's Parliamentary Companion 1982*, London, Dod's Parliamentary Companion Ltd.
ETZIONI, A. (Ed.) (1969) *The Semi-Professions and Their Organisation*, New York, Free Press.
FLEXNER, A. (1915) 'Is social work a profession?' in *Proceedings of the National Conference of Charities and Corrections*, New York, Hildman Publishing.
GOODE, W.J. (1969) 'The theoretical limits of professionalization', in ETZIONI, (Ed.) *The Semi-Professions and Their Organisation*, New York, Free Press.
GOSDEN, P.H.J.H. (1972) *The Evolution of a Profession*, Oxford, Blackwell.
HARRIS, K. (1982) *Teachers and Classes. A Marxist Analysis*, London, Routledge and Kegan Paul.
HILTON, J. (1934) *Goodbye Mr Chips*, London, Hodder and Stoughton.
ILLICH, I. (1973) 'The professions as a form of imperialism', *New Society*, 13 September, pp. 633–5.
ISIS (1982) *Annual Census 1982. Statistical Survey of Independent Schools*, London, Independent Schools Information Service.
JENKINS, J. (1982) 'Industry across the curriculum at Malvern', *Education*, 19, November, pp. 396–7.
JOHNSON, T. (1972) *Professions and Power*, London, Macmillan.
JOHNSON, T. (1977) 'The professions in the class structure', in SCASE, R. (Ed.) *Industrial Society: Class, Cleavage and Control*, London, Tavistock.
KALTON, G. (1966) *The Public Schools*, London, Longmans.
LEGGATT, T. (1970) 'Teaching as a profession', in JACKSON, J.A. (Ed.) *Professions and Professionalisation*, Cambridge, Cambridge University Press.
MARSHALL, T.H. (1965) *Class, Citizenship and Social Development*, New York, Doubleday.
MARX, K. (1974) *Capital, Volume I*, London, Lawrence and Wishart (first German edition, 1867).
OZGA, J.T. and LAWN, M.A. (1981) *Teachers, Professionalism and Class*, Lewes, Falmer Press.
PARSONS, T. (1954) 'The professions and social structure', in *Essays in Sociological Theory*, Glencoe, Free Press.
SALTER, B. and TAPPER, T. (1981) *Education, Politics and the State*, London, Grant McIntyre.
SCOTT, J. (1982) *The Upper Classes*, London, Macmillan.
THOMPSON, E.P. (1980) 'The business university', in *Writings by Candle-light*, London, Merlin Press (originally published 1971).
WAKEFORD, J. (1969) *The Cloistered Elite. A Sociological Analysis of the English Boarding School*, London, Macmillan.

WALFORD, G. (1982) 'Science, society and the public schools', paper presented at the Histories and Ethnographies of School Subjects Conference, St Hilda's College, Oxford, 20–22 September.

WALFORD, G. (1983a) 'Girls in boys' public schools: A prelude to further research', *British Journal of Sociology of Education*, 4, 1, p. 39–54.

WALFORD, G. (1983b) 'For thine is the kingdom, the power and the glory: Women in boys' public schools', paper read at Women and Education Group, Bristol, 2 March.

WALFORD, G. (1985) *Life in Public Schools*, London, Methuen.

WEINBERG, I. (1967) *The English Public Schools*, New York, Atherton.

WILENSKY, H.J. (1964) 'The professionalisation of everyone?', *American Journal of Sociology*, 70, pp. 137–58.

Parents, Sons and Their Careers:
A Case Study of a Public School, 1930–50

Christine M. Heward, University of Warwick

In a recent analysis Brian Salter and Ted Tapper have argued that the most notable contemporary development in the public schools is the rapidly growing emphasis on individual academic achievement measured by public examination results. They have explained this by examining the changing social context of the public schools, in particular parental pressure and the requirements of careers in industry and commerce. They suggest that changing structural and ideological relationships of public schools have been studiously ignored in previous analyses. Salter and Tapper attribute this failure to the alluring nature of the total institution model and long-held pervasive stereotypes about elite education.[1]

This chapter uses new evidence from an intensive case study of a Woodard school, which has retained particularly rich archival sources, including letters from parents to headmasters. Through access to these sources generously granted by the school and the patient cooperation of old boys and staff it has been possible to interrelate manuscript, oral and printed sources. Detailed evidence about hitherto neglected aspects of education at a particular public school has thus been revealed.

By using this new evidence and further conceptual development of Salter's and Tapper's model of structural relations, this chapter shows that the emphasis on examination success, encouraged by parental pressure and career requirements, has long historical roots in at least one section of the burgeoning public school community of the nineteenth century.

The analysis and explanation of educational developments require a model of changing educational, structural and ideological relations. Weber advanced such a model in his theory of bureaucratization. He argued that the growth of industrial capitalism engendered greater complexity which required stable and reliable administrative organizations staffed by trained professional officials. Accordingly an important historical development in all capitalist economies was the abolition of hereditary privileges in government and its replacement by recruitment through competitive examinations. In this way the educational ideals of a leisured and cultural gentlemanly elite were supplanted by technical expertise.

Bureaucratic administrative organizations have become more widespread, their authority legitimated by reference to written rational procedures. They are characterized by a specialist division of labour, a hierarchy of authority and standardized, codified procedures.[2]

Nineteenth-Century Developments

Weber's view was that these general political developments had been retarded in England because of the outstanding reliability of the ruling aristocracy. Perkin has suggested that in England in the nineteenth century the rapidly expanding middle classes were the pugnacious protagonists of the ideology of free and open competition, epitomized by examinations. The aristocratic ideology gradually accommodated to these notions in the second half of the nineteenth century.[3] Honey has argued that the growing importance of examinations following the Cardwell and Trevelyan Northcote reforms signalled the professionalization of the upper classes. The Empire rather than the Church became the goal of younger sons. Oxford, Cambridge and the public schools introduced examinations. Professionalization and bureaucratization of their client groups were just as important as the gentrification of the middle classes in the public schools in the second half of the nineteenth century.[4]

Certainly the Taunton Commission, reporting on educational provision for the middle classes in 1867, was very much alive to the growing importance of education and of success in examinations to middle-class parents attempting to ensure successful careers for their sons. Unlike the upper classes who could bestow wealth upon their offspring, the middle classes 'have only education to look to keep their sons on a high social level'.[5] The Commission divided the middle classes into three groups according to the career and consequent type and length of education they desired for their sons. The higher stratum, men of substantial independent means, wanted a classical education to 18 for their sons in preparation for university entrance. The second stratum of business and professional men wanted a modern curriculum of languages, mathematics and science until 16 to prepare their sons to enter business, or be articled in a profession. The lower middle classes and superior artisans wanted education to 14 in very good reading, writing and arithmetic.[6]

All three groups had difficulties in finding the kind of education they required at a price they could afford. According to the Commission, the first group 'are compelled to seek ... the education they require, in boarding schools ... generally ... of a very expensive kind.'[7] The most powerful opponents of the 'modern' curriculum were the school masters, who saw the classics as the only vehicle of a liberal education.

The commissioners conducted extensive investigations in three types of school — grammar, private and proprietary. They found the 780 endowed grammar schools languishing. 'Two hundred years of revolution in men's intellects and children's training, the reformation of religion and the upgrowth of science'[8] had largely passed them by. They were in urgent need of reform. The terms of their endowment, enforced by the Eldon Judgement in 1805, had effectively prevented modern influences from touching them.

Of the 2000 private schools, Bryce investigated those in Lancashire where he found that 'honest incompetence and successful charlatanism alternate with good and solid work.'[9] The private schools had little to commend them except that their commerical nature ensured that parents' demands for modern subjects were felt and that the things upon which parents insisted were 'tolerably certain to be well done.'[10]

The Commission was, however, somewhat more complimentary about the small group of new proprietary schools. Their foundation sprang from parents 'seeking to have their children educated in the way they themselves preferred'.[11] According to Fitch, the most successful were the religious proprietary schools which taught modern subjects, having discarded 'fancy classics', namely Greek.[12] They had the added advantage of cheap but good school masters.[13] Among the most impressive of this type of school were those founded by Canon Nathanial Woodard. Woodard was a high churchman, who by diligent fund raising founded a network of schools to provide 'cheap Church of England public school education for the middle classes'.[14]

Saint Oswald's College, Ellesmere

St Oswald's College, Ellesmere, opened on 8 September 1884 with seventy boys. In Canon Woodard's hierarchy it was a second-grade school built of brick, unlike Denstone, the first-grade school in the Midland division, which was of similar architectural design but built of stone. The fees were very low, twenty guineas, little more than the cost of food. The masters' lack of salary was augmented by their religious devotion to their task. Table 1 shows that the intake during the first four years was overwhelmingly middle-class. Farmers' sons were the largest single group with 30 per cent. The sons of Church of

Table 1. Fathers' Occupations of Entrants, 1884–88

	Number	*Percentage*
Group 1. Farmers		
1 Farmers, landowners, bailiffs, stewards	101	30
Group 2. Professional		
1 Church of England clergy	51	15
2 Bank managers, solicitors, accountants, architects	25	7
3 Doctors, vets, chemists	16	5
4 Docks superintendents, ships masters	10	3
5 Teachers and school masters	11	3
6 Architects, surveyors and engineers	—	—
		33
Group 3. Business and Commercial		
1 Tradesmen, merchants, grocers, drapers, carpenters	60	18
2 Manufacturers and works managers	15	5
3 Hoteliers, innkeepers, publicans	12	4
4 Agents and travellers	8	3
		30
Group 4. Miscellaneous		
1 Clerks	14	4
2 Servants	3	1
3 Expatriates, Indian Police and colonial officers	2	—
4 Miscellaneous	5	2
5 Illegible	2	—
		7
Total	335	100

England clergymen were a further significant group, accounting for 15 per cent. The college was divided approximately equally between the sons of professional men, businessmen and farmers.

The picture of life at the college, recounted in the early magazines, is one of order, regularity and serious purpose in religion, study and games. The curriculum was a careful combination of traditional and modern studies. Latin was its peak but English and mathematics were almost as important.

Competition through examinations was the cardinal organizing principle of academic work at the college. The first term broke up on 19 December 1884, after four days of half-yearly examinations. The term ended with an entertainment and farce after which the headmaster addressed the school. Carefully setting the tone of his new school, he 'mentioned the need of pulling up the standard of learning gradually but steadily in the College and after distributing the Latin form prizes to the winners, he ended by wishing us all a happy vacation in proportion to the energy with which each had worked in the half.'[15]

This stress on serious application to study and the importance given to academic success won immediate recognition. In its first year three Oxford men were appointed to examine the school in all aspects of the curriculum. A. Lowe, late scholar of Lincoln College, examined the Latin, French and Greek. He reported 'the creditable way' the examinations '. . . have been done speaks well of the school . . . the papers of the higher boys are excellent, the competition close.'[16]

The school was organized into a finely graded hierarchy which emphasized the importance of academic study and examination success. Every half year a list of college members was published in the magazine, in which each boy was accorded his particular individual status. Three principles determined a boy's place in the ranking — social class, age and his mark in Latin. The servitors were domestic servants who received three hours' instruction a day, a salary of £5 a year and a certificate for academic success.[17] The servitors' list was at the end, ranked according to their Latin marks.

Boys were ranked by form, which usually accorded closely with age. Older boys enjoyed high status and younger ones none at all. Within the age grading, rank was determined by Latin examination marks. By this means the virtues of competition and serious application to academic work were combined into a hierarchy regulated by educational and social principles.

From the outset the college entered its senior pupils for the

Oxford local examinations. At this period there was a number of different examination systems attempting to establish themselves nationally as reliable tests of education for employers. The record of 100 per cent pass and of high placings of particular candidates from St Oswald's in these prestigious national examinations was exultantly proclaimed in the college magazines.

The modern influence upon the curriculum was strongly felt from the outset. In 1888 shorthand was introduced. On 22 October 1888 the Provost of the Society of St Nicholas presented the Oxford Local certificates. After praising the staff and boys on their success, he pointed out the practical value of shorthand.[18]

The Provost also gave further official encouragement to modern curricular emphases, for in 1889 the subject for his English Essay Prize was Electricity.[19] Prowess in the English language won high praise at St Oswald's. In 1890 the magazine duly reprinted the school's English examiner's fulsome praise. He had found 'the spelling faultless ... March's essay on the Age of Elizabeth a model.... All candidates used appropriate language and many sentences were almost epigrammatic in their terseness.'[20] It is difficult to gauge the effects of the academic contest upon the boys. Certainly the editor of the magazine in 1890 took it in his stride. '*Tempus adest* is the prevailing feeling with many of us just now, for is not this the season in which we are wont to see visions and dream dreams of long lines of examiners, racking their own brains for questions intended in no long time hence to torture ours? Oxford locals loom like a cloud on the horizon and beyond them we sometimes catch glimpses of a pleasant prospect — six weeks holiday. But we anticipate.'[21]

It is clear that St Oswald's was preparing boys for middle-class careers, through its modern curriculum, stress on serious study, examinations and competition. The evidence in the school magazines about the careers of early old Ellesmerians is highly selective, favouring those who had entered universities. Success in examinations also received favourable notice. In one edition in 1905 news of thirteen old boys is given. Three were at Durham University and three at Oxford. One of the latter passed eighth in the military entrance examination for university candidates. Two were in the medical profession. One was an assayer in a Birmingham firm of refiners. One was a railway inspector in Buenos Aires. Another was a gunner in the 1st Orkney R.G. Artillery Volunteers and the last a lecturer in mining with Durham County Council.

An analysis of boys' intended careers given in the headmaster's register between 1890 and 1905 is shown in Table 2. It suggests a move by sons away from farming and business towards the professions. These intended careers show the influence of the school in the popularity of holy orders and the professions in general.

The ethos of the school was a blend of religious piety, diligent study and toughness in games. The ideal of service to the community was strongly emphasized in the elaborate daily rituals of this Anglo-Catholic educational community. Team games, where individuals dedicated themselves to the success of the team, celebrated similar values and ideals. Rugger and cricket, the essential tests of public school manliness, were very important from the school's foundation. In the early days teams from St Oswald's had difficulties finding suitable opponents. The process of establishing relations

Table 2.   Boys' Intended Future Careers, 1890–1903

	Number	Percentage
Group 1. *Farmers*		
1 Farmers, landowners, bailiffs	24	10
Group 2. *Professional*		
1 Holy orders	39	17
2 Bank managers, solicitors, architects, civil servants	41	18
3 Vets, medicals, chemists	21	9
4 Docks superintendents, ships masters	3	1
5 School masters	6	2
6 Architects, surveyors and engineers	21	9
		57
Group 3. *Business and Commercial*		
1 Commercial — no further indication	49	21
2 Tradesmen, grocer, butcher, etc.	7	3
		24
Group 4. *Miscellaneous*		
1 Clerks	9	4
2 Going abroad	1	—
3 Armed services	6	2
4 University	3	1
5 Miscellaneous	4	2
		9
Total	234	100

with other public schools, so important in cementing the position of a school in the public school hierarchy, was slow.[22]

The school also gave an excellent preparation for the prolonged academic study tested in a series of examinations required to enter professions like the Church and medicine. Compared with other public schools at this period, Ellesmere, striving to be accepted as a recognized public school, does seem to have been more middle-class in its intake and more seriously intellectual and religious in its outlook.

Between the Wars

In this period there was an increase in the central control of the many examining bodies which had grown up piecemeal in the nineteenth century. This led to greater uniformity of standards.[23] In 1918 the School Certificate and Higher School Certificate examinations were introduced. Two important concepts were enshrined in these regulations, that of a liberal education and of graded advanced study for university entrance.

Subjects were grouped, and to 'pass' the School Certificate one had to gain five passes in certain groups including English language and mathematics. Seven credits gained matriculation exemption which satisfied university entrance requirements. This attempt at standardization found ready acceptance with schools, universities, employers, parents and professional bodies. Entry into more and more professions required 'a good School Certificate'.[24]

The gradual reform and introduction of statutory control in different professions since 1850 ensured that by 1930 most had minimal ages and educational qualifications for entry and a considerable training period.[25] Training varied from the lengthy part-time training in banking and accountancy to five years' university education needed in medicine. In some, promotion also depended on further examination success, as in the prestigious fellowships of the medical profession, or the successive grades in the civil service. Some were regulated by a council of senior members of the profession.[26] A number of professions were organized in a hierarchy of seniority, with an associated ladder of promotion for the ambitious to scale, from curate to archbishop, for example.

From the middle of the nineteenth century, leading occupations, like medicine, were under increasing pressure to organize and control their own training and practice. In order to do this they introduced bureaucratic controls including specialization, hierarchies of authority, rules, procedures and examinations. They had thus begun the process of 'professionalization', a course of action since emulated by many lesser occupations.[27]

It was the bureaucratization and professionalization of leading professions which led to the notion of a career as a systematic preparation and training followed by regular progress to a senior position in an established and respected occupation.

By the inter-war period the course of careers in a large number of middle-class occupations was sufficiently regular and systematic for a literature of Careers Guides to develop. In 1926 *The Problem of a Career Solved by Thirty Six Men of Distinction* was published.[28] It described the entry, training, remuneration, promotion, career prospects and attractions of a wide variety of openings in the armed services, business and professions, and science. It was written with considerable authority by men who had attained eminence in their fields and dedicated rather curiously to the Prince of Wales, who did not have that particular problem to solve.

Table 3 shows the extent to which the thirty-six careers described in the Guide had acquired particular bureaucratic characteristics. Business and farming were the two major areas open to those who wished to avoid the constraints of bureaucratized careers with their competitive examinations and promotion ladders. The most important characteristic of all the careers stressed by the writers was the possibility of an independent and secure source of income.

After a secure income, service to the community was undoubtedly seen as the most important characteristic of any future career. 'It should be the duty and pride of every successful man to assist others less fortunately placed and there are many ways in which a solicitor can and ought to help those who have been unhappy in their lives', wrote Sir George Lewis on the satisfactions of a career as a solicitor.[29] Service to the community led more certainly to a respected position within it. For this reason the professions were in many ways more attractive than business and farming. Alfred Salmon, Chairman of Lyons corner shops, was painfully aware of these niceties,

> ... although some professions, such as that of doctor or surgeon, may appear more directly of service to the individual, it has to be remembered that the very life of a community, particularly of the present-day English community, depends on commerce, so that I think no one need

Table 3. Bureaucratic Characteristics of Thirty-Six Careers in 1926

	Fees	Income Stipend or salary	Profits	Exams or entry qualifications	Formal training and exams	Professional association or register	Promotion ladder
Navy commissions		✓		✓	✓		✓
Army commissions		✓		✓	✓		✓
Metropolitan police		✓		✓	✓		✓
Civil Service — administrative		✓		✓	✓		✓
executive		✓		✓	✓		✓
Local government		✓		✓			✓
Social service		✓					
Politics and public life							
Church of England priesthood		✓		✓	✓		✓
Roman Catholic priesthood		✓		✓	✓		✓
Non-conformist churches ministry		✓		✓	✓		
Law: the bar	✓			✓	✓	✓	✓
solicitor	✓			✓	✓	✓	✓
Medicine and surgery	✓			✓	✓	✓	✓
Dental surgery	✓			✓	✓	✓	
Veterinary science	✓			✓	✓	✓	
Science		✓		✓	✓		
Teaching		✓					✓
Art: drawing and illustration							

	Music	Architecture	The stage	Journalism	Literature	Accountancy	Banking	Insurance	The Stock Exchange	Business	The Dominions	Engineering	Marine engineering	Farming	Merchant Marine
		∨				∨	∨					∨			∨
		∨				∨	∨					∨	∨		∨
		∨				∨	∨					∨	∨		∨
									∨	∨				∨	
						∨						∨	∨		∨
		∨				∨									

be deterred from entering the business world by fear that he will not serving his fellow men.[30]

In the period between the two world wars, Ellesmere responded to the pressure of increasing bureaucratization in the careers its pupils sought to enter in a number of ways. In 1927 a sixth form was established to cater for the increasing number of boys staying at school to gain matriculation exemption and Higher School Certificate.[31]

In 1935 Reverend R.A. Evans-Prosser became headmaster. He was a classicist and staunch representative of the Woodard tradition, having previously been an assistant master at Ellesmere. He immediately embarked upon an ambitious building programme. A large new dormitory, changing rooms, squash courts and science laboratories were all completed before the outbreak of war in September 1939. Evans-Prosser was keenly aware of the school's market position in competition with local grammar schools. He fully understood the importance of careers and examinations to the parents he was trying to attract. The new science laboratories were particularly important in this regard. He told the Old Ellesmerians' dinner on 26 November 1938, in the Grosvenor Hotel, Manchester, that 'the new science building would make Ellesmere one of the best equipped schools in the country and would encourage boys to stay on and take up medicine and biology. The new dormitory would increase the capacity of the school.' He went on to remind the audience 'of the opposition of the luxurious secondary schools, which were being built out of the rates.'[32]

The Pressure from Parents

Evans-Prosser's model of his school was essentially that suggested by Salter and Tapper. He was concerned with the importance and effects of a highly competitive social context upon his school. He was trying to attract parents to send their sons by providing education which would gain entry to the careers they desired for them. Thus parental pressure and career requirements are the two key factors in both models.

The headmaster was made aware of parental pressure by the letters he received from parents. Some of these have been retained by the school in a unique archive of correspondence, containing some 2000 letters, which give valuable insights into the ways in which parents saw their son's careers. Their hopes and fears for the future were mixed with their knowledge of suitable careers and their assessment of their son's abilities.

Three subjects dominated the headmaster's correspondence from parents: money, careers and health. By far the most garrulous correspondents were the clergy and widows. Impecunity forced them to write begging letters giving full accounts of their circumstances. The farmers took up their pens much less frequently. They sometimes delegated the correspondence with the school to their wives. Their letters were often mis-spelt, ungrammatical, written on sheets from exercise books or bill heads.

Parents planned their sons' careers very carefully indeed. They were aware that ensuring an established position in a middle-class occupation for their sons required a long-term strategy, spanning the years from childhood through youth into manhood. Schooling was a part of a continuous and integrated process of maintaining, possibly improving, the family's social position, lifestyle and values in the next generation. The most important requirement of their sons' school was that it should give the right academic preparation for entry to the career that they had in mind.

The school should also reflect and inculcate values similar to those of home. The social standing of the other pupils and the school in general had to be similar to their own. Many of their ideals for their sons were concentrated in their notion of manliness. They wanted their young sons to be transformed from childhood into proud manhood. They summed up their attitude to the school at the end of their sons' school days with 'you made a man of him'.

The crucial importance of a career is illustrated by the initial enquiry made by the wife of an agricultural merchant in January 1939:

> The Larches,
> Deepworth.
>
> January, 18th, 1939
>
> The Principal.
>
> Dear Sir,
>
> Would you be so kind as to forward me a Prospectus of the College and all particulars of the curriculum. I have a small boy aged 9, now attending the Deepworth Grammar School, whom I have thought of sending to a boarding

school if he could be so educated and brought out to earn a good living. He seems to have a very definite bent for engineering at present and is fairly clever in things electrical.

Yours faithfully,
Mrs C. Thompson[33]

School Fees

Decisions about a son's education involved not only choosing a suitable opening for him and preparing him for it. In families with several children the kind of education they were to receive, its timing and cost had to be considered. Long-term plans of the financial commitments involved were all important. The clergy were always hard pressed financially. Even with the considerable reductions in fees they received at Ellesmere they found it a severe financial strain. A Nottinghamshire incumbent, enquiring in 1938, proposed to send his son to Ellesmere in September 1939. He outlined his long-term strategic problems in some detail.

How are you going to deal with me in the matter of fees? Of course, I should propose to keep him at Ellesmere until he became ready for some profession, perhaps the Royal Navy, or medicine (or as it may work out). My little girl will most likely be entered at Abbots Bromley — while I have another boy to deal with later on — if the first goes on all right, no doubt he would follow his brother, in due course.[34]

School fees were the single most important and persistent problem for parents and the school. Parents tried to do the best they could for their sons within their means. The headmaster in his turn was trying to build up the school's reputaton. He pursued a vigorous policy of expansion. In offering fee reductions he had to judge how much parents could pay without getting into difficulties during their son's schooling. The basis of his calculations was the amount required to run the school. Both parties walked a tightrope, which often required careful negotiations.

Having received the prospectus, Mrs Thompson wrote back immediately saying: 'My husband and I will discuss the matter more fully when he comes home, but meanwhile I am just afraid that the fees will overtax his present resources, much as I would like to send the boy to you.'[35] Like many other parents she was anxious to stress the value they placed upon their son's education. She continued: 'but I will try very hard to let him come to you ... if we can manage it, as I feel it would be the very best thing we could do for him and we do earnestly wish to give him the best chance in life.... We will do all we can to further this end.'[36] To supplement the family's slender resources Edward sat the scholarship examination. Although he was unsuccessful the headmaster offered the family a fee reduction of £20. They continued to hesitate. Further correspondence from Mrs Thompson cajoled a further reduction of £5 from the headmaster. They decided through the 'very kind help and generosity' of the headmaster to send Edward to Ellesmere in September 1939. To do so 'we shall sacrifice much', his mother said.[37]

Many parents undoubtedly found the commitment to paying the fees for a number of years a strain. Queries about the bill, pleas for special consideration and attempts to postpone payment are common subjects of correspondence from parents. The proper management of their finance was essential for middle-class pride and self-respect. Debt was a very sensitive issue indeed. A handful of parents did contract debts to the school which they continued to pay several years after their sons had left the school. A dentist in a nearby market town owed the school £76 when his son left in 1934. The debt was halved by regular small payments. When the payments ceased the headmaster wrote a curt note reminding the dentist that 'a man in your position'[38] should be able to pay such a debt. The dentist replied equally tartly that threats of proceedings would 'only humiliate' him.[39]

The War and Its Consequences

The Second World War, which began in September 1939, severely disrupted the carefully laid plans of many parents for their sons' futures. The lives of young men were increasingly regulated and controlled as conscription was extended. Amid the uncertainty and increasing bureaucratic controls parents tried to maintain a long-term view of their sons' careers after the war. The difficulties were formidable. Boys were liable for conscription just as they were beginning their professional training. Disruption and uncertainty affected most parents, some catastrophically. At the outbreak of the war property values plummeted. One London estate agent 'lost over a thousand pounds in a fortnight'.[40] In an acrimonious correspondence about fees he rebuked the headmaster: 'Remember, it is not very easy for a person who has never had any financial responsibility or the management of a firm, and who is sitting comfortably in the country, to visualise the conditions of a professional business in London at the present time.'[41]

The ever-anxious Mrs Thompson also found her long-term financial strategy for her son's future undermined by the outbreak of the war. Days before her son was due to start at his new school she wrote to the headmaster: 'I am so afraid that if the war lasts as the Government seems to suggest for three years, that we shall be badly hit. . . . I should have to send Edward for six months and then be forced to bring him back. . . .'[42] The headmaster reassured her and Edward Thompson entered the school in September 1939.

There were several boys in the school whose parents were in the Far East. The boys were under the care of guardians in Britain, with whom they spent their holidays and exeats from school. They had not seen their parents since the beginning of the war. In the Japanese advance of 1942 their families lost everything. In April 1942 one guardian wrote to tell the headmaster that his ward would have to leave the school. His 'mother and two sisters have arrived in England on a refugee ship from Singapore in a penniless condition. The father is somewhere, the last seen of him was on the docks at Singapore. He by the way is now in the army, a Captain in a Pioneer Battalion.'[43]

In all these cases the boys remained at the school, although it is unclear from the correspondence how they were supported. The school seems to have taken a benevolent attitude. Such actions were an established part of the school's tradition. In the period before the war the school had taken in a number of Jewish refugees at substantially reduced fees.

Curriculum and Examinations

After their ability to provide for their sons' education parents' next concern was whether their sons were being prepared to enter a suitable career. The subjects their sons were studying and their success in them were frequent subjects of correspondence to the headmaster.

Parents began their vigilance of their sons' career preparation at an early age. At this period Latin was still required for entry to many university courses. It had also figured prominently in the education of many parents.

James Porter was eleven when he entered the school in 1943. In

October 1944 his father, a bank clerk in Manchester, wrote to the headmaster of his disappointment:

> to learn that my son ... has ceased to take Latin ... his last year's report was poor ... may have been due to ... time ... in the sick room.
>
> I do feel very strongly that Latin is an essential subject, and that without it choice of career later will be restricted. Could you possibly arrange for Latin lessons to be resumed?[44]

The requirements of the curriculum and examinations became more elaborate as entry to professional training drew nearer. The Reverend George Foukes Smyth, the Nottinghamshire incumbent discussed above, sent a spate of instructions to the school about his son's studies after he gained his School Certificate in 1946.

> The question of John's future is bothering me ... he will be conscripted in the early part of 1948. The ground he covers in the intervening time ... will have a determining effect upon the course of his career.... My finances will not enable me to support John at a residential university; but I am anxious that he should take a degree.... I suggest that he might read for the Matriculation Examination of Dublin University ... he has ... the idea that he has a vocation for the priesthood.... This leads me to ask you if he may begin ... Greek with as little delay as possible ... to offer Greek for matriculation?[45]

In January 1947 Father Foukes Smyth gave notice that his son would leave at the end of the term despite his previous plan that John should stay until the summer to sit the Higher School Certificate examination. He could not afford the fees for both his sons and a daughter. Father Foukes Smyth made strenuous efforts to find ways to ensure his son's future success despite his own impecunious position. Later the same month he informed the school of an ingenious scheme to ensure his son's education at a fee he could afford. The abbot of the Anglo-Catholic community at Nashdom had agreed to accept John as a guest. There he was to be taught Greek and general science, although the community had no laboratories. Father Foukes Smyth had been given an undertaking that his son would gain matriculation exemption for the Northern Universities if he passed these two subjects.[46]

Failure in the all important examinations caused parents considerable anguish. Weaker candidates were sometimes advised by the school to concentrate on the minimum number and spread of subjects to ensure success.[47]

Trevor Jones entered Ellesmere in 1941 when he was 11. His father was a Lancashire businessman, whose business became very erratic during the war and the family had difficulties in paying his fees. Mr Jones had high ambitions for his son. He intended Trevor to stay at Ellesmere 'until he has passed his School Certificate Examination and I am anxious that he should remain to take his Higher School Certificate Examination prior to undertaking a University course.'[48] Trevor took his School Certificate in July 1946 and failed. His father, duly incensed, told the headmaster,

> I am satisfied that he has devoted to [sic] little time to serious study in the past and has concentrated to [sic] much on prowess in games.
>
> He left home last week with no doubt in his mind as to my own views on his failure and has given me a solemn promise to really work for success in his next effort.
>
> I am sure that he realises that the next few months are vital to his future and I am convinced that with the right guidance that he will make good.
>
> We have in mind a career in Dentistry or Engineering as a possible target. . . .[49]

Trevor failed again in December and his father wrote disconsolately to the headmaster,

> It has been a disappointment to me that he has not shown any particular aptitude for scholastic learning but I feel also that he has perhaps developed to [sic] great a prowess for sport to the detriment of his lessons.
>
> I had visualised a university career but in view of his failure in examinations this must now be eliminated from our minds.[50]

Edward Thompson's parents, in contrast, were surprised that their son passed the School Certificate at the first attempt. His mother wrote, 'we were very pleased that he passed at all this year. We hardly expected him to.'[51] As we saw above, they had planned a professional career for their son from a very early stage. By the time their son had reached the School Certificate they had changed their plans from engineering to agriculture and wished Edward to go to university although they did not want to 'force our ideas upon him'.[52] In order to enter university Edward required good enough marks in his School Certificate to gain exemption from the university's own matriculation examinations, matric exemption as it was known. The Thompsons were very concerned about Edward's second attempt at the School Certificate. They therefore applied pressure to the school and their son. Mrs Thompson wrote to the headmaster that Edward's 'French bothers him a bit and he feels he will again fail in it.' She asked the headmaster if he could have extra coaching in his weak subjects.[53] Like Mr Jones she was concerned that her son should 'concentrate more on his lessons and do better next year'. She felt that he was 'somewhat easy going ... I suppose it is difficult to make a young boy see that these next years are so important.' Her method of applying pressure to her son was less direct than that of Mr Jones. She asked the headmaster to talk to Edward about the matter.[54]

The 'Old-Boy' Network

Examination passes alone did not ensure a successful professional career. Both parents and the school had access to networks of relationships which they used to further their sons' careers. Tony Case, an oral informant, decided, on the basis of a book about the legal profession, to make it his career. He gained a good enough School Certificate to get exemption from Part 1 of the Law Society's examinations. His father asked the family's bank manager to which of the town's solicitors his son should be articled.[55] His entry to the legal profession was immediately effected through the network of local professional relationships.

Trevor Jones's father inveighed against the emphasis upon sport in his son's schooling. Sport, however, often cemented the network of relations between educational institutions and the professions. Reverend R.A. Evans-Prosser, the headmaster at this period, was an extremely keen sportsman. He particularly enjoyed rugger, squash and tennis. He was a county squash player, who regularly beat his pupils. He used his reputation as a sportsman and his network of educational and professional relations in the interests of his pupils' careers.

Michael Owen came from South Wales where his father was in business. He entered the school in 1945, apparently destined for the medical profession. Michael had a successful career at Ellesmere. He became a prefect and member of the first Rugby fifteen. As at all public and grammar schools at this period there was a very strong emphasis on sport at Ellesmere. All the oral informants confirm that the captain of the first fifteen represented the acme of success, admired from afar by all the younger boys at the school.

At some time during his schooldays Michael's future career was changed from medicine to law. The headmaster wrote to a firm of solicitors in Bristol, who apparently already had an articled clerk from Ellesmere.[56] The principal of this firm was Secretary of Bristol Law Society and arranged an articled clerkship for Michael. His entrance to the law faculty of Bristol University was also arranged, provided he passed two subsidiary subjects in the Higher School Certificate. Unfortunately, he was only successful in one subject and commenced his articles, but not the university course.[57] If sport had contributed to his failure he did not regret it. For the headmaster's reputation in sport was an important element in the professional network, which he had enabled Michael to enter. Michael wrote several letters to the headmaster from Bristol saying how much he was enjoying the work and thanking the headmaster for his help. His principal had played rugger for Somerset. He remembered the headmaster's name well and sent his kindest regards. Michael enjoyed sport. In his letters to the headmaster he enquired about the school's results. Sport also cemented his own school and budding professional relations. He met another old Ellesmerian in Bristol and they played squash together.[58]

The War Continues

The Second World War greatly increased the problems of parents attempting to organize their son's future careers. The lives of young men were subject to increasingly severe regulation as conscription was extended. Professional and commercial life was disrupted. The universities also faced increasing difficulties because so many of their staff and potential students were in the forces. Competition, disruption and uncertainty about the future made planning a career of consistent progress towards an established position very difficult indeed. Parents continued to try to ensure suitable careers for their sons as best they could given the circumstances. Some abandoned or modified their original plans. Others redoubled their efforts, attempting to circumvent the problems.

G.D. Foster, a bank manager in a nearby market town, sent his son to the school in 1935. In June 1940 he wrote to the headmaster about the importance of his son's approaching School Certificate examinations because he wanted his son to go on to Cambridge in 1941. 'You will appreciate that this war will naturally make a great deal of difference to all parents, but we do not want our boys not to have the opportunity they would otherwise have.'[59] His son passed the School Certificate and Mr Foster was pleased and thanked the school for the 'careful teaching he must have had'.[60] The events of that summer changed his plans for his son's future and he continued his letter: 'it was my intention to send him to you for at least another year, and afterwards on to Cambridge, but this terrible war has upset everything.'[61] The evacuation of Dunkirk on 29 and 30 June 1940 was followed by the Battle of Britain and the beginning of the Blitz on 8 September. Because of 'the great uncertainty of what will happen after the war', David Foster accepted a proffered position and started his career in banking in September 1940.[62]

The ending of the war did not bring an end to parents' problems about their sons' careers. Indeed the flood of returning servicemen increased the competition for university places. Servicemen were given preference over young applicants. Conscription continued. Mrs Thompson was keenly aware of all these difficulties as she made frenetic attempts to ensure a place for her son in an agricultural college. She may well have believed that the peace declarations would end conscription and bring a speedy return to the kind of conditions she had known before the war. She clearly believed the Labour landslide of 1945 had contributed to her problems. She wrote to the headmaster: 'this present Government are making things so very difficult and so upsetting for young men and boys and parents also.'[63] Her hopes rested on the coming examinations. She viewed her son's prospects with alarm,

> ... if he should fail ... there will be nothing for him, but conscription straight away. I feel then that his seven years with you at Ellesmere, (which incidentally have been happy years) will in great measure have been lost.[64]

For Mrs Thompson it seemed a dolorous prospect indeed.

Sons' Reactions

Boys had a variety of reactions to the culture and expectations of their family and school. Some conformed, accepting the values and expectations, and in many cases pursuing the kind of successful career their parents envisaged. John Foukes Smyth wrote to the headmaster immediately after he left Ellesmere.

> I am sorry I cannot return this summer but I must train for the priesthood.... Now I have the world to face, but with the strong foundation of a thoroughly satisfactory schooling ... I hope that in later years I may always continue in the Faith, *pro patria Dimicans*[65]

— the school motto — through faith in the fatherland. After National Service he trained for the priesthood.

Edward Thompson also continued to pursue the career mapped out for him at school. He sought entrance to agricultural college after completing his National Service

Not all the boys sought careers which would bring them ultimately to a comfortable and respected position in the community. A number were inspired by the hero cult, fed by the veneration of the Captain of the first fifteen and the importance of figures like Captain Oates in the schoolboy literature of the period. The ideals which led so many school boys to a noble death in the First World War were reinterpreted in the Second World War. After the Battle of Britain in the summer of 1940 members of the Royal Air Force became the new heroes. Joining the Royal Air Force became the ambition of many young men anxious for adventure and full of zeal to serve their country.

How many rebelled or rejected the pressure of school and family it is impossible to say, for it is not recorded in any accessible way. Those who have kept in touch with the school were successful. For the most part, they enjoyed their school days. The history of public school 'failures' has yet to be written.

Conclusion

Pressure for academic achievement in the public schools has quickened and become more pervasive. It has long historical roots among those sections of the middle classes who rely upon education as a most important means of ensuring the family maintains or improves its social position from one generation to the next. To achieve this end parents make vigorous efforts to enable their sons to enter a career which will give a secure and comfortable income with improving long-term prospects. The professions which enjoy widespread respect within the community are often the first choice of parents.

From the middle of the nineteenth century the professions were reformed. Careers began to be organized along bureaucratic lines. In particular, examinations became more widespread and important. Middle-class parents planned their sons' education and future careers with great care. In some cases the lengthy financial obligations involved were a strain. Parents placed particularly strong pressure upon the school about their sons' curricula and examination success. Failure caused considerable concern. A number of parents applied intense pressure to their sons to succeed. Parents also used their own networks of contacts and that of their sons' school to further their sons' careers.

In response to greater competition for careers and increasing regulation of the lives of young men during and after the Second World War, parents redoubled their efforts to ensure their sons' success. Sons made a variety of responses to the culture and expectations of parents and school. Some conformed, becoming successful professionals or businessmen. Some wanted to be heroes and joined the Royal Air Force. Others may have rebelled or dropped out. But of them we know nothing.

This study has provided strong historical evidence to support Salter and Tapper's model of the relationships of public schools to their structural context and especially to the importance of parental pressure within that context. This new evidence suggests that the process of professionalization and its associated examinations has long historical roots and was of growing importance within the public school community. Between 1935 and 1950 Reverend R.A. Evans-Prosser was attempting to expand his school and to increase its prestige so that it enjoyed an established position within the clearly defined hierarchy of public schools. To do this he made sure that the school appealed to parents by having a good record in the subjects and examinations required for successful middle-class careers.

The Second World War and its aftermath rapidly accelerated the historical process of professionalization and increased the regulation of young men's lives. Examinations became very important indeed. As John Rae and Salter and Tapper themselves suggest,[66] the last two decades have seen a further quickening of these historical processes. They are now of greatly increased importance in those schools which dominate the public school hierarchy. Ellesmere was attempting to establish itself within the more populous middle rungs of the hierarchy during the period when professionalization became crucial for the success of schools at that level.

Acknowledgements

I would like to thank the Headmaster and Governors of Ellesmere College for their generous assistance in making their archives available to me so freely and Richard Taylor, formerly Head of the History Department, for his help and encouragement. Alison Negus and Fleur Waite patiently translated my manuscript into typescript.

Notes

1 SALTER, B. and TAPPER, T. (1981) *Education, Politics and the State: The Theory and Practice of Educational Change*, London, Grant McIntyre, pp. 161–80.
2 GERTH, H.H. and MILLS, C.W. (1958) (Eds) *From Max Weber: Essays in Sociology*, London, Oxford University Press; WEBER, M. *Theory of Social and Economic Organisation*, Illinois, Free Press.
3 PERKIN, H. (1969) *The Origins of Modern English Society 1780–1880*, London, Routledge and Kegan Paul, pp. 291–339.
4 HONEY, J.R. de S. (1977) *Tom Brown's Universe: The Development of the Public School in the Nineteenth Century*, London, Millington, pp. 151–3.
5 *Schools Inquiry Commission*. Report of the Commissioners appointed by Her Majesty to inquire into the education given in schools in England, not comprised within Her Majesty's two recent commissions on popular education and on public schools (Chairman, Lord Taunton), 3966, 1867, I, p. 18.
6 *Ibid.*, pp. 16–20.
7 *Ibid.*, p. 17.
8 *Ibid.*, p. 104.
9 *Ibid.*, p. 284.
10 *Ibid.*, p. 302.
11 *Ibid.*, p. 310.
12 *Ibid.*, p. 320.
13 KIRK, K.E. (1937) *The Story of the Woodard Schools*, London, Hodder.
14 HEENEY, B. (1969) *Mission to the Middle Classes: The Woodard Schools, 1848–1891*, London, SPCK.
15 *The Ellesmerian*, 1885, 1, 1, p. 8.
16 *Ibid.*, p. 11.
17 *Ibid.*, 1886, 2, 2, p. 27.
18 *Ibid.*, 1888, 4, 6, p. 85.
19 *Ibid.*, 1889, 5, 5, p. 65.
20 *Ibid.*, 1890, 6, 5, p. 60.

21 *Ibid.*, 1890, 6, 3, p. 30.
22 JOHN HONEY's view is that recognition by other public schools is the cardinal mark of any public school. HONEY (1977) op. cit., pp. 238–95.
23 ROACH, J. (1979) 'Examinations and the secondary schools 1900–1945', in *History of Education*, 8, 1, pp. 45–58.
24 PETCH, J.A. (1953) *Fifty Years of Examining: The Joint Matriculation Board 1903–1953*, London, Harrap, pp. 80–99 and 182–200.
25 MILLERSON, G. (1964) *The Qualifying Associations: A Study of Professionalisation*, London, Routledge and Kegan Paul, pp. 120–47; CARR-SANDERS, A.M. and WILSON, P.A. (1964) *The Professions*, London, Frank Cass, pp. 307–18.
26 MILLERSON (1964) *op. cit.*, pp. 148–80.
27 *Ibid.*, pp. 9–25.
28 CAIRNS, J.A.R. (1926) *The Problem of a Career Solved by Thirty Six Men of Distinction*, London, Arrowsmith.
29 *Ibid.*, p. 142.
30 *Ibid.*, p. 257.
31 At Speech Day, 21 October 1933, the headmaster told the assembled company that there was 'no such thing as a boy of sixteen with a Public School education. It was the last two years that trained the boy, the years from sixteen to eighteen, in the qualities of leadership for which one looks to the public schools.' *The Ellesmerian*, 1933, 44, 225, p. 11.
32 *Old Ellesmerian Chronicle* (1939) 54, pp. 127–8.
33 All the names of parents and boys have been changed to preserve anonymity. 83–13–29, 18 January 1939.
34 19–20–66, 17 February 1938.
35 83–13–29, 18 January 1939.
36 18–13–29, 20 January 1939.
37 18–13–29, 15 June 1939.
38 83–82–66, 14 June 1939.
39 83–82–66, he replied by writing on the bottom of the headmaster's letter of 14 June 1939.
40 33–82–9, 23 September 1939.
41 33–82–9, 27 September 1939.
42 82–13–29, 13 September 1939.
43 74–82–66, 10 April 1942.
44 74–82–66, 5 October 1944.
45 19–20–66, 28 September 1946.
46 19–20–66, 20 January 1947.
47 Nigel Dale 1943–47, oral evidence.
48 74–99–2, 15 May 1946.
49 74–99–2, 29 September 1946.
50 74–99–2, 22 May 1947.
51 24–13–29, 21 September 1945.
52 24–13–29, 21 September 1945.
53 24–13–29, 21 September 1945.
54 24–13–29, 21 September 1945.
55 1947, oral informant.
56 56–20–83, 11 November 1948.

57 56–20–83, 18 October 1949.
58 56–20–83, 18 October 1949.
59 60–60–66, 15 June 1940.
60 60–60–66, 14 September 1940.
61 60–60–66, 14 September 1940.
62 60–60–66, 1 October 1940.
63 24–13–29, 19 May 1946.
64 24–13–29, 19 May 1946.
65 19–20–66, 11 April 1944.
66 RAE. J. (1981) *The Public School Revolution*, London, Faber, pp. 154–62; SALTER, B. and TAPPER, T. (1981) *Education, Politics and the State: The Theory and Practice of Educational Change*, London, Grant McIntyre, pp. 161–80.

Evaluating Policy Change: The Assisted Places Scheme

Geoff Whitty, King's College, University of London
and
Tony Edwards, University of Newcastle

For most of the time since the Fleming Committee (1944) recommended their 'closer association with the general educational system', the public schools have generated controversy rather than political action. The only partial exceptions to this lack of action have occurred since the Labour Party in 1973 became committed to a policy of elimination, not integration. That commitment was accompanied by a marking of the steps by which 'reduction and eventual abolition' were to be achieved. The next Labour government made the first move by announcing that the direct grant list was to be phased out from September 1976. It then tried to restrict the use of independent schools by LEAs to cases where they could demonstrate an 'absolute shortage' of equivalent places in their own schools. In sharp contrast, the Conservative Party committed itself to an 'improved' version of the direct grant system which had initially been proposed by direct grant school representatives at the Headmasters Conference.[1] The return of a Conservative government in 1979 therefore brought an abrupt reversal of policy. The announcement of an Assisted Places Scheme was Mark Carlisle's first significant action as Secretary of State; the necessary legislation was included in the 1980 Education Act, and the first assisted pupils entered the 229 participating schools in September of the following year.

This paper arises from our current research into the origins, operation and effects of this Assisted Places Scheme.[2] It is not a preliminary report of 'findings' because it is much too early in the scheme and the research project for such an exercise. Our aim is rather to identify some problems in evaluating the scheme and to explore the possibilities for undertaking research of value to the development of policy on such a politically controversial educational issue. We trust that the research itself will not be marked at the end by the characteristics so deplored by a leading defender of the public schools — 'an unnecessary obscurity of language, an almost compulsory concern with the obvious, heavy work with the data (and) a subjective and "progressive" conclusion.'[3]

The Assisted Places Scheme is intended to help 'able children from modest backgrounds' to enter independent schools of high academic reputation through means-tested assistance with school fees. The participating schools include almost all the 119 direct grant schools which chose not to be absorbed into an academically non-selective public sector after 1976. They also include schools which, although among those recommended by the Fleming Committee and the First Public Schools Commission Report (1968) for 'association' or 'integration', have not in practice had more than a slight relationship with the public sector. Fee remission is arranged directly between central government and schools, and the selection of pupils between parents and schools. The scheme thus provides, for those who qualify for it academically and financially, an alternative to the maintained system over which the LEAs themselves have no formal control.[4] In areas where the maintained schools are comprehensive, it provides one of the few ways in which academic selection at 11+ or 13+ can be made available to able children from families with low incomes. Some 5500 places have been offered each year, although the numbers taken up have been substantially lower — 4243 in 1981 and 4417 in 1982. Despite this apparently limited scope, the scheme has a potential importance far beyond the numbers currently involved in it. It is increasingly being heralded as a success by its sponsors, and so as worthy of being extended.

In what follows, we shall first outline our initial reasons for choosing the scheme as a worthwhile area of research, and then explore some problems in establishing the criteria by which to evaluate its operation. We then briefly describe how we are conducting the research at various levels of detail, and consider some of the difficulties already encountered. Finally, we identify themes emerging during the study and discuss ways in which they might be further explored so as to inform the continuing debate on the desirability and feasibility of providing a 'bridge' between the state and the independent sectors of education by this or other means.

Reasons for Studying the Assisted Places Scheme

Despite its limited scope, the announcement of the scheme revived and highlighted longstanding arguments about academic selection, the functions of the independent schools, and how they complemented or endangered the public sector. In the controversy which surrounded its launching, it was easy to discern advocates and critics presenting their arguments in terms of such concepts as 'freedom', 'opportunity' and 'social justice' which have also featured in much broader controversies about social policy. At the same time, some of the arguments were more specifically concerned with the socially divisive effects attributed to academic selection or the academic costs attributed to its abandonment — concerns which have dominated debates about comprehensive secondary education. To this extent, the scheme seemed to crystallize some of the central issues about the nature of secondary schooling and its relationship to the future shape of British society.

The scheme also provided, partly because of its limited scope, an unusual opportunity to trace a highly controversial piece of educational legislation from its inception through to its implementation, and to explore empirically whether the consequences predicted by its proponents and opponents were realized in practice. We did not imagine, however, that those consequences could be studied in a social vacuum, since the effects of any policy are clearly dependent upon how it articulates with other prevailing features of the social formation. We have therefore tried to locate the scheme in the context of previous attempts to link the state and independent sectors and the historic role of the public schools in class formation and reproduction in British society.

Finally, we felt that the study could make some contribution to current debates within the sociology of education. Many of the concepts employed in the controversy surrounding the scheme were concepts that have helped to shape a good deal of sociological theory and research and were likely to direct analysis of data generated by the project itself. We did not expect that research on a limited topic such as this, even when set in its broader context, could be used to confirm or refute the varieties of functionalist, Marxist, Weberian and pluralist theories that have characteristically been used (often at high levels of abstraction) to account for the relationships between education, the state and society. We did have some hopes, however, that the data we gathered could help us to interrogate the plausibility of some middle-range theories that figure in the contemporary sociological literature on education. For example, the data might well be relevant to claims about the role of a scholarship ladder in enhancing equality of opportunity, in the recruitment of elites, and in legitimating the existence of academically and socially differentiated forms of educational provision.[5] While the broader theories from which such claims are derived are clearly not of the kind which would be seriously damaged or decisively strengthened by such an empirical exercise in itself, it might well have some value in conjunction with similar analyses of specific policies.[6]

Developing Criteria for Assessing the Scheme

Much of our initial interest lay in the relationship between the claims made for and against the scheme at the time of its inception and its actual operation and effects. Some of the predictions were both confident and specific — for example, that 'able children from our poorest homes' would once again have the opportunity of attending academically excellent schools.[7] Others stated quite precisely possible alternative outcomes — for example, that 'a Scheme designed to attract working class children who would otherwise go to a poor neighbourhood comprehensive may simply attract middle class children who would otherwise go to a good comprehensive.'[8] However, many of the issues which were raised during the controversy surrounding the scheme reflect irreconcilable philosophical differences which cannot be subjected to empirical testing. Thus much of the debate expressed predefined positions on the relative claims of freedom and equality to inform the structuring of society. Even if it were possible to come to some conclusions about the extent to which either of these 'goods' was being enhanced by the scheme, no research could adjudicate between their resepective merits. What we have done is to locate supporting and opposing arguments within the context of these broader philosophical positions and within the ideological repertoires of the various political parties.

Even in its proponents' own terms, there are no straightforward ways of investigating how far the scheme promotes or restricts 'freedom'. Thus it might be claimed that its existence increases freedom of choice for parents of able pupils. Yet if there were evidence that its operation reduced the standard of provision for able children within the maintained sector, this might support the conclusion that overall there had been a reduction in freedom of choice. The example illustrates the way in which philosophical and empirical considerations sometimes come together. Advocates of the scheme have often insisted that the only relevant criteria for judging its success or failure are the benefits which it may bring to the individual children who receive assistance, and that its critics seek to subordinate the needs of individuals to the supposed needs of the educational system.[9] But to focus entirely on pupils who have received assisted places without regard to possible consequences for the public sector would itself be vulnerable to the charge of a politically biased restriction of view. More generally, the notion of a clear confrontation between individual freedom and social justice is highly contentious.[10] As Harvey has argued, the concept of social justice can be interpreted in so many ways that it has been used to justify political and economic arrangements as different as Marxism and monetarism.[11] From the latter perspective, the scheme itself might be defended as strengthening private provision and as directing state aid to individuals rather than to institutions; insofar as this helped to increase overall levels of wealth in society, then even the least well off would receive more benefits in the long run than in an apparently more 'equitable' system. From a more meritocratic perspective, the scheme could be seen as contributing to national productivity through the sponsorship of talent and the creation of human capital.[12] Such claims are impossible to test, given the range and complexity of influences at work inside and outside the educational system.

Yet, despite the complications we have outlined, some issues raised by supporters and critics of the scheme do seem susceptible to empirical investigation. The most obvious example is the extent to which it has reached its target group, able children with parents of 'modest means', whether it has done so more effectively as it has become better known and as some participating schools have vigorously publicized its opportunities, and whether it has done so more successfully than the financially less discriminating direct grant arrangements which it partly replaced.[13] Over time, it may also be possible to study some of its effects on the participating schools, and on state primary and secondary schools. To what extent, for instance, has it made it possible for the independent schools to recruit more academically selective intakes? With more difficulty, it might be possible eventually to trace effects on examination results. We can also enquire whether the return in some parts of the country to a fairly substantial 'scholarship' system has also produced a return to 11+-style coaching in some primary schools. In state secondary schools, we can investigate effects on intakes and on how teachers, parents and pupils perceive the merits of particular types of school, and also whether parental interest in the scheme is related to the prevailing pattern of state provision in particular areas. Finally, and crucially of course, we are interested in testing the claim that assisted place pupils will gain tangible benefits (individually or as a group) in relation to their peers in the state sector. This is the crucial question because advocates of the scheme have insisted that it 'complemented' the state sector by providing academic opportunities difficult to maintain in 'schools catering for the majority', while its critics have argued that it represented an unjustifiable expenditure of public money without any check that the assisted pupils needed to move from the public sector.[14] These have been the considerations which have shaped our decisions about what evidence to collect. In all cases, however, we have to be wary of mistaking short-term effects for long-term consequences.

Even here, time-scale is not the only complicating factor to be considered in interpreting our data. Other complications appear if we look more closely at one specific claim made about the impact of the scheme on the public sector, that it would be disastrous for the maintenance of academic sixth forms in comprehensive schools. Thus the National Association of Head Teachers estimated that by the time it was fully in operation, the proportion of 'academic sixth form material' creamed off would be as high as 30 per cent.[15] Supporters of the scheme have tended to reduce this estimate to a level nearer 20 per cent, but have also argued that the effect on individual state schools would be small in that the individuals involved would almost certainly be drawn from a wide geographical area (as was true of the more 'academic' direct grant schools) and so would otherwise have attended a large number of different schools.[16] The validity of claim and counter-claim is not difficult to assess within a local area by identifying the schools from which assisted place pupils are drawn and the secondary schools they would otherwise have attended, and we have been surprised that neither the DES nor the Independent Schools Joint Committee has monitored this aspect of the scheme's operation. Even so, any conclusions would be complicated by the fact that other, notably demographic, changes are currently threatening the viability of state school sixth forms, and that in this situation even a numerically slight 'creaming' effect could be educationally significant. If, on the other hand, a particular LEA is attempting to tackle the problem by introducing sixth form colleges, the effects of the scheme would probably be less than if it were trying to maintain full-range comprehensives. Yet given the academic quality and scope of sixth form provision in some of these colleges, a significant part of the original justification for the scheme would be brought into question. Thus even if we establish the extent of the 'creaming' process (and some assisted place pupils would have attended independent schools anyway by other means), then those findings have to be interpreted in relation to a great deal of other evidence.

The Scope and Methods of Data Collection

In collecting our data, we have chosen to work on three levels — nationally, in selected areas, and in individual schools. We have therefore tried to focus on individuals and schools affected by the scheme while maintaining in view its broader contexts.[17]

At the national level, we have made an historical analysis of the relation of the scheme to previous attempts to link the public and private sectors, and a sociological analysis of its relationship to other aspects of contemporary social policy. There has also been a more detailed study of its origins, its inclusion in Conservative Party policy, and the debate which surrounded its announcement, all based on both documentary analysis and interviews with some of those centrally involved. Some of this 'preparatory' work is continuing and being revised.[18] Statistics on the distribution of assisted places, their take-up and the levels of financial support being made available to parents are either already published by the DES and through the ISJC's annual surveys or are being obtained in confidential form. The distribution of places is highly significant in relation to initial claims that priority had been given to inner-city areas without selective maintained schools, and that the nature of local provision in the public sector had been carefully considered. Given the historic concentration of public schools in the south of England, and of direct grant schools in and around London, Manchester, Liverpool and Bristol, an equitable selection of schools and allocation of places was bound to be a formidable task.

Our local studies cover four separate areas. Two are in the north and two in the south of England, and they include urban, suburban and semi-rural catchments. While their choice may have begun with their geographical accessibility to the research team, the most significant factor has obviously been the willingness of schools and LEAs to cooperate with the research. As will be discussed more fully in the following section, levels of cooperation have varied so much between and within the local study areas that this has been the major determinant of the particular independent schools within which the operation of the scheme is being studied in depth.

Within each of the four areas, we hope to interview the heads of all the independent schools participating in the scheme. The interviews are open-ended and tape recorded. They cover such matters as the academic record of the school, its reasons for participating in the scheme, its present and (especially in the case of former direct grant schools) recent relations with local LEAs and maintained schools, the selection of assisted pupils and the opportunities which the school is seen as offering them. While much of the information obtained in this way has to be used in conjunction with documentary evidence, the interviews give direct access to the most significant 'gate-keepers' of the scheme. By arousing interest in the research, and perhaps by establishing some confidence in its conduct, they have also served to prepare the ground for making contact with pupils and with parents.

Within the study areas, we have also requested the cooperation of LEAs and their schools. In one area, all primary school head-teachers were contacted by letter about the number of pupils known by them to be interested in taking up assisted places. The prevailing impression was that little was known about the scheme, though some of the more informed responses were followed up. We hope to investigate examples of special preparation of pupils for entrance to independent schools, while recognizing that in some LEAs primary schools have been asked not to provide even basic information about the scheme to parents or information about pupils to independent schools.

In those independent schools chosen for intensive study, interviews are being conducted with staff, pupils and parents. Pupil interviews involve similar numbers of assisted and feepaying pupils within the same year groups. These interviews are semi-structured, and include questions about home and primary school, reasons for choosing their present school and their opinions of it, plans for higher education and employment, hobbies and other interests, and any continued contacts with friends from primary school. Where the parents also agree to be seen, the interviews are much longer and extend from precoded items on their own education and occupation to open-ended questions about their preference for an independent school, their reasons for rejecting alternatives, and their more general views on (for example) the 'openness' of British society.

Where the LEAs permit it, approaches are being made to state secondary schools within the local study areas, and similar interviews conducted with staff, pupils and parents. In some cases, these would have been the schools attended by our assisted place sample if the scheme had not been in existence, and will be the schools attended by former friends from primary school. This component of the research will enable us to make detailed comparisions between the characteristics and career trajectories of assisted place holders, fee-payers in the same schools, and state secondary school pupils from the same local areas.[19] Though there are severe problems in making meaningful comparisons between the academic 'careers' of assisted place holders and what they 'might have done' in a school otherwise available to them (the difficulty of doing so was empha-sized to us by several independent school heads, and we needed no persuading), we can realistically make some 'systemic' comparisons of resources, curriculum, subject choice and ethos in schools in the two sectors.

In all the data collection which we have outlined, equal attention is being given to girls and boys. That might have been taken for granted had several major studies of social origins and educational destinations not focused entirely on boys, and had not the functions and prestige of boys' 'public' schools not dominated debate about the entire independent sector. At least before the sixth form stage, most schools participating in the scheme are single-sex and so, within the constraints imposed by schools' willingness or reluctance to take part in the research, we have tried to focus equally on girls' schools and boys' schools, girl and boy pupils.[20]

Some Methodological Problems

The negotiation of access has been an enduring preoccupation of the research team so far. A controversial policy innovation of this kind engenders such loyalty and hostility that its gatekeepers are unusual-ly inclined to doubt whether any research can be impartial and unusually concerned to discover the views of the researchers them-selves. Some previous work on public schools has also made the independent sector especially suspicious of research with a sociolo-gical orientation.[21] Our own efforts to gain co-operation have been made at several levels, though the structure of the sector has meant that the main points of contact have been with individual schools and their heads. Nevertheless, the evident and understandable interest in the project displayed by national bodies such as the Independent Schools Joint Committee, the Headmasters' Conference and the

Girls' Public Day Schools Trust has undoubtedly influenced the responses of some schools to our approaches. For example, one head who at an early stage offered to help the research 'in any way' subsequently withdrew his offer when HMC advised caution. More recently, however, the HMC Assisted Places Committee has encouraged its members to cooperate, while recognizing that the decision must rest with individuals. In a few cases, the grounds for refusing cooperation have been not so much the politically sensitive nature of the scheme but rather what is perceived as the impossibility of any systematic comparison of schools or types of schools in the opportunities they offer. The controversy surrounding several recent studies of both comprehensive schools and non-selective in comparison with selective schools might well seem to support this scepticism.[22] However, it seems to us difficult to justify in principle in the context of a scheme the essential defence of which is that it offers opportunities to able pupils in schools with established academic reputations which they would be unlikely to find within the public sector. Much more readily understandable is the unwillingness of some heads to allow any enquiry which might seem to make assisted place pupils an object of special attention and so hamper their equal treatment. In our negotiations with schools, we have tried to make clear that cooperation may extend from an interview with the head supplemented by information about the working of the scheme to the unrestricted access to pupils and parents which some schools have felt able to offer subject only to the agreement of the individual parents themselves.

Other anxieties have emerged more or less intensely at different stages of the research. Many advocates of the scheme are rightly concerned about the danger mentioned earlier of drawing conclusions from short-term evidence. We have tried to be sensitive to this concern, for example, by excluding from detailed study the first cohort of pupils to enter the scheme because they are likely to be untypical in several respects. We have also undertaken to monitor the progress of the scheme, and of the pupils involved in it, beyond the initial three years of SSRC funding. Another concern, that our findings might be used prematurely or out of context for politically motivated purposes, was an especially sensitive issue in the early years of the scheme when the possibility of a Labour election victory put its immediate future in jeopardy. We have a steering committee to advise on avoiding this danger. We recognize, however, that an important reason why independent schools have recently become more willing to cooperate in the research has been their renewed self-confidence in the aftermath of the 1983 Conservative election victory. At the same time, there is an evident wish to evaluate the progress of the scheme, and in particular its success in reaching its target groups.

In some ways, LEAs and their schools have posed even more formidable barriers to investigation. The fact that the scheme is free from LEA control, together with the total opposition to it displayed by most Labour-controlled authorities, have made some of our negotiations difficult from the outset. To some LEAs, research into how the scheme works is seen as implying support for it or at best as giving publicity to something which they would prefer to see ignored. One Labour authority has made this position explicit: since it is opposed to the Assisted Places Scheme, it sees no reasons why it should devote time to research into the Scheme. Its Chief Education Officer has made public claims about the disastrous effects which can be expected, yet apparently has little interest in whether or not his predictions prove correct. We recognize that recruitment to an authority's schools might be adversely affected if it were made publicly obvious that they were being harmed by the scheme and that, to this extent, our research might inadvertently help to confirm one of its critics' main predictions. In this case, however, crying wolf in advance on the part of the chief officer might have just the same effect with much less evidence to justify the cry. On much more general grounds, we would argue that neither liking nor disliking a policy is a good reason for simply assuming its effects, and that research such as our own might help to take debate about one piece of legislation beyond a mere exchange of hitherto unsubstantiated claims. At present, three Labour-controlled and four Conservative-controlled LEAs are giving us some access to schools.

The fact that at different times (and occasionally at the same time) our research could be viewed suspiciously by the independent sector and by Labour LEAs raises the ethical question of what stance the research team should declare in the course of negotiating access. To be viewed with distrust by a left-wing Labour authority was sometimes seen as a recommendation by independent school heads, as was also true in reverse. Assumptions have also been made on the basis of the researchers' past connections with independent schools, or past publications, or views on other educational issues where these were known. While obviously necessary not only to gaining and maintaining access but also to the whole coherence of the research design, a non-partisan stance in a variety of contrasting contexts has been difficult to keep. This is especially so for members of the team who, in their 'private' capacities, were initially inclined to the claims of either the scheme's advocates or its critics. We have often been asked directly for our own views. Initially, it was relatively easy to characterize them as merely lay opinion and so as irrelevant to the exercise. Inevitably, however, they are shaped increasingly by reflections on the research data. While making no claim whatsoever to be engaged in action research, the team has not attempted either to adopt the classic positivist stance by refusing to discuss the project with informants, In some cases, this can bring conflict between the researcher's belief in feeding his or her reflections back into the research context and a concern that to do so might affect the operation of the scheme in its local situation. For example, some comments on the possibility that places were not going to their intended recipients produced in one school some changes in how the scheme was advertized. The letter to primary school heads already mentioned may have drawn the attention of some to arrangements they had previously known little or nothing about. The danger of inadvertent sponsorship or opposition has therefore to be kept constantly in mind.

Some Emerging Themes

A number of issues have emerged or become more sharply defined since the Assisted Places Scheme came into operation upon which the evidence we have been gathering may throw some light. We intend to analyze that evidence with a view to informing the ongoing debate. Of particular concern are the social backgrounds of those gaining places, the effects of their doing so on the life chances of other pupils, and the more general question of how the scheme changes the systemic relationship between the state and the independent sector.

At the individual level, there have been claims that some pupils are benefiting who could not be held to 'need' assistance in any accepted sense of the term 'need'.[23] It is likely, however, that parents who abuse the scheme financially are almost certainly a small minority whose only significant function may be to supply ammunition to its critics. Far more interesting in our view is the composition of that group which is clearly financially eligible for assistance with fees and choosing to take advantage of it. The frequency of one-parent families is already well-established.[24] Much less certain, partly because of the rather different occupational categories employed, is the representation or possible under-representation of manual working-class parents. Their participation in the scheme is vital to many of the claims made in its defence in 1979–80. If it transpires that a high proportion of assisted place holders come from 'submerged' middle-class backgrounds already high in cultural capital, then a major justification for withdrawing children from the public sector would be called into question. This would still be the case even if the lists of entrants revealed that many able children from financially modest backgrounds were taking up places. The scheme would then be a further example of an initiative ostensibly designed to enhance equality of opportunity for working-class children which was, in practice, taken most advantage of by middle-class parents — in this case educationally if not financially equipped to do so. If this were shown to be the case, it would be important to monitor the official response to see whether or not policy was adjusted with a view to reaching the 'missing' target group, or whether pronouncements about the progress of the scheme revealed subtle changes in its rhetoric of legitimation.

At the systemic level, the development of the scheme has coincided with cuts in resources for the maintained sector, school closures, and rising demands for a return to grammar school forms of secondary education.[25] It has therefore been argued that the scheme is providing a means whereby some parents who feel that their children are being denied opportunities previously available in the public sector can now take their children out of it. It may in the process be removing from that sector some of those parents who would otherwise be most critical of diminishing resources and articulate in being so, thus reducing some of the most articulate pressures for change. For some of these parents, the fact that the Assisted Places Scheme is state funded may make the transition to private education a less traumatic step than it might otherwise have been and thus help to break down the moral as well as the financial disincentives to the use of the independent sector. For many parents, the ending of selection within the maintained sector may also provide a justification for a resort to private education. In the absence of any widespread resurgence of maintained grammar schools, the abolition of selection seems likely to have contributed to a greater legitimation of the independent sector than might otherwise have occurred. Our interviews with parents will therefore need to probe these issues extremely carefully.

Whatever the outcomes of our detailed investigations, it seems unlikely that our research will establish unequivocally that one set of

empirical claims has turned out to be valid and another set invalid —
though that is a possibility to which we must always remain open . It
may rather be that, at the end of the day, our study will bear out
many of the central claims made by both the advocates and the critics
of the scheme, Insofar as the advocates have argued their case largely
in terms of increased opportunities and advantages accruing to the
participants in the scheme, while the critics have concentrated on the
disadvantages for the state system and the individuals remaining in
it, this is not as paradoxical as it might seem. Yet if this were to be
the case, it might seem that the research had provided little by way of
clarification of the issues raised in the controversy over the scheme.
Nevertheless, if the research were to establish that the opposing
groups involved in the controversy both had good grounds for the
empirical claims they had made, it would at least become clearer that
the development of a coherent policy in this area necessarily involves
a choice between fundamentally conflicting principles. This, in turn,
would suggest that the recent politicization of the question of the
future of the public schools may not have been as inappropriate as
has often been suggested by those who mourn the passing of the era
of relatively peaceful coexistence between the two systems.

Notes

1 The emergence of this sharp contrast in policy is traced in RAE, J. (1981)
The Public School Revolution, London, Faber, pp. 50–85. See also the
Labour Party's (1980) discussion document *Private Schools*, London.
2 We acknowledge the support of ESRC for this research, which has been
funded 1982–85.
3 HOWARTH, T.E. (1969) *Culture, Anarchy and the Public Schools*, London,
Cassell, p. 19.
LEAs were initially allowed to block the transfer of pupils to independent
schools at 16+ if they could claim that sixth form provision in their own
schools would suffer. The government removed this 'veto' in 1983.
5 As academically comprehensive schools have come to predominate in
the public sector, so the independent schools have increasingly been
presented as essential to the preservation of high academic standards and
to the training of occupational elites; see, for example, the book by
Howarth already cited, the *Black Paper* of 1975, and the Independent
Schools Information Service (ISIS) (1976) publication, *Selection: Modern
Education's Dirty Word*, London.
6 This point is elaborated in EDWARDS, T., FULBROOK, M. and WHITTY,
G. (1984) 'The state and the independent sector: Policies, ideologies and
theories', in BARTON, L. and WALKER, S. (Eds) *Social Crisis and
Educational Research*, London, Croom Helm. Since the writing of that

paper, Mary Fulbrook has moved to a lecturing post at University College, London. We are grateful for her help in the initial planning of the present article.

7 RHODES BOYSON, writing in the *Daily Mail*, 25 June 1981.

8 Editorial, *Conference* (the journal of HMC), February 1982.

9 The following comment from a *Conference* editorial, February 1983, is a recurrent theme in statements by representatives of the independent sector: 'We must repeat, again and again, that this is a scheme to assist not schools, nor school teachers, nor head teachers, but children who need help.'

10 The competing claims of 'freedom' and 'social justice' provide the main theme of the (1974) ISIS pamphlet *The Case for Independence,* London.

11 HARVEY, D. (1973) *Social Justice and the City,* London, Arnold.

12 Until recently, it has been this view, with its associated concern for individual opportunity, which has predominated in argument on behalf of the scheme from within the independent sector. It is possible that, in the changing ideological climate, arguments based on monetarist economic and social principles will gain increasing importance in the future. See EDWARDS, T. *et al.* (1984), *op. cit.*

13 Towards the end of the direct grant system, in the late 1960s, a national average of 61 per cent of pupils had all their fees paid by LEAs and only the fees for the 'residuary' places left over to be allocated by the school governors were means-tested. In addition, per capita grants from central government represented an indirect subsidy so that even parents paying 'full' fees were paying only 58 per cent of the economic costs; see GLENNERSTER, H. and WILSON, G. (1970) *Paying for Private Schools,* London, Allen Lane, p. 46. In the Assisted Places Scheme, all places are means-tested and there are no per capita grants.

14 The claim is clearly made in ISIS (1981) *The Case for Collaboration,* London, while the counter-argument was the main reason for John Rae's opposition to the scheme from within the independent sector; see *The Public School Revolution, op. cit.* pp. 178–83, and his article 'What future for the private sector?' *The Times Educational Supplement,* 17 September 1982.

15 Letter in *The Teacher,* 4 February 1980. When the scheme was first announced, Neil Kinnock frequently attacked it as a means of 'pirating scholastic talent from state schools' (*The Guardian,* 29 September 1979), while a circular to the heads of all independent schools from the Labour Party's National Executive continued the metaphor by referring to them as 'a gang of poachers' (Editorial, *Conference,* February 1982).

16 This counter-claim was made by one of the architects of the Scheme, James Cobban, *The Sunday Times,* 8 June 1980, and by Mark Carlisle in *The Times Educational Supplement,* 15 February 1980.

17 A similar concern to keep individuals in view is evident in CONNELL, R. *et al.* (1982) *Making the Difference: Schools, Families and Social Division,* Sydney, Allen and Unwin.

18 It is reported more fully in EDWARDS, T. *et al.* (1984), *op. cit.*

19 Such comparisons within the *same* area may constitute an improvement on the methods of analysis used by CONNELL *et al., op. cit.*

20 The most obvious contrast here is with HALSEY, A.H. *et al.* (1980) *Origins and Destinations*, Oxford, Clarendon Press. It is not surprising, however, that significantly fewer girls have taken up assisted places.

21 LAMBERT, R. *et al.* (1968) *The Hothouse Society*, London, Weidenfeld and Nicolson attracted particular criticism.

22 For example, RUTTER, M. *et al.* (1979) *Fifteen Thousand Hours*, London, Open Books; the attacks by Caroline Cox and John Marks on the National Children's Bureau study — STEEDMAN, J. (1980) STEADMAN, E. (1980) *Progress in Secondary School*, London, National Children's Bureau.

23 See, for example, the report in *Education*, May 1982.

24 The 1982 survey carried out on behalf of the Independent Schools Joint Council included a firm statement that 'the biggest single group of beneficiaries ... was the single-parent families, followed by the unemployed' (*The Guardian*, 24 November 1982).

25 At the time of going to press, such schemes had been floated by Conservative councillors in a number of LEAs, including Solihull and Richmond-upon-Thames. However, few, if any of these schemes look likely to reach the stage of implementation.

Images of Independent Schooling: Exploring the Perceptions of Parents and Politicians*

Ted Tapper, University of Sussex
and
Brian Salter, University of Surrey

The survival of independent schooling in Britain is dependent upon the ability of the schools to attract a sufficient number of parents to pay the fees that enable them to meet their costs, and upon a willingness of governments to permit their continued existence. The purpose of this chapter is to elucidate those images of independent schooling that encourage parents to pay fees and that persuade political parties to pursue particular education policies.[1] The chapter will then examine the extent to which those images are supported by the realities of schooling. Our aspirations are straightforward, if ambitious: to persuade parents to consider more carefully whether their purchase of independent schooling is worthwhile, to encourage politicians to formulate their educational policies either on the basis of their general principles or on a clearer understanding of educational realities rather than wishful thinking, and to urge social scientists to refine their understanding of the process of class reproduction.

Although these bold opening propositions can be qualified (for example, a few independent schools have substantial endowments which cushion them financially), they are not without merit. Few independent schools would be able to survive for very long unless enough parents were persuaded of the wisdom of fee-paying. The schools may be able to influence the educational values of their prospective customers (rather than vice versa) but in the final analysis

* The Arts Research Support Fund of the University of Sussex made available various small grants to facilitate the research for parts of this chapter. Some of the data first appeared in Tapper T. (1984) 'The politics of independent schooling: Assessing the policy assumptions', *Teaching Politics*, 13, 1, January, pp. 95–104. This present article is a prelude to our forthcoming book, *Power and Policy in Education: the Case of Private Schooling*.

it is the parents' willingness to pay fees that keeps them in business.

In the present context the political threat may ring hollow, but direct grant status has been phased out within the last ten years and it could be argued that the resolve of the Labour Party to abolish — albeit gradually — the independent sector has never been firmer. Both the present leader, Neil Kinnock, and the deputy leader, Roy Hattersley, have made unequivocal commitments.

Parental Perceptions

Thanks to the reminiscences of numerous old boys we are only too well acquainted with the daily routine of public schools, especially those boarding institutions apparently cast forever in the mould of past decades.[2] But it is much more difficult to discover why parents should persist in exposing their children to such environments.

The most substantial piece of pertinent work was undertaken by Bridgeman and Fox in 1977.[3] Their survey consisted of 330 parents (167 mothers and 163 fathers) whose children were attending one of three preparatory schools of differing prestige. Bridgeman and Fox concluded that their parents fell largely into one of two categories: 'traditionals' and 'pragmatists'.[4] The former, well-established members of the traditional upper class, excluded the possibility of their children attending maintained primary schools. They were locked into a well-defined educational model in which their children moved from a prestigious preparatory school to a boarding secondary school and then to an Oxbridge college. The 'pragmatists' had opted out of the state system because of specific grievances which if remedied could result in a changing of parental minds. One has the impression that 'pragmatists', perhaps swayed somewhat by financial considerations, will oscillate between the independent and maintained sectors. Thus their daughters may be educated in state schools and their sons privately, or they make use of state controlled primary and junior schools but then send their children to independent secondary schools. Such oscillation may also be a response to the differential quality of state schooling, so residential changes could result in different decisions.

Although these parents differ in terms of their loyalties to the state and independent sectors, there is considerable overlap as to why they have chosen private preparatory schools in preference to state primary schools.[5] The majority of these reasons fall into one of two categories: educational variables and socio-cultural variables. The negative view of the experience of schooling within state schools (size of classes, high rate of teacher turnover, insufficient incentive for children to stretch themselves, and insufficient emphasis on formal learning) is very pronounced. The concern with the socio-cultural climate of the maintained primary schools (insufficient teaching of good manners, limited stress upon hard work, insufficient emphasis on correct speech, and too many rough children) is somewhat less marked but nonetheless it evokes widespread concern.[6] Although the 'traditional' parents are more likely to stress the interrelationship between schooling and character training it appears to be the more socially marginal members of the 'pragmatists' who are most worried by the prospect of contamination by proletarian social mores. Whereas many 'traditional' parents view schooling as part of the process of social reproduction in the broadest sense of the term (the moulding of character, the creation of a social network, and the opening up of future opportunities), so many 'pragmatic' parents seem to feel that their children are acquiring a number of valuable personal resources some of which may be highly esoteric and few of which are necessarily integrated.

For these parents to create an image of the independent schools (most succinctly stated: '. . . they think private schools are educationally "better" '[7]) means that they also create images of the maintained schools. In fact the images of one help to define the images of the other. As some parents are in a position to choose between the two educational sectors one would expect this interaction between images, but what is significant about Bridgeman's and Fox's survey is that even those parents who have no intention of using the maintained schools are also prepared to justify their behaviour by their negative images of them. In similar fashion many parents who have neither the intention nor the financial resources to send their children to independent schools undoubtedly construct images of them. In view of the fact that many of these parents, on both sides of the schooling barrier, inhabit closed educational worlds it would be interesting to know how they construct their images. In particular what are the sources of information available to them and what are the means by which they sift and test that information? Inasmuch as parents are determining the schooling of their own children it could be argued that the consequences of acting on the basis of poorly constructed images are insignificant. However the impact of individual decisions is accumulative and, to carry the argument to an extreme, independent schooling may simply be the product of irrational consumer preferences!

The Political Parties: Policies and Perceptions

This section of the paper will focus upon how the two main political parties in Britain, the Conservative and Labour Parties, have viewed the independent sector of schooling since the 1944 Education Act. Our attention is restricted to these two political parties because of their monopoly of government since 1944. In examining the basis of the Labour Party's policy towards the independent sector we have made considerable use of the party's 1980 publication, *Private Schools*.[8] Although described as a discussion document, the pamphlet represents the culmination of a major policy initiative by the party. It is a comparatively lengthy review of a particular policy issue, the end product of a lot of time, energy and expertise.[9] Furthermore, because of its inevitably directed discussion of future policy options it has formed the basis of the Labour Party's current policy proposals as seen in subsequent annual conference motions, the 1983 General Election Manifesto, and the TUC-Labour Party Liaison Committee statement entitled 'Private Schools'.[10] There is no parallel concentration of thinking on the part of the Conservative Party; indeed Mrs Thatcher has purposefully refrained from the formulation of detailed policy proposals in favour of the forceful presentation of broad principles. In examining Conservative Party policy we have been forced therefore into an analysis of a wider range of material: policy statements, general election manifestos, the speeches and writings of leading party figures, and Central Office publications (including those of the Conservative Research Department).[11]

Since the 1944 Education Act the Labour Party's policy on private schooling has travelled through three distinct phases. Until the late 1950s the dominant faction in the party believed that the private schools would wither on the vine as parents abandoned them for an improving state sector. Rather than pursue an electorally damaging line, the main task was to increase the resources available to the maintained sector so improving its quality as it expanded in response to the demographic trend. The private sector was a diversion that was best ignored. With the passage of time it was impossible to sustain such optimism for the evidence demonstrated that, regardless of the qualities of the maintained schools, the independent sector retained the loyalty of a large segment of the British middle class, so reinforcing one of the Labour Party's traditional charges that the public schools were central to the process of class reproduction.

A shift in Labour Party policy owed as much to new educational ideas as to the conservatism of the British middle class. Whereas at one time Labour governments were motivated by the idea that the state should provide the means that enable all children, regardless of their social origins, to climb to the top of the educational ladder (that is, to provide equality of educational opportunity) it was later argued that schooling should enable children to develop their intelligence. In the language of the time there was a shift from a 'weak' to a 'strong' definition of equality of educational opportunity.[12] To pursue this new objective in an educational context which explicitly favoured those with either wealthy parents and/or with high intelligence (as measured by the 11+ examination) was patently absurd, for it imposed severe limits upon what the unfavoured majority could realistically hope to achieve regardless of their ultimate potential.

In this second phase, notwithstanding the ever louder voice of the abolitionists, the Labour Party was committed to integrating the two educational sectors.[13] Circular 10/65 issued by the first Wilson Government argued for a universal system of secondary education organized along comprehensive lines, while Tony Crosland, as Secretary of State for Education and Science, created the Public Schools Commission whose terms of reference explicitly included the directive to consider ways in which the independent schools could be integrated into the maintained sector.[14] Integration floundered on three rocks: selection, independence and finance. Those more hostile to the independent schools were not prepared to concede that they should have the right to select their non-fee-paying pupils, for they feared (probably correctly) the perpetuation of academic and social selection if the individual schools retained this right. On the other side of the coin, few independent schools were prepared to sacrifice the almost complete autonomy in the management of their internal affairs for what would be for them the contraints of voluntary aided status. The very formidable financial problems stem from the fact that it is invariably more costly to fund places in the independent sector and that to do so deprives the maintained schools of both scarce resources and possibly of pupils who would have a positive influence upon their character.

It is our contention that Labour Party policy moved into its third and present phase in response to the intractable problems surrounding integration rather than because of any fundamental ideological shift within the party. But it has to be admitted that as these problems grew so did discontent within the party at large at the Parliamentary Labour Party's failure in the period 1974–79 to implement conference and manifesto pledges. Although the intensification of the latter malaise has been closely linked to the leftward drift of the Labour Party, even a right-winger like Shirley Williams moved to a more radical position in despair at the failure of integration.[15] What also has to be recognized is that a sophisticated group of officers and co-opted individuals, who had never been noted for their sympathy towards the private sector, were now directing their attention to the problem, the end result of which was the discussion document, *Private Schools*. Much play in interpreting policy changes has been made with Roy Hattersley's speech to the 1973 Autumn Conference of the Incorporated Association of Preparatory Schools in which he said that 'competitive education, which allows the few to leap further and further ahead, ensures that the less fortunate fall further and further behind. That is why the pursuit of equality of opportunity had to be replaced by the pursuit of equality itself.'[16] However, this is little more than a reiteration of the established theme that equality of educational opportunity is a limited goal and that schooling should stretch the talent of those who fail to ascend the educational ladder.

The present policy also owes much to the fact that when last in government the Labour Party's attempt to integrate the direct grant schools into the maintained sector ended up reinforcing the independent sector! The Second Report of the Public Schools Commission (the Donnison Report) recommended that direct grant status should be abolished and that the schools should be integrated into the maintained sector as comprehensive secondary schools with voluntary aided status.[17] This recommendation was pursued by the Labour government from 1974 and direct grant status was phased out from September 1976. Unfortunately, as far as that government was concerned, approximately two-thirds of the ex-direct grant grammar schools opted for independent status. Of those that joined the maintained system the majority had been controlled by the Roman Catholic Church, had admitted a high percentage of free place pupils and were located in northern conurbations. This is not the kind of experience to encourage political parties to think in terms of reformist strategies.

Although policy towards the independent sector has changed over time, the view of private schooling upon which those policies have been based has remained fairly consistent.[18] The party's evaluation of independent schooling draws upon three interrelated sets of observations on the class composition of the schools, on the experience of schooling they impart, and on their links to the most powerful, prestigious and wealthy sections of British society. The very negative influence of private schooling, in the Labour Party's view, follows from these observations. The schools select their pupils both academically and socially, they expose them to a narrowly academic curriculum and in the process impart socio-cultural experiences which at the very least help to insulate them from their peers. Little of this would matter were it not for the fact that the schools maintained close links with the British ruling class so that their pupils dominate the commanding heights of this society.[19] It is accepted by the Labour Party that this view applies mainly to the prestigious end of independent schooling, that is, the public schools, but to some extent the whole of the sector is tarred with the same brush.

What, in the Labour Party's opinion, are the consequences of these alleged facts? The independent sector is viewed as an agent of class reproduction, selected by many parents for base reasons of social snobbery rather than because of purely educational advantages that private schools may bestow. The character of the British class structure is considered to be the partial product of the selective intake of the independent schools and their subjection of that intake to esoteric educational and socio-cultural experiences. The damage perpetrated by the latter experiences is especially profound because they have permeated the educational system at large. In the words of the discussion document: 'But our fundamental opposition to private schooling arises from the knowledge that their educational influence has resulted in attempts by parts of the maintained sector to emulate their narrow academic character and has endowed private schools with unearned and unfair reputations of educational superiority.'[20] Not only has this experience of schooling led to damaging educational consequences but also its political and industrial repercussions have been equally pernicious. The discussion document claims that the private schools pride themselves on instilling 'in pupils a sense of leadership, of self assuredness and of superiority in order to run the country for those lesser mortals who have not had the "benefit" of a private education.'[21] This is described as 'the characteristic arrogance of such a system' which 'has no place in a democratic country in the twentieth century'.[22] The political right frequently castigates the public schools for sapping the entrepreneurial spirit of the British bourgeoisie, while in parallel fashion the political left has argued that their curriculum (narrowly academic, overburdened by the classics, and biased against applied sciences and vocational studies) is entirely inappropriate to the needs of a modern industrial society. According to this criticism, although the public schools may be successful at replenishing the British ruling class, the price the nation as a whole pays for this is a slow but sure decline into industrial oblivion.

Although the Labour Party's case against the private sector is all-encompassing, even in the making of it there is considerable ambivalence. On the one hand the schools are castigated because of the kind of educational experiences they offer, and the social impact of those experiences, yet on the other hand it is recognized that there may be substance to the claim that they offer a superior education. For as the discussion document notes, 'Perhaps the most obvious division between private and maintained schools is the superior facilities that parents can buy for their children in many of the public schools: expansive playing fields; well stocked libraries and — in recent years — new or modernised laboratories.'[23] In terms of the values that schools inculcate, the discussion document in fact argues that the two systems are not that far apart: 'Implicit in the claims of the public schools is that they have a virtual monopoly in developing self-confidence and leadership. Manifestly this is not true. Any school system strives to encourage maturity, common service, responsibility, co-operation and honesty. Indeed there are the fundamental values of the comprehensive system.'[24] The tension within the party's critique of private schooling is a result of the attempt to portray it as a privileged form of schooling but not necessarily one that is superior in educational terms.

The Conservative Party has consistently argued the case for private schooling; party conferences ritualistically reiterate their support for the principle that parents have the right to purchase schooling for their children. The provision of concrete assistance has however been more circumspect but nonetheless welcome to the independent schools. For example, in the early days of her tenure at Elizabeth House Mrs Thatcher increased the capitation grant for the direct grant schools and her last government put into effect the Assisted Places Scheme. In spite of the different attitudes towards private schooling on the part of the two main political parties, it is the issue of selection rather than independence which has aroused the more bitter controversy since the 1944 Education Act. However the initial Tory response to Circular 10/65, strongly influenced by Sir Edward Boyle, the Shadow Minister for Education, was pragmatic. The party opposed the imposition of a uniform pattern of secondary education upon the local authorities but was wise enough to recognize the unpopularity of early secondary school selection and of the 11+ examination in particular. Between 1965 and 1970 the Conservative Party evolved the following guidelines on secondary school reorganization: that local authorities should be allowed to develop their own plans, that comprehensive schools should if possible be purpose-built, that large schools should be avoided, that selection within schools was inevitable, and that it was possible for grammar and comprehensive schools to coexist successfully. Indeed Sir Edward Boyle argued at the 1965 party conference that neighbourhood comprehensive schools in the large cities could not fully serve the interests of the brightest working-class children and that some grammar schools should be retained for this purpose.[25]

By the late 1960s there was growing opposition within the Conservative Party towards its educational goals in general and towards its policy on grammar schools and selection in particular. This came to a head at the 1967 conference when the platform's motion was approved by a small majority only after a formal count. The position of Sir Edward Boyle was further undermined when the parliamentary backbench committee on education swung to the political right albeit temporarily, in November 1967. It was no surprise, therefore, that he should quit politics for university administration, to be succeeded as shadow minister by the redoubtable Mrs Thatcher. She purposefully made it her concern to move the educational debate from established issues (especially how schooling should be formally organized) onto new territory. This change in emphasis occurred in a wider context which was questioning many of the post-war developments within the British educational system. The most dramatic, some would say melodramatic, expression of this malaise was found in the Black Paper publications. It was the breakdown of the established political consensus, and the accompanying attack upon the main thrust of theory and practice, that enabled the proponents of private schooling to assume a more aggressive posture.

Under the auspices of Mrs Thatcher the Conservative Party argued that it was important to establish educational priorities, and subsequently top billing was given to the replacement of older primary schools through a major building programme.[26] She also maintained that the formal character of the educational system was far less important than the experience of schooling. The latter concern was invariably expressed in the everyday language of preserving educational standards. Although a traditional strain in Tory educational thinking, it was promoted with a new sense of urgency in the 1970s partly because it was sensed that parents were worried about the impact of educational change upon the quality of schooling (and therefore it was an issue with potential electoral mileage) and partly because of fears for the character of schooling engendered by specific policies of the 1974–79 Labour government (that is, the abolition of direct grant schools and the imposition of a universal system of comprehensive secondary schooling through legislation).

The Labour government's phasing out of direct grant status (which was to take effect from September 1976) was a critical development because it was seen by the Tory Party as an attack upon centres of educational excellence that for decades had provided children, many from families of modest means, with a highly relevant schooling. The party's initial response was a pledge by the then shadow minister, Mr Norman St John Stevas, to restore direct grant status (in fact to place it on a legislative basis) and to re-open the direct grant list with the obvious intention of increasing the number of direct grant schools.[27] Over a time these options were replaced by the party's embracing, and eventual enacting, of the Assisted Places Scheme. The Conservative Party's defence of the direct grant schools stemmed partly from the belief (as reiterated by Sir Edward Boyle to the 1965 conference) that many comprehensive schools were incapable of offering bright children an education commensurate with their ability and/or aptitude, that there should be at least a residue of grammar schools for the talented tenth. In view of the declining number of maintained grammar schools it was increasingly obvious that only the private sector could provide that alternative to the comprehensive schools.

One of the strong themes in the educational thinking of the Conservative Party is that an independent sector is required in order to provide a reference point for the maintained schools. The critics may claim that all the party really wants is a rod with which to beat the maintained schools, but if there is less diversity of provision then, according to Conservative educational spokesmen, there will be less variety of practice and fewer opportunities to compare practice. From the mid-1970s a second traditional strand (that is, in addition to the stress on academic excellence) which was promoted with a new sense of urgency, was the need to maximize parental choice and parental influence upon those decisions which affect the schooling of their children. The consequence was a reinforcement of the party's commitment to independent schooling. As we have discussed earlier, the promotion of parental influence stemmed from the belief that this was a viable means of stimulating desirable educational experiences, that the character of schooling had for too long been determined by bureaucrats, teachers and sociologists. Implicit in this thinking is the idea that educational practice in independent schools is so much more acceptable because they are subject to the pressures of the marketplace and that if the same influence can be brought to bear upon maintained schools (via vouchers or open enrolment) they will also be forced to improve or perish. In policy terms these ideas have been reflected in the parental charter and the Assisted Places Scheme.

Tory educational policy, although always committed to the maintenance of the independent sector, has elevated its importance in recent years. The party's disaffection with the maintained sector has meant its turning to independent schooling to find a model of acceptable practice. The direct grant grammar schools, phased out by a Labour government, were seen as bastions of an academic excellence which had been made available to a broad spectrum of the community, while the traditionally independent schools were modernizing their practices apparently in response to the demands of parents. In contrast with the self-doubts of the Labour Party over educational policy, the Conservative Party grew in confidence as it became more aggressively critical of the status quo and more prepared to contemplate radical alternatives.[28] Norman St John Stevas, the party's Shadow Minister for Education between 1975 and 1979, could rightly claim that as time passed so the educational debate was increasingly located upon territory that had been carved out by the Conservative Party.[29]

Educational Realities

If a measure of social divisiveness is the class composition of a school's pupils, then the independent schools are undoubtedly socially divisive. All surveys reveal that most pupils in independent schools have fathers with middle-class occupations whereas the majority of pupils in maintained schools have fathers with working-class occupations.[30] Bald labels however describe complex patterns of schooling and disguise subtleties in the process of class reproduction. While confirming the general picture, Halsey's study (*Origins and Destinations*) shows that middle-class parents (the 'service' and 'intermediate' categories) are more prepared to use the state primary than the state secondary schools and that there are differences in class composition between the three kinds of private secondary schools, that is, HMC schools, direct grant schools and independent non-HMC schools.[31]

Of greater importance is the fact that a significant majority of parents in all eight of Halsey's occupational groupings use the maintained, rather than the private, schools. Only 32.7 per cent of parents in class 1 send their children to private primary schools (35.7 per cent of the same parents send their children to private secondary schools) and even this figure drops sharply for class 2 parents (14.3 per cent send their children to private primary schools and 15.6 per cent to private secondary schools).[32] Moreover in terms of educational scatter (that is, attendance at differing kinds of secondary schools) the survey data reveal '... that the class of higher grade professionals, managers and proprietors is the one with greatest educational scatter.'[33] This leads him to the cryptic conclusion that 'classes, we must always remind ourselves, are not castes.'[34] What these figures do suggest is that if there is educational apartheid in the British educational system, then much of the problem must exist within the maintained sector simply because that is where the overwhelming majority of schoolchildren of all class backgrounds are educated.

The private sector's function of class reproduction is complicated not simply by its own internal divisions, and the relationship of the class structure to those cleavages, but also by movement into and out of independent schooling across generations. Halsey's survey reveals that in those families in which at least one of the parents had some experience of private schooling less than 50 per cent (47.7) actually sent their own children to similar secondary schools, whereas 11.7 per cent of those families in which one or both parents had attended state selective schools and 3.1 per cent of those families in which both parents had attended non-selective schools sent their children to private secondary schools.[35] This demonstrates that there has been considerable intergenerational drop-out from the private sector and a smaller percentage movement (but for a larger number of parents) into it. It is our contention that such information necessitates a refinement of the charge that the private sector is socially divisive.

Given this transference across the two educational systems, most parents will have direct contact with at least the state sector of schooling; there are few of Bridgeman's and Fox's 'traditionals'. Furthermore, although it may be surmised that parents who were privately educated would prefer selective as opposed to non-selective state schooling for their children, over a fifth of them in Halsey's survey (21.1 per cent) had to be satisfied with the latter.[36] With the phasing out of the maintained and direct grant grammar schools it is possible that the intergenerational movement between the two systems will decline. Those parents who sought free places at direct grant schools via the state primary schools no longer have this incentive to use them (although the introduction of the Assisted Places Scheme has complicated the picture somewhat), and other parents may not be prepared to allow their children to attend comprehensive schools although they would have found a grammar school education perfectly acceptable.

In recent years the number of day pupils, as opposed to boarders, has been more buoyant in the independent schools.[37] Day school fees, which like boarding fees have tended to increase more rapidly than the rate of inflation, may be beyond the means of most working-class families but are probably within the reach of the lower middle class (Halsey's 'intermediates'), especially when the incentive to have one's children educated privately is high and both parents are working. As far as we are aware there are no trend data on the class composition of the independent sector, but in view of its changing characteristics (more day pupils, and a comparatively greater expansion at the less expensive and prestigious end of the market) it is probable that the balance of middle-class parents making use of the private schools has shifted from (in Halsey's terms) the 'service' to the 'intermediate' class.[38]

The preoccupation with the interaction between the private schools and the class structure is understandable but unfortunately appears to have ruled out any discussion of their wider social characteristics. The fact that the independent sector educates, often in single-sex schools, a significant percentage of those girls who subsequently go up to university and/or pursue professional careers has passed almost unnoticed. The Labour Party's discussion document, for example, lacks a single reference to the education of women in the private sector; its concern is with the class structure alone as if this precluded the consideration of other social issues. Finally, it has to be mentioned that many of the independent schools are religious foundations (Methodist, Roman Catholic and Jewish as well as the more common Anglican establishments). One would like to know how successful these foundations are at retaining a particular set of religious values over time, how this influences their more general mores, and how this influences the cohesiveness of the British ruling class. Again British social science has conspicuously failed to consider these problems.

If the charge that the private schools are socially divisive is to carry real weight it has to be demonstrated that they not only recruit very selectively but also socialize their pupils in ways that intensify the differences between them and their peers; in other words, they inculcate very distinctive experience of schooling. In this part of the chapter we will examine recent changes in public school education concentrating upon the socio-cultural and academic values they attempt to impart. Our focus is upon the public schools (boys' boarding schools that recruit their pupils nationally and belong to the Headmasters' Conference). It is our contention that these schools form a model for much of the independent sector (where they go, the others will be required to follow), and they best illustrate the inevitable consequences of the necessary entanglement if they are to maintain their preeminence in a wide network of institutions.[39] Furthermore, it is against the public schools that the charge of creating social divisiveness has been most often levelled; they are considered responsible for the creation of a leadership cadre bound together by its own special mores.

In order not to repeat at length work we have published elsewhere, what follows is essentially an encapsulation of previous argument.[40] The past physical isolation of the public schools has been steadily eroded by closer contacts with parents (even those who favour boarding education are likely to select a school within easy commuting distance), with the neighbourhood (a mutual sharing of facilities with local state schools and the undertaking of social welfare activities in the community), and with the public at large (note the incessant media attention and above all the TV series on Radley College). The traditional socio-cultural values have likewise been modified extensively. The strength of the old house system, with its prefects and personal fags, has been diluted as much by economic necessity as by anything else.[41] Games and team spirit are still important but compulsion is less strident and the choice of activities much wider. The combined cadet force remains an honoured institution at many schools but its pursuits are for the genuinely committed rather than for all regardless of their tastes. Attendance at chapel may no longer be on the wane, as in the heady days of the sixties and early seventies, but today it would be much more difficult to describe it, as others have done in the past, as the essential school ritual. Finally, much of the old value system assumed the need to perpetuate a masculine world; this is less true today given the willingness of many boys' schools to accept girls as pupils.

The change in the socio-cultural environment has been matched by a new, and some would say regrettable, emphasis upon examination success.[42] Whereas the traditional public school was reputed to turn out well-rounded, Christian gentlemen, today's public school product is much more likely to be an aggressive, well-qualified specialist. Although this may be regretted by some, the changed nature of the curriculum has found general favour. The grossly inflated position of the classics has been punctured to the point where the present-day sixth form is dominatd by the maths and science scholars, invariably receiving their schooling in new, well-equipped laboratories. Accompanying this trend is an expansion of the arts which has done much to dispel the image of the public schoolboy as a philistine.

In spite of the above changes, it is still possible to maintain that the independent sector imparts an experience of schooling which cements social divisions, but it is impossible to make that argument in the terms that it has been made in the past. In view of the changes we have noted, the schools can scarcely be described as training a future ruling class which is totally out of tune with the needs of contemporary Britain. Although pupils in the independent sector, and the public schools in particular, may be socially selective, they are not isolated from the main societal currents, It can be plausibly argued that the schools have successfully identified those currents and that they have taken the necessary measures to ensure that their pupils compete effectively in terms of their demands. So much so that it is our contention that this was picked up by those members of the Conservative Party with an interest in educational issues and propagated far and wide.[43] The extent to which the private schools still maintain a distinctive experience of schooling is dependent upon developments within the maintained sector. The implication of the above argument is that the private sector has lost its educational peculiarity while responding to academic pressures that are most concretely expressed in terms of examination success. We will shortly argue that the maintained schools, in spite of considerable media publicity to the contrary, have also been forced to travel along the same path. So there is a genuine convergence of the experiences of schooling.

Of course it is conceivable that schools may organize themselves differently without significantly influencing the socio-cultural pursuits of their pupils, for these may originate from outside the schools, and the best they can do is accommodate them. The source of the culture would then be the class structure, and divergences in cultural activities would depend upon the character of the class system. What is required, therefore, is information on how pupils actually behave rather than how either parents or schools think they should behave, or how politicians imagine schools try to influence pupil behaviour. We have analyzed some of the data collected for the National Child Development Study (NCDS) by the National Children's Bureau (NCB) in order to throw some light upon this problem.[44] The suggestion is that the character of the class system is not such as to prevent many aspects of the youth culture from cutting across school boundaries.

The differences shown in Table 1 are as anticipated and the same cultural activity, although its form remains constant, may contain an enormous variety of material. Television programmes, to note the obvious, vary greatly in cultural terms. But in spite of this caveat the overlap in the pursuit of socio-cultural activities by these 16-year-old adolescents, drawn from the two schooling sectors, is marked. If, in spite of these data, independent schooling is creating a cultural milieu which reinforces the distinctiveness of the class origins of its pupils, then it is necessary to know the specific areas in which this is pursued and what impact it actually has upon the behaviour of pupils. In *Origins and Destinations* it is argued that by the time schoolchildren are due to sit externally controlled examinations the working-class

Table 1. *Frequency of Involvement in Various Socio-Cultural Pursuits (percentages)*

	Often	Sometimes	Hardly ever/never	No change
Reading				
Maintained	23	47	25	4
Private	40	43	15	3
Sports				
Maintained	38	35	24	3
Private	46	33	17	5
Watching TV				
Maintained	65	29	5	1
Private	52	39	8	1
Dancing				
Maintained	39	31	25	5
Private	26	34	31	10
Voluntary Work				
Maintained	8	30	46	16
Private	7	31	45	18

Note: Full data in these analyses were available for approximately 12,000 children; 1974 is the date of the most recent follow-up of the sample.

pupils in selective schools have been sufficiently enculturated that they can compete on equal terms with middle-class pupils, in other words, what cultural capital the latter may possess is employed most effectively when entry to the selective schools, and survival within them, are determined.[45] What the National Child Development Study suggests is that Bourdieu's notion that cultural capital is divided along class lines needs to be re-evaluated in the light of the fact there are powerful forces within contemporary society (such as segments of the media and those firms that produce goods and services for young people) which have a vested interest in promoting a youth culture that cuts across class lines.

We have already argued that the experience of schooling within the independent sector now stresses more than ever before the importance of academic success. As the private schools were moving in this direction so in the maintained sector the secondary schools were being reorganized along comprehensive lines which meant the phasing out of those grammar schools which had offered some working-class children the chance of an academic education. It is part of contemporary educational folklore, fully supported by influential and vocal segments within the Conservative Party, that many comprehensive schools are incapable of catering for their brighter pupils. This undoubtedly affected the general educational climate, and Bridgeman's and Fox's survey on why parents choose private schooling reveals the stress 'the pragmatists' place upon a narrow understanding of educational standards. The cause of the independent sector was undoubtedly boosted (at least in the short run) by the move towards a comprehensive system of maintained secondary schools, as it was subsequently reinforced by the abolition of direct grant status. Parents have been presented with an image of a maintained sector which is constantly in turmoil and failing in educational terms which has been contrasted with a private sector which is stable and educationally respectable. Is it any wonder that those 'pragmatic' parents who could afford the fees drifted towards the independent schools?

The debate about the academic differences between schools has concentrated primarily upon the examination performance (O-level and A-level GCEs, and GSEs) of pupils in the selective secondary system (grammar and secondary modern schools) and in the non-selective secondary system (comprehensive schools). It is not a debate which directly affects the independent schools, for the question is about the influence of selection rather than independence. However, many schools in the independent sector (especially the more prestigious establishments) are academically as well as socially selective and it is evident that many parents who pay fees do so in the expectation of enhanced examination results. The only sensible conclusion that can be drawn from varying studies of the impact of secondary school organization upon examination performance is that it remains to be proven that in terms of the national picture it has any significant influence whatsoever.[46] Once one attempts to compare like with like, by controlling for variables such as social background and ability of the pupils, then the differences thrown up by the raw data patterns evaporate rapidly.

Is there anything about the character of independent schooling to suggest that its inclusion in the research would substantially alter the general picture? We believe that this question must be answered in the negative. This is not to deny that individual schools of all kinds may — for better or worse — influence the examination performance of their pupils, nor to deny that small groups of individuals may be consistently influenced by the organization of secondary schooling. But these qualifications, as important as they may be, do not alter the general conclusion that it remains to be proven that the organization of secondary schooling has a significant impact on the examination performance of pupils.

The assumption that the organization of secondary schooling influences the examination performance of pupils stems from the belief that differing kinds of schooling are committed to contrasting educational values. Again without denying the likelihood of individual school variations (which are likely occur within all types of school), it must stated that there is little evidence to substantiate this and some evidence to the contrary. Based on a sample of forty-five secondary schools, located in the south-west of England and compared in 1968–69 and 1978–79, King discovered there was a general movement towards entering pupils for more external examinations, controlling their schoolwork more closely, and offering better careers guidance.[47] These changes have been accompanied by a closer monitoring of pupils' behaviour so that there are more rules regulating the general bahaviour of children around the schools in cloak-rooms and corridors. Although lateness is less often automatically sanctioned, persistent lateness more often leads to punishment. Systems of regular detentions are more common.[48] Furthermore, even when apparently radical innovations are introduced it cannot be assumed that the school is then committed to new goals. As Ball shows in his study of Beachside Comprehensive, the move towards mixed ability teaching was motivated primarily by the desire to increase the social control of teachers by undermining those anti-school cliques that emerge within a streamed school.[49] Ball himself notes that the educational outcomes are unlikely to be different in view of the underlying conservative motivation for change.

To sustain more forcefully our argument that the independent and maintained sectors offer a similar experience of schooling, we have analyzed a further body of information from the National Children's Development Study which illustrates how pupils evaluate varying aspects of their schooling. Of course children's responses do not describe the experience of schooling as it actually is, but presumably it is those responses which one is attempting to mould.

The distributions (see Table 2) suggest that pupils, in both the maintained and private sectors, feel reasonably positive about their

Table 2.   *Responses to Schooling (percentages)*

	Very true or partly true	*Can't say*	*Untrue or partly untrue*
I feel school is largely a waste of time			
Maintained	11	9	79
Private	3	3	94
I'm quiet in class and get on with my work			
Maintained	60	11	29
Private	64	10	26
I think homework is a bore			
Maintained	54	16	30
Private	38	17	45
I find it difficult to keep my mind on my work			
Maintained	36	10	54
Private	35	8	57
I don't like school			
Maintained	30	14	55
Private	20	13	68
I am always willing to help teacher			
Maintained	59	18	22
Private	59	20	21

schooling. The differences are in the anticipated direction but are not so large as to imply, even remotely, that these children are relating to their schooling in fundamentally different ways.

If the independent schools are to act as effective agents of social reproduction then their alleged social divisiveness (biased pupil recruitment patterns and peculiar socializing experiences) has to be a critical variable in ensuring that their ex-pupils succeed in obtaining a grossly disproportionate share of those jobs to which most income, power and status accrue. One of the central charges levelled at the public schools in particular is that they are integral to the process by which a closed ruling class perpetuates itself over time. In spite of the persistence of this claim, it is exceedingly difficult to discover conclusive supporting evidence. It is a well-documented fact that many of the so-called top posts in Britain are filled by those who attended public schools,[50] but to examine the schooling of those who hold positions of wealth and power inevitably gives a very slanted view of what happens to all the products of the public schools. A few may dominate the nation's more exalted ranks but most must end up as respectable members of the bourgeoisie (or worse) for these are simply insufficient opportunities at the top to accommodate them all. There is also a danger in assuming that the domination of particular positions by public school boys is per se a measure of the importance of those positions — which is as good a way as any of proving one's case.

A more significant problem is the failure to establish a causal relationship between schooling and membership in one of the factions of the ruling class. There is no evidence that schooling exercises a significant *independent* influence when it comes to determining who will belong to the commanding heights of this society.[51] Much of the literature on this relationship concludes with little more than wishful thinking. This is perfectly illustrated by Glennester and Pryke: 'But it is difficult to believe that a public-school education counts for nothing. Parents who pay high fees to send their children to these schools obviously believe that it is important, or they would not waste their money.'[52] But perhaps they have more money than sense and are indeed mistaken in their belief!

In view of the existing vagueness, it is necessary to explore the possible contribution that schooling can make to an individual's job chances. Bourdieu has argued that ruling elites in France are a product of the interaction of cultural and economic capital.[53] Without denying the influence of either of these forms of capital, we would like to suggest the additonal relevance of social capital which can be defined as an individual's network of social relations.[54] It is this form of capital which the independent sector, especially the public schools, are particularly good at either creating or cementing. It is created for those individuals for whom a public school education represents a mobility channel, and cemented for those individuals for whom is it is an established part of their family lifestyle. All the similarities in the world in terms of cultural style, including formal academic attainments, do not make for equality in the distribution of social and economic capital.

What we are tentatively suggesting, therefore, is that the public schools provide a convenient institutional context for the obtaining and augmenting of social capital. If they were abolished it would prove difficult to create an institutional network that was as convenient. The state system of schooling would undoubtedly disperse the critical individuals far too widely and the Oxbridge colleges probably exercise their influence too late in the life cycle to perform such a function effectively. Moreover the Oxbridge experience is available to only a part of the ruling class and what is required for this purpose is an institutional framework which is more all-embracing. It is this that the public schools currently provide.

Social capital is a resource that can work to the advantage of those who possess it at all levels of the class structure, but within any particular class stratum its influence is variable. Bourdieu has argued that cultural capital is of increasing importance in determining an individual's class position, but there are still certain occupations, for example politics and stockbroking, which have resisted this trend and for which the possession of the right social capital is undoubtedly important. However, as time passes there are probably fewer occupations which are open to those with only the right social capital; even politicians and stockbrokers have experienced the benefits of economic resources — personal or institutional. If the public schools are more critical to the transference of social than either cultural or economic capital, then this would suggest they exercise a declining influence over entrée into the ruling class. Nonetheless, it must be remembered that the public schools (if not the independent sector as a whole) provide the context for the interaction of *all* those varying forms of capital which result in class power. Within their confines are to be found a large number of individuals who either already possess, or are in the process of acquiring (with economic capital as the possible exception), those resources necessary to make it to the top in this kind of society. Thus we have a new variant of the critical mass theory. In this version the disproportionate presence of all those forms of capital which are the prerequisites to class dominance interact to ensure the inevitable — the perpetuation of a class-based soceity. But schooling per se is a catalyst rather than a crucial determinant in its own right. If it is to be removed in its present form either a new alchemist is required or a different process of social reproduction will evolve.

Conclusions

It is impossible to make definitive conclusions regarding the effectiveness of independent schooling. The ultimate experiment, in which the same individual repeats his or her schooling, is not feasible and individual circumstances vary so much that all generalizations contain numerous exceptions. What parents value will differ, so what appears to be an irrational decision to some may be perfectly reasonable to others. It must also be remembered that parents are making decisions about the schooling of *their own children* and as most parents want to do the best by them they may well be enclined to ignore the general picture in the belief that their circumstances are special. All they may gain is peace of mind, but this alone may be worth the expense. Perhaps the policies of political parties must be evaluated differently, as parties are obliged to consider carefully current realities, as well as the probable consequences of implementation, before formulating their policies. But political parties have their own ideological traditions to come to terms with and electoral credibility demands some semblance of internal unity. The public school question touches upon the ideological soul of both the major British political parties and this must not be lost sight of when evaluating their educational policies.

In spite of the mitigating factors, neither parents who purchase independent schooling, nor the political parties responsible for regulating it, are apparently motivated by a clear understanding of educational realities. On the basis of his survey, Halsey concludes that those parents who are keen that their children should win a competitive place at a private secondary school gain no advantages (in these terms) by sending them to private preparatory schools rather than state primary schools: 'Is the parent who aspires to send his son to one of these schools well advised to spend his money on primary-school fees or can he 'take the Cash and let the Credit go? Our unambiguous answer to the anxious parent is that he should take the cash. It transpired that in all probability the respondent's type of primary education was highly correlated with various *unmeasured* attitudes and values held by the parents and thus acted as a proxy for them.'[55]

In terms of the effects of secondary schooling, the general conclusion of the relevant research is that on average it has little independent impact upon examination results. Halsey has claimed, however, that for the parents of *less able* children it may make more sense, if the parents are concerned with examination results, to pay for private secondary schooling. This conclusion was reached, however, by making comparisons between the minor private schools and the secondary modern schools, apparently assuming that they are composed of a roughly similar body of less able children.[56] This is an exceedingly dangerous assumption for even non-HMC independent schools may be quite selective in academic terms. That the middle-class parents at the non-HMC independent schools were prepared to keep their children in schooling somewhat longer than the equivalent parents of the secondary modern pupils may simply reflect the fact that, as they were more able children in the first place, they were benefiting more from their schooling.

If parents are more concerned with the socio-cultural values to which their children will be exposed, we have made the point, with the help of data provided by the National Children's Bureau, that pupils in the two sectors seem to relate to their academic work in very similar terms and hold in common several socio-cultural pursuits. Although the independent sector is still socially selective, it seems unable to isolate its pupils from the pressures of a very pervasive youth culture. It may be anecdotal evidence but it can scarcely be of comfort to parents, who imagine their children are cosseted safely in the confines of their independent boarding schools, to have read on the front page of *The Times* that recently twelve pupils have been expelled and five others suspended from Stowe School 'after teachers uncovered a drugs ring' and that 'one boy has been expelled and six others severely disciplined at Eton College for vandalizing Eton parish church.'[57] Obviously this is not typical behaviour of independent schoolboys but neither it is typical behaviour of any secondary school pupils.

The Labour Party in its over-preoccupation with the class intake of the independent sector is apparently unable to formulate any coherent definition of what constitutes social divisiveness. Instead it proposes in the short-term a strategy (one of financial squeeze) which would probably do little more than restrict even further the class intake of the private schools, which is as good a way as any of creating a self-fulfilling prophecy. Responding to the pressures of their institutional network, the independent schools have been exposed to an increasingly demanding academic ethos. The narrowly academic interpretation of schooling which the Labour Party believes the independent schools are imposing on the educational system at large originated from outside the private sector and has claimed it as its foremost victim. Even if the private schools are socially divisive, they can no longer be seen (undoubtedly to the chagrin of some parents) as training a future ruling class through the inculcation of esoteric socio-cultural values. Neither is there any evidence that the private schools exercise an independent influence upon an individual's job chances. We have argued that private schooling is within itself an important form of social capital but more significantly it provides a very convenient institutional framework within which those who already possess economic, social and cultural capital can interact. In other words, the schools form the marketplace in which types of capital are exchanged and accumulated.

In the conclusion to *Origins and Destinations* the authors call for the abolition of private schooling, not simply on the expected and decidedly dubious grounds of their class-discriminatory role and the alleged superiority of the state schools at 'identifying and selecting talented boys',[58] but also because they '. . . exact their uncalculated but enormous toll of reduced political pressure from middle-class parents, of stimulus from expert teachers and response from motivated children. The private market starves the comprehensives of the resources they need to attain high standards.'[59] No evidence is presented to demonstrate that the private sector has a greater proportion of either expert teachers or motivated children (and by implication casts aspersions on teachers and children in the state schools), and the authors fail to discuss how the political pressure of middle-class parents works in practice. It has to be remembered that their own evidence shows, by a large margin, that all social classes use the maintained schools in preference to the independent sector. If there is a resource problem, then one needs to know why this marginally additional middle-class pressure is so vital to resolving it. If the independent schools do have better resources, this may be in spite of rather than because of their middle-class clientele. Reluctant parents may have been persuaded to pay for congenial schools (through fee increases) by those who teach within them and who are naturally keen on improving their working conditions. By way of an historical example the reform of the nineteenth century public schools appears to have owed little to parental pressure and much to crusading headmasters. Finally, and this is a point with wide ramifications, it is extremely unlikely that if the independent schools were abolished their pupils would then be distributed evenly thoughout the maintained sector. There is every chance that differences between maintained schools would widen somewhat, including whatever differences result from the class composition of catchment areas.

The Conservative Party is no less misguided in its attitude towards the independent sector. Much of its policy is based on the assumption that the academic standards of all too many comprehensive secondary schools are abysmally low, whereas most of the evidence points to the fact that the organization of secondary schooling has little impact upon examination performance. Some comprehensive schools may be failing their bright working-class pupils but there is no guarantee that these same individuals will take advantage of the Assisted Places Scheme by moving into the independent schools. The fact that the scheme recruits bright working-class children is not a sign of its success — it is a necessary but not a sufficient prerequisite. What has to be proven is that these children are then given a more enriched educational experience, with more concrete payoffs, than they would have obtained if they had remained in the state sector. The scheme will certainly pick up mainly working-class children (the income scale ensures this), and the means of selection adopted by most of the independent schools will filter out the able, but it is exceedingly unlikely that few of them will do much better in terms of examination results than if they had remained in the state sector. If this should occur, then the Conservative Party will have created another self-fulfilling prophecy, this time a real rather than a hypothetical one.

The purpose of this chapter has not been to suggest that the independent schools should be either abolished or retained. The object has been to test out those reasons which persuade parents to purchase private schooling and those assumptions upon which the educational policies of the two main political parties are founded. We have argued that educational realities do not support either those reasons or those assumptions. The political parties would do better if they restricted themselves to the statement of general principles (that is, the Conservative Party's belief that parents have the right to purchase schooling for their children if they so desire, and the Labour Party's belief in the universal state provision of social services), for their respective views of schooling are woefully inadequate.

Although parents and political parties may be misguided in their understanding of educational realities, these failings are small in comparison to how British social science has understood independent schooling. Overwhelmingly preoccupied with the class composition of the schools, it has failed to explore how the experience of schooling within the independent sector has changed over time and the implications of this for the process of class reproduction. The research is by and large narrow in its scope, outdated in its observations, and unsophisticated in its analysis — most decidedly a suitable case for treatment.

Notes

1 We have examined the educational policies of the Labour and Conservative Parties because of their control of government since the 1944 Education Act. The SDP-Liberal Alliance is struggling to discover its customary middle way in a policy area which does not readily allow such an alternative. As such it does offer distinct possibilities for policy analysis.
2 Probably the best sociological study in this tradition, although one that is now dated, is WEINBERG, I. (1976) *The English Public Schools: The Sociology of Elite Education*, New York, Atherton Press. For an update of this work see SALTER, B. and TAPPER, T. (1981) *Education, Politics and the State*, London, Grant McIntyre, Chapter 8.
3 The paucity of such work is explained partly by the problems of gaining access: BRIDGEMAN, T. and FOX, I. (1978) 'Why people choose private schools', *New Society*, 29 June, (pp. 702–5). For a more recent survey which conveys a similar pattern of responses see Fox's contribution to this volume, pp. 45–64.
4 These are our terms and not theirs.
5 In our opinion Bridgeman and Fox exaggerate the differences they found.
6 *Ibid.*, p. 703.
7 *Ibid.*, p. 702.
8 THE LABOUR PARTY (1980) *Private Schools* (a Labour Party Discussion Document).
9 The creation of the Labour Party's current policy toward the independent sector will be considered at length in our next book.
10 Even a cursory comparison of the latter statement with the section entitled 'Future policy options' (pp. 35–50) of the discussion document reveals the extent of the overlap.
11 One recent interesting publication (*Independent Schools: Speakers Notes*, compiled by the Conservative Independent Schools Committee, 1983) illustrates the powerful commitment of at least a segment of the Conservative Party to the independent sector.

12 For a discussion of such ideas and one that was particularly pertinent for the Labour Party see CROSLAND, C.A.R. (1956) *The Future of Socialism*, London, Jonathan Cape, Chapters 10–12.

13 We are using our own terms to clarify the history of the Labour Party's policies. Some members of the party would see integration as the means of abolishing the private sector.

14 The PUBLIC SCHOOLS COMMISSION (1968) *First Report*, Volume 1, London, HMSO, p. vii. The precise wording is as follows: 'The main function of the Commission will be to advise on the best way of integrating the public schools with the state system of education.'

15 A position she has modified.

16 The full text of the speech, delivered at Cambridge in September 1973 to the Autumn Conference of the Incorporated Association of Preparatory Schools is reprinted in the ISIS *Newsletter*, 3, September 1973, pp. 1–4.

17 The PUBLIC SCHOOLS COMMISSION (1970) *Second Report*, Volume 1, London, HMSO, pp. 11–12, para. 1.

18 Note we are interchanging the terms 'private schooling' and 'independent sector'. As we discuss later the public schools form a part of the independent sector.

19 THE LABOUR PARTY, *op. cit.*, pp. 9–32.

20 *Ibid.*, p. 5.

21 *Ibid.*, p. 15.

22 *Ibid.*

23 *Ibid.*, p. 13. Note the sentence moves from considering the private schools in general to the public schools in particular.

24 *Ibid.*, p. 14.

25 Conservative Party Conference, 14 October 1965 (3rd Session: Education).

26 This was the Department's major goal while she was Secretary of State for Education during the period of the Heath Government.

27 See his speech to the Conservative Party Conference, 7 October 1975, (1st Session: Education).

28 Those self-doubts were manifested most concretely by Callaghan's launching of the Great Debate, although this clearly served a broader political purpose.

29 In his speech to the Conservative Party Conference, Blackpool, 11 October 1977 (1st Session: Education).

30 HALSEY, A.H. *et al.* (1980) *Origins and Destinations: Family, Class and Education in Modern Britain*, Oxford, Clarendon Press, pp. 36 and 52–3. For reasons of style we henceforth invariably refer to this as Halsey's study but we are fully cognisant that the book was very much the result of a team effort.

31 *Ibid.*, pp. 51–2.

32 *Ibid.*, p. 51.

33 *Ibid.*, p. 71.

34 *Ibid.*

35 *Ibid.*, p. 76.

36 *Ibid.*

37 Although the 1983 ISIS census reveals a slight trend in the opposite

direction: ISIS (1983) *Annual Census*, p. 7, Table 3.

38 Although these may be the very parents who are deserting the independent schools in the present harsh economic climate.

39 This is a highly controversial point. It could be argued that the prestige
end of the independent sector was forced to change in recent years by
pressure that percolated upwards. The striving for examination success
was, for example, allegedly first emphasized by those schools taking the
children of grammar school educated parents who were intent on
escaping the comprehensive secondary schools. Obviously there is
room for more theorizing and empirical work on this very point. It is
possible that complementary pressures were at work, and it should not
be forgotten that membership of the Headmasters' Conference has
always been partially dependent upon the academic reputation of the
headmaster's school.

40 SALTER and TAPPER, *op. cit.*, pp. 161–78.

41 For example, it is cheaper to feed the school as a whole rather than by
houses.

42 The regret is expressed most frequently by the headmasters of the
smaller boarding schools who still value highly the character training
aspects of schooling: SALTER and TAPPER, *op. cit.*, pp. 178–86.

43 See, for example, BOYSON, R. (1975) *The Crisis in Education*, London,
Woburn Press, pp. 144–9.

44 We wish to thank the National Children's Bureau for making the data
available to us but we accept full responsibility for the interpretations
made. We wish to thank also ISIS for a small grant which enabled us to
obtain the data.

45 *Op. cit.*, pp. 75–8.

46 This is a contemporary intellectual and political minefield. By purposefully restricting our attention to selection we avoid conflict with
Rutter who has argued for the importance of internal school organization: RUTTER, M. *et al.* (1979) *Fifteen Thousand Hours*, London, Open
Books. It is impossible, however, not to take issue with Caroline Cox
and John Marks because they have argued that selection does have a
bearing upon examination results (COX, C. and MARKS, J. (1981) 'Real
concern: An appraisal of the National Children's Bureau report on
"Progress in Secondary Schools" by JANE STEEDMAN', *Centre for Policy
Studies*, London; MARKS; J. *et al.* (1983) *Standards in English Schools — An
Analysis of the Examination Results of Secondary Schools in England for 1981*,
London, National Council for Educational Standards). Our claim that
the case is 'not proven' rests upon the quantity and strength of the
opposing literature: STEEDMAN, J. (1980) *Progress in Secondary Schools*,
London, National Children's Bureau; STEEDMAN, J. (1983) *Examination
Results in Selective and Non-Selective Schools*, London, National Children's Bureau; GRAY, J. *et al.* (1983) *Restructions of Secondary Education*,
London, Routledge and Kegan Paul, Chapter 15; GRAY, J. and JONES, B.
(1983) 'Disappearing data', *The Times Educational Supplement*, 15 July, p.
4. The DES statisticians also appear to be less than happy with the work
of Cox and her co-researchers: WILBY, P. (1983) 'Official rift on
comprehensives', *The Sunday Times*, 9 October, p. 4.

47 KING, R. (1981) 'Secondary schools: Some changes of a decade', *Educational Research*, 23, 3, p. 174.

48 *Ibid.*

49 BALL, S. (1981) *Beachside Comprehensive*, Cambridge, Cambridge University Press, pp. 288–90.

50 BOYD, D. (1973) *Elites and Their Education*, Slough, NFER.

51 In terms of promoting social mobility the Social Mobility Group at Nuffield College, Oxford has laid great stress upon the influence of the changing character of the class structure rather than schooling. GOLDTHORPE, J. *et al.* (1980) *Social Mobility and Class Structure in Modern Britain*, Oxford, Clarendon Press. For further general support of our interpretations see: HEATH, A. (1981) 'What difference does the old school tie make now?' *New Society*, 18 June, pp. 472–4.

52 GLENNERSTER, H. and PRYKE, R. (1973) 'The contribution of the public schools and Oxbridge: I "Born to Rule"' in URRY, J. and WAKEFORD, J. (Eds) (1973) *Power in Britain*, London, Heinemann, p. 225.

53 BOURDIEU, P. and PASSERON, J.C. (1977) *Reproduction in Education, Society and Culture*, London, Sage.

54 For a discussion of the importance of social networks upon job opportunities see GRANOVETTER, M. (1974) *Getting a Job: A Study of Contacts and Careers*, Cambridge, Mass., Harvard University Press.

55 HALSEY *et al*, (1980) *op. cit.*, p. 211.

56 *Ibid.*, p. 212. In general terms the findings of Halsey, Heath and Ridge support our interpretation, a point reinforced — for the most part — by their contribution to this reader. Where we differ is in terms of the policy implications which suggest that for all the value-free pretensions of the methodology of political arithmetic personal prescription always gains the upper hand.

57 *The Times*, 17 June 1983, p. 1

58 But *not*, if their secondary modern/independent non-HMC school comparisons are to be taken at face value, at enabling them to obtain more externally controlled examination passes.

59 HALSEY *et al.* (1980) *op. cit.*, p. 213.

Notes on contributors

Sara Delamont	Senior Lecturer, Department of Sociology, University College, Cardiff.
Tony Edwards	Professor of Education, Department of Education, University of Newcastle.
Greg Eglin	Senior Lecturer in Management Education, Faculty of Management, North East London Polytechnic.
Irene Fox	Senior Lecturer, School of the Social Sciences and Business Studies, Polytechnic of Central London.
A.H. Halsey	Professor of Social and Administrative Studies, Director of the Department of Social and Administrative Studies and Fellow of Nuffield College, University of Oxford.
Anthony F. Heath	Fellow of Jesus College and Lecturer in Sociology, University of Oxford.
Christine M. Heward	Lecturer in Education, Department of Education, University of Warwick.
John M. Ridge	Lecturer in Sociology, Department of Social and Administrative Studies, University of Oxford.
Brian Salter	Senior Research Fellow, Department of Adult Education, University of Surrey.
Ted Tapper	Lecturer in Politics, School of English and American Studies, University of Sussex.
Geoffrey Walford	Lecturer in Sociology, Social and Technology Policy Group, University of Aston.
Geoff Whitty	Lecturer in Education, Faculty of Education, King's College, University of London.

Subject Index

academic attainment, 5, 6, 16, 20–1, 23–34, 41, 51, 57, 58, 59, 60, 67, 71–5, 128–9, 137–62, 176, 189, 199–200, 201, 203
see also examinations
A-levels, 4, 21, 23–39, 57, 91, 97, 107, 129, 132, 195
see also examinations; O-levels
Assisted Places Scheme, 3, 6–7, 38, 46, 49, 61–2, 91, 163–78, 191, 203
Association for Science Education, 116
Association of Governing Bodies of Girls' Public Schools, 11
Australia, 41

Battle of Britain, 157, 158
Beachside Comprehensive school, 196–7
binary system, 107–8
Black Papers, 47, 91, 176, 187
boarding schools, 5, 11, 19, 36, 43, 45–6, 47, 51, 55–60, 65–86, 118–19, 125, 130, 131, 139, 180, 191
Boarding Schools Corporation, The, 19
Boyle, Sir Edward, 186–7, 188
Bristol, University of, 156
Bristol Law Society, 156
Britain, *passim*
bureaucratization, 137–62
Burnham Scale, 130

Business Education Council, 107
Butler, R.A., 18, 45

Callaghan, J., 205
Cambridge, University of, 34–8, 98, 115–16, 118, 121, 123, 129–30, 132, 138, 157, 180, 199
Canterbury, 21–2
Cardwell reforms, 138
careers
see occupations
careers officers, 92–108
Careers Service, 91, 102, 108
Carlisle, M., 163
Centre for Contemporary Cultural Studies, 154
Certificate of Secondary Education (CSE), 20, 87, 104
Charterhouse, 11, 18
Clarendon Commission, 11, 12
classroom participation, 4, 65–85
'commercial' schools, 2, 9
see also public schools
comprehensive schools, 5–6, 16, 19–20, 23, 26, 30–1, 35, 45–63, 87–110, 115, 118, 120, 164, 168–9, 172, 183, 186–7, 188, 191, 195, 206
see also maintained schools
Conservative government, 10, 13, 18, 42, 54, 163
see also Conservative Party; Heath government; Thatcher administration

Author Index

Acker, S., 103, 104, 108
Adelman, C.
  see Walker and Adelman
Apple, M.W., 130, 133
Ashton, D.N. and Field, D., 87, 97, 108
Atkinson, P., 81, 83, 85
Atkinson, P. and Delamont, S., 82, 85

Ball, S.J., 196–7, 207
Bamford, T.W., 11, 42
Barnes, D., 79, 85
Barron, G., 89, 108
Barton, L. and Walker, S., 176
Bell, R. *et al.*, 88, 108
Bellack, A.A. *et al.*, 79, 85
Bennett, N.D. and Eglin, G.J., 107, 108
Berg, I., 88, 108
Bernstein, B., 77, 80, 84, 85
Bohn, M.J.
  see Super and Bohn
Bott, E., 49, 63
Bottomore, T.B., 89, 108
Bourdieu, P., 5, 7, 66, 77, 80–4, 85, 91, 100, 108, 195, 198–9
Bourdieu, P. and Passeron, J.C., 207
Bowles, S. and Gintis, H., 89–90, 100, 107, 108
Box, S.
  see Ford and Box
Boyd, D., 1–2, 7, 63, 133, 207

Boyson, R., 177, 206
Braverman, H., 127, 133
Bridgeman, T. and Fox, I., 180, 181, 190, 195, 204
Bryce, 139
Bucher, R. and Strauss, A., 113, 134
Bullivant, B., 79, 85
Burgess, R., 85
Burnet, J.F., 134

Cairns, J.A.R., 161
Carlisle, M., 177
Carr-Sanders, A.M. and Wilson, P.A., 161
Centre for Contemporary Cultural Studies, 63
Cobban, J., 177
Coleman, J.S., 33, 43
Connell, R. *et al.*, 177
Coulson, M.A. *et al.*, 100, 108
Coulthard, M., 76, 85
Cox, C. and Marks, J., 178, 206
Cox, C.B. and Dyson, A.E., 63, 91, 108–9
Crosland, C.A.R., 18–19, 43, 205

Dancy, J.C., 32–3, 134
Deem, R., 104, 109
Delamont, S., 5, 65–86
  see also Atkinson and Delamont
Delamont, S. and Duffin, L., 85
Delamont, S. and Hamilton, D., 76, 85
Denzin, N., 69, 85

217

Jackson, J.A., 134
Jenkins, J., 133, 134
Johnson, T., 112, 134
Jones, B.
  see Gray and Jones
Jones, K., 63
Judge, H.G., 43

Kalton, G., 134
Karabel, J. and Halsey, A.H., 7, 85, 108
King, R., 196, 207
Kinnock, N., 1, 8, 177
Kirk, K.E., 160

Labour Party, 62, 109, 204, 205
Lambert, R., 47, 51, 57, 63
Lambert, R. *et al.*, 178
Larkin, R.W., 79, 86
Lawn, M.A.
  see Ozga and Lawn
Leggatt, T., 112, 113–15, 116–17, 134
Levitas, M., 87, 91, 109
Lewis, Sir George, 145
Lewis, P.
  see Dingwall and Lewis
Llewellyn, C.
  see Goldthorpe and Llewellyn
Lockwood, D.
  see Goldthorpe and Lockwood
Lowe, E., 141

Mack, E.J., 11, 42
Marks, J.
  see Cox and Marks
Marks, J. *et al.*, 206
Marsden, D., 47, 48–9, 56, 57, 64
Marshall, T.H., 112, 134
Marx, K., 134
Mehan, H., 76, 86
Meux, J.
  see Smith and Meux
Millerson, G., 161
Mills, C.W.
  see Gerth and Mills
Musgrave, P.W., 100, 109

National Children's Bureau, 43
Newman, B., 100, 109
Newsom Commission, 11, 18, 32, 38, 51
Nichols, T., 108

Old Ellesmerian Chronicle, 161
Ozga, J.T. and Lawn, M.A., 114, 124, 126–7, 133, 134

Parsler, R., 85
Parsons, T., 112, 134
Passeron, J.C.
  see Bourdieu and Passeron
Perkin, H., 138, 160
Petch, J.A., 161
Pryke, R.
  see Glennester and Pryke
Public Schools Commission, 42, 43, 205

Raby, L. and Walford, G., 99, 109
Rae, J., 6, 8, 11–12, 21, 32, 36, 38, 40–1, 42, 44, 51, 57, 63, 159, 162, 176, 177
Reid, I. and Wormald, E., 103–4, 109
Ridge, J.M.
  see Halsey *et al.*
Roach, J., 161
Robbins Report, 109
Roberts, K., 100, 109
Roberts, K. *et al.*, 49, 63
Roweth, B., 97, 104, 109
Rubenstein, D., 60, 63
Rubenstein, D. and Stoneman, C., 63
Rutter, M. *et al.*, 178, 206

Salaman, G.
  see Esland and Salamen
Salmon, A., 145, 148
Salter, B.
  see Tapper and Salter
Salter, B. and Tapper, T., 6, 8, 132, 134, 137, 148, 159, 160, 162, 204, 206
Scharlieb, M., 66, 86